Dangerously Sleepy

Dangerously Sleepy

Overworked Americans
and the Cult of Manly Wakefulness

ALAN DERICKSON

PENN

UNIVERSITY OF PENNSYLVANIA PRESS

PHILADELPHIA

HD
5124
.D 36
2014

Published by
University of Pennsylvania Press
Philadelphia, Pennsylvania 19104-4112
www.upenn.edu/pennpress

Printed in the United States of America
on acid-free paper
10 9 8 7 6 5 4 3 2 1

Library of Congress Cataloging-in-Publication Data

Derickson, Alan.
   Dangerously sleepy : overworked Americans and the cult of manly wakefulness /
Alan Derickson. — 1st ed.
      p. cm.
   Includes bibliographical references and index.
   ISBN 978-0-8122-4553-0 (hardcover : alk. paper)
   1. Hours of labor—United States—History. 2. Shift systems—United States—
History. 3. Men—Employment—United States. 4. Men—United States—Attitudes.
5. Sleep deprivation—Health aspects—United States. 6. Sleep deprivation—Social
aspects—United States. I. Title.
   HD5124.D36 2014
   331.25'60973—dc23   2013011243

For Margaret Ellen

Contents

Preface

One thing is absolutely certain in America: the quality and quantity of sleep obtained is substantially less than the quality and quantity that are needed. Over the past century, we have reduced our average nightly total sleep time by more than 20 percent. Today, cultural and economic forces combine to create a 24-hour society in which millions of Americans— either chronically or intermittently—obtain insufficient sleep as a result of workplace and lifestyle determinants. A convincing body of scientific evidence and witness testimony indicates that many Americans are severely sleep deprived and, therefore, dangerously sleepy.

—National Commission on Sleep Disorders Research, 1993

American society harbored many dangerously sleepy people long before the landmark report of the National Commission on Sleep Disorders Research. This book explores the making of a restless nation by concentrating on the fraught historical relationship between sleep and work—the two biggest time commitments of most adults throughout the modern era. Indeed, America's well-known pattern of overwork sets it apart from all other advanced, affluent societies. While employees in other prosperous nations saw their working time decline in the late twentieth century, the average worker in the United States saw his or her time on the job increase by over 160 hours per year. This trend reduced the time left for sleeping and other forms of rest. In the 1990s, 24 percent of American workers slept six hours or less a day. By 2007, 30 percent of the workforce fell into that short-sleep category, with employees in the manufacturing and transportation sectors exceeding the overall average. Almost half the nation's night-shift workers get by on a sleep allowance of six hours or less. This book seeks to uncover some of the damage inflicted by inadequate recuperative rest due to working time.[1]

The sheer duration of time at work is one of two critical temporal factors in workers' sleep loss. The arrangement of time also takes a toll. The spread of nonstandard work schedules—night work, rotating shifts, split shifts, weekend assignments, and other disruptive arrangements—has had a powerful impact on the quality and quantity of unconscious rest. The acceleration of globalization and the growth of a 24/7 economy in the twentieth century have put more Americans to work at all times of the day and week. At present, about one in five full-time employees juggles working, sleeping, and other activities under one of many alternatives to the customary, but ever-less-standard, daytime weekday schedule. The balancing act for several million members of the workforce involves holding more than one job. In addition, a growing number of workers have contingent employment in consulting, contracting, or other temporary placements more likely to involve unpredictable and demanding nonstandard hours. This book digs up many of the roots of these diverse plans and makes clear that their deleterious effects have been present and, to a limited degree, evident from the outset.[2]

Focusing on work-induced sleep loss illuminates a fundamental cultural influence that has operated to extend wakefulness excessively, particularly among men. Wakefulness as a measure of masculinity is a facet of the history of gender in America that has received no attention at all. Recent gender studies have pursued many facets of male experience and identity, often fixing on dramatic expressions such as extreme muscularity and myriad forms of aggression. But mundane manly stamina, as displayed by persevering through long days or nights on the job, has thus far gained little notice. Fulfilling the familiar male breadwinner role entailed a daily dedication to struggle to maintain consciousness as a basic test of strength. For many American men, winning bread meant losing sleep.[3]

Men erected standards of sleepless commitment to work that they have often found difficult to meet. But it appears that the difficulties have been much steeper for a sizable share of the women who have entered the paid workforce in large numbers since the mid-twentieth century. Although male customs and values of overwork and wakefulness presumed little or no responsibility for household maintenance, employers and domestic partners have seldom made accommodations for employed women's second shift of tasks at home. Employed mothers, along with other women workers, continue to face a predicament set up long ago by men functioning under the very different circumstances of the breadwinner-homemaker model. Commenting on the spread of extreme jobs, Sylvia Hewlett, founder of the Center for Work-Life Policy, observed, "If an older generation of working mothers had difficulty coping with fifty-hour workweeks, surely their younger peers are having an even more difficult time managing sixty-plus-hour workweeks along with a slew of additional performance pressures." Unreasonable expectations about their ability to forego sleep indefinitely have served to reinforce barriers to opportunity for many women. Although this study focuses on men's overwork, it does aim to help place the plight of working women in contemporary America in historical context. Work-and-family scholar Joan Williams recently argued that her colleagues should be "focusing attention not on women's differences but on the masculine norms that make those differences seem so important." Noting that "workplaces are gender factories where men forge and enact their masculinity," Williams pointed specifically to norms of overwork and sleep deprivation widely promoted as ideals of manliness.[4]

This book contributes to our understanding of American history in two significant ways. First, it expands the horizons of historical scholarship on the impact of work on health. The literature on occupational safety and health in the United States up to this point has centered on toxins like lead, asbestos, and silica, as well as on other hazards like radiation and threats of traumatic injury, which tend to be confined to the workplace proper. This project builds on recent work on less strictly occupational risks like fatigue and work-related tuberculosis. My purpose is to introduce temporal terms of employment like scheduling and cumulative hours spent on the job into the discussion of the history of workers' health, expanding the domain beyond the hazardous conditions caused by chemical, physical, and biological agents of disease.[5] Second, this is the first full-length study to make the history of sleep and wakefulness practices in America its principal subject. Thus far, only a handful of works have delved into any aspect of the history of unconscious rest. Admittedly, my foray into an expanse of virtually unexplored territory has severe limitations. I seek only to illuminate the sleep practices related to a few kinds of male-dominated work that exhibited exceptional levels of sleep deprivation: the result is neither comprehensive nor representative.[6]

More than mere inconvenience or minor discomfort is at stake here. Workers forced to do without enough sleep over an extended period of time disproportionately suffer serious ill effects, some of which were unrecognized or vastly underrecognized until quite recently. The vulnerability of the drowsy or unconscious worker to accidents on the job or on the way home stands out as the best-understood risk. Overextended employees with diminished vigilance and sluggish reactions incur traumatic injuries at an elevated rate. Leading sleep scientist David Dinges concluded that "fatigue has contributed to serious incidents and accidents in industrial operations, nuclear power plants, and in virtually all modes of transportation. . . . Many of these accidents involved human errors by personnel who often had inadequate sleep and/or were working the night shift." Such catastrophic events as the Three Mile Island accident and the grounding of the *Exxon Valdez* have demonstrated the potential for disaster when employees attempt to function while deprived of sleep.[7]

Although not as self-evident as the link between somnolence and accidents, the role of sleep loss in producing chronic disease has been established by researchers for numerous disorders. These include ulcers and other gastrointestinal ailments, depression and other psychiatric conditions, heart attacks and other forms of cardiovascular disease, and diabetes and other metabolic disturbances. Some evidence links short sleep to elevated rates of cancer. In addition, biomedical science has demonstrated that existing in a prolonged state of either drowsiness during the daytime or insomnia at night due to nonstandard working time is, in itself, a work-related disease, commonly called shift work sleep disorder. According to the American Sleep Disorders Association, the sleep of shift workers tends to be unrefreshing, largely because it is curtailed by one to four hours per day. The experiential result is commonly a persistent foggy state of consciousness that generates irritability, damaged social relationships, impaired work performance, and an overall reduction in alertness to one's surroundings. Although the prevalence of this condition is not known with any precision, the American Academy of Sleep Medicine has estimated that its victims number in the millions. This book attempts to capture some moments of the dawning awareness of this disorder over the course of the past century. This exploratory study primarily aims to suggest that sleep deprivation in the American workforce has constituted a significant health problem for the past century, even though the full breadth and depth of that phenomenon have been and still are quite imperfectly understood.[8]

Public and private authorities in America have denied or minimized the deleterious effects of short sleep and have defined dangerous sleepiness in the narrowest terms. The first section of the book examines the broad cultural and political forces that have shaped values and practices related to sleeplessness. Prominent elite men, especially celebrity entrepreneurs from Thomas Edison to Donald Trump, have aggressively propounded the notion that sleep is not only a waste of valuable time but a sign of unmanly weakness. The evolution of public policy has reflected changing gender roles, with supposedly weak female employees initially meriting the solicitude of the state and then joining their male counterparts in the freedom to work endlessly. Accordingly, regulations setting real limits on hours affect only a very small number of occupations whose practitioners may pose a danger to the general public. Woven together, these cultural and political influences have fostered the general disposition that real men need little sleep, and certainly do not need the government to tuck them into bed.

The second section of *Dangerously Sleepy* offers case studies of male-dominated occupations plagued by sleep difficulties. These cases of working-class consciousness under duress come from abiding sites of endemic (and in all probability, atypically extreme) deprivation—transportation and manufacturing. Today, over a third of employees in those sectors get less than six hours' sleep a day. At the turn of the twentieth century, steelworkers faced a weekly rotation from a twelve-hour day shift to a twelve-hour night shift, with the wrenching transition of a twenty-four-hour stint called the "long turn." At the same time, Pullman porters toiled up to four hundred hours a month, always at the beck and call of rail passengers. Since the 1920s, most long-haul truckers have faced long and irregular hours on the road, often with no fixed schedule. All three groups found themselves trying to gain respite in inhospitable places, putting up with what I term discommodations. All three dealt with variants of the misery known as flexploitation, as employers demanded not just machine-like regularity of work behavior but, beyond that, a superhuman adaptability. Each group tried in its own way to alleviate onerous terms of employment, adopting strategies that mixed individualism and collectivism, self-reliance and alliance building, accommodation and resistance. The volume concludes by pondering the possibilities for reforms that would promote a more healthful relationship between work and sleep, changes that might grant employees in America the same entitlement to limited working time now bestowed on horses, mules, and oxen in parts of this country, if not the same rights enjoyed by citizens of most other prosperous societies.[9]

Chapter 1

Sleep Is for Sissies:
Elite Males as Paragons of Wakefulness

Sleep is an absurdity, a bad habit. We can't suddenly throw off the thraldom of the habit, but we shall throw it off.
—Thomas Edison, 1914

Sleep is for sissies!
—Shelley Ross, ca. 2005

Denigration of the critical need for rest has deep roots in American culture. For more than two centuries, a chorus of influential voices, virtually all male, has proclaimed sleep a vice and sleep deprivation a virtue. This attitude has remained both prevalent and relatively constant up to the very recent past. To be sure, some in elite circles have contested this dismissive stance and defended moderation. But on balance, potent promoters of sleep deprivation have done more to shape values and assumptions. The resulting habitus has governed thinking on sleeping time for the American workforce in the modern age.

Americans have long striven to emulate those who have won (or at least appear to be winning) the race of life. Even in the preindustrial era, important figures in the business community decried the amount of time squandered at rest. With the onset of industrialization, time discipline tightened, and allocating scarce time to dozing came under tougher criticism. As Max Weber observed, by the early twentieth century the business corporation had displaced the military as the preeminent institution instilling discipline in modern society. Accordingly, throughout the past century, corporate leaders occupied a highly privileged position in setting norms for rest, mainly through self-reports on their own behavior. Luminaries in other major

realms of endeavor joined captains of industry in casting aspersions on those
who lay unconscious when they could be up and doing. The pronouncements
and practices of the successful received extensive and usually adoring attention from the mass media. A recurrent theme in this discourse of heroic
wakefulness has been the unmanly weakness associated with indulging in a
reasonable amount of sleep.[1]

During the preindustrial and industrializing eras, moral opposition to
any idleness informed a Protestant work ethic that celebrated perseverance at
one's vocational calling and implicitly denigrated sleep as a form of idleness.
As anthropologist Matthew Wolf-Meyer has observed, influential Puritan
cleric Cotton Mather "equate[d] sleep with the avoidance of divine service
and a lack of consciousness of one's earthly obligations." Protestant values
and the ready availability of opportunities for white men drove the strenuous pursuit of social and economic advancement in the eighteenth and nineteenth centuries. Many advanced, and some of the biggest winners and those
who closely studied their habits were happy to share the secrets of success.
In explaining the rags-to-riches formula, business leaders and their admirers
repeatedly commended sleep deprivation as a significant asset in personal
strategies of upward mobility. These narratives spoke of male experience to a
male audience, capitalizing on opportunities to portray sleep as an effeminate
indulgence.[2]

Probably the most famous American of the eighteenth century, Benjamin Franklin, was a wealthy publisher and popular author before he became
an inventor and Founding Father. His *Poor Richard's Almanack* was a huge
best seller in annual editions from the 1730s through the 1750s, outselling the
Bible and eventually appearing in over a hundred reprint editions in seven
languages. The almanac's maxims constituted a compendium of instructions on the way to get ahead, predicated on the fundamental assumption
that qualities of personal character—integrity, diligence, thrift, industry, and
the like—were the main determinants of upward mobility. Franklin's wide-
ranging advice on self-discipline naturally extended to rest and wakefulness.
The most famous piece of advice, of course, was this 1735 contribution: "Early
to bed and early to rise makes a man healthy, wealthy and wise." Reinforce-
ment of the first part of that recommendation came seven years later: "He that
riseth late must trot all day, and shall scarce overtake his business at night."
In his own life, Franklin from early young adulthood embraced not extreme
sleeplessness but rather moderation. In the 1730s he followed a schedule that
called for sleeping from ten P.M. to five A.M. as part of a comprehensive plan

for every hour of the day. This plan and its rationale were set forth in an autobiography that went through fifty-five editions between 1794 and 1833 and reached a wide audience of young working-class men, among others. While residing in France in the 1780s, the whimsical old statesman amused himself and readers of the *Journal of Paris* with a fanciful proposal that the city's residents sleep from eight P.M. to four A.M., at which time the ringing of all local church bells would awaken them, with cannon fire as an additional alarm, if needed. In both his minor and major writings, Franklin emphasized the virtues of moderate amounts of sleep, upholding a standard in the range of seven to eight hours a day in a way that balanced rest and wakefulness.[3]

However, this embodiment of American success also undercut his basic message by casting sleep in a negative light. The 1741 edition of *Poor Richard* carried this harsh exhortation and admonition: "Up, Sluggard, and waste not life; in the grave will be sleeping enough." Two years later, the almanac told its readers that "the sleeping Fox catches no poultry." In *Poor Richard Improved*, Franklin sharpened the point further by noting "how much more [time] than is necessary" was lost to sleep by those who forgot those two maxims. His admiring sketch of John Calvin, the leading formulator of the Protestant ethic, pressed the critique further: "He . . . slept but very little; and as his whole time was filled up with useful action, he may be said to have *lived* long, tho' he died at fifty-five years of age, since *sleep* and *sloth* can hardly be called *living*." It is not clear which association was meant to be more damning—sleep and death or sleep and sloth.[4]

In the period before charismatic capitalists came to dominate the popular imagination in lifestyle matters, military leaders held a more privileged position as role models. In the early nineteenth century, Napoleon fascinated Americans. *Gunn's Domestic Medicine*, a popular manual, extolled the sleep pattern of the French emperor. The guide to self-care and healthful living approvingly reported that Napoleon slept only four hours a night when engaged in an active military operation and five hours at less exciting times. Using an alarm watch, Napoleon arose at two A.M. to begin his day. John Gunn held that anyone could follow a similar schedule by applying himself to breaking old habits and forming new ones. Over the course of the nineteenth century, alarm clocks came into common use to cut sleep and enforce abstemious routines.[5]

Clock time became a central component of the time discipline necessitated by industrialism. Employers had to drill masses of workers recruited to the textile mills and other early production sites from agrarian backgrounds.

On the farm, natural rhythms based on the availability of daylight and the changing seasons had always governed work activities. The quest to impose mechanical time relied not only on clocks but also on general alarms. Factory and plantation bells alerted workers to arise before dawn and begin preparing for their responsibilities. Managers sanctioned employees who nodded off on the job. In Philadelphia cotton mills in the 1830s, for example, historian Cynthia Shelton found that "children would often fall asleep at their jobs and had to be struck or strapped to be kept awake." Masters saw themselves as inculcating in their subordinates a stricter discipline that would become internalized as self-control, a virtue deemed essential to economic progress. But across the class divide, many workers saw only a hard authoritarianism, deep exploitation, and challenges to ethnic and occupational customs; and they often resisted vigorously. In this initial stage, the struggle was over setting and meeting novel standards of regularity. Workers were to resemble as closely as possible the tireless machinery that drove innovative production processes. Sleep practices were expected to complement metronomic regularity in performance on the job. In many industries and occupations, this expectation of mechanical reliability remains the primary criterion of self-management.[6]

In some lines of work, however, an additional requirement soon appeared on the horizon. Advancing industrial capitalism increasingly needed not merely workers as dependable approximations of machines but workers as acrobats, possessed of boundless agility and flexibility in maintaining their alertness. Of the several organizational and technological factors that prompted this intensification of work discipline with its powerful implications for sleep practices, probably none was more important than the advent of electric lighting. Artificial illumination by candles or other means had permitted some work between sunset and sunrise, but the feasibility of regular night shifts and other extended operations increased enormously after 1880 with the availability of affordable, durable forms of lighting using incandescent-bulb lamps. Although it is beyond the scope of this study to consider the full range of transformative change that electric lights brought to American ways of life, it is necessary to consider the rethinking regarding sleep that occurred in elite circles in the wake of this historic innovation.[7]

Thomas Edison created much of this bright new world. With regard to the changing relations of work to sleep, the inventor of practical incandescent lighting was not only the father of the night shift. He also took a prominent part in criticizing and even ridiculing sleep as an inefficient and immoral indulgence. This was a role for which he was uniquely qualified by stature and experience. Edison was perhaps the most famous and widely admired American of the late nineteenth and early twentieth centuries, a hybrid celebrity renowned for his imaginative genius and his entrepreneurial acumen. Authority to hold forth on the topic of sleep rested on his well-established personal practices, constituting a sort of heroic wakefulness. A tireless self-promoter whose greatest invention was himself, Edison spent considerable amounts of his own and his staff's energy in publicizing the idea that success depended in no small part on staying awake to stay ahead of the technological and economic competition. As the founder of General Electric, he had a vested interest in any wakefulness that sold light bulbs. But beyond that, Edison saw himself as a man on a mission to enlighten American men on his approach to self-advancement through endless work and minimal sleep. To that end, he cooperated with numerous journalists in varied revelatory exercises and exhibitions. Long after his death in 1931, he remained the paragon of modern sleeplessness to legions of journalists, historians, and other commentators. No American has done more to cast sleeplessness in hegemonic terms. None did more to frame the issue as one of a simple choice between productive work and unproductive rest: the wizard stayed up not to play but to create value in the laboratory.[8]

Edison ascended to prominence with the invention of the phonograph and with his substantial contribution to the invention of the telephone in the 1870s. To enhance further his growing reputation, he made himself readily accessible to the press. In April 1878, the *Chicago Tribune* presented a rhapsodic report on a "wonderful genius." The newspaper noted Edison's "willingness to work at all hours, night or day," his unwillingness to interrupt his work "for more than a few hours two or three times a week" during his 1873 honeymoon, and his policy of selecting subordinates based on "their physical endurance." In perfecting a printer for stock prices, Edison "gave himself scarcely any time for sleep," at one point toiling nonstop for sixty hours to overcome a design defect. In this early installment of the saga of superhuman sleeplessness, the hero did admit to dozing for thirty hours or more to recuperate from extended wakeful spells, a practice that would disappear from future narratives. In November 1878, *Potter's American Monthly* lauded the man with 150 patents as "an incessant worker, taking neither food nor sleep when the fever of a great invention is upon him." That same month, *Scribner's Monthly* prefaced a piece with a drawing of the inventor strolling in the dark. The caption read, "Three A.M.: Going Home

from the Shop." Eight months later, *Scribner's* disclosed that Edison celebrated a breakthrough on telephone sound transmission "by forgetting all
about his supper and remaining at work until the dawn of day reminded
him that sleep as well as science demanded a portion of his time." This initial
wave of publicity introduced a theme that would be extended and embel-
lished for half a century.[9]

Uncritical media attention soared in the wake of Edison's work on electric lighting. In late 1879, he made the most dazzling individual discovery in
this monumental project—finding a durable filament to sustain incandescent light. Unable to rest on his laurels, Edison and his team forged ahead
over the course of the following decade to invent and develop for practical
application a comprehensive practical system for generating, distributing,
and using electric power for illumination. To that end, he and his coworkers repeatedly engaged in marathon work sessions with only minimal rest
breaks. These exertions were not kept a secret from curious members of the
press, whom Edison continued to host with charming good cheer and apparent modesty. He indicated his preference for working at night and admitted his tendency to become so absorbed in his research that he often
kept at it all night. In 1885, Sarah Bolton's *How Success Is Won* reported on a
sixty-hour sleepless stint of problem solving and conveyed the estimate that
the inventor had worked eighteen hours a day for the past ten years. Bolton
marveled at Edison's capacity for nocturnal diligence and his ability to sleep
soundly in a chair. She proclaimed him "the very embodiment of concentration and perseverance." In 1889, *Scientific American* published an interview
in which Edison claimed that he seldom slept more than four hours a day,
a claim that *Ladies' Home Journal* and *Godey's Lady's Book* passed along to
their readers. This interview also gave a glimpse of the investigator as a stern
manager of his nocturnal operations: "At first the boys had some difficulty
in keeping awake, and would go to sleep under stairways and in corners.
We employed watchers to bring them out, and in time they got used to it."
Adaptability had already become the watchword in the embryonic stage of
industrial research and development.[10]

Just as Edison set the pace for his employees and showed the way to success for adult men in general, he served as a role model for the nation's male
youth. Imparting lessons of sleep discipline to the young had been a theme in
the American popular literature since Franklin wrote his autobiography for
the purpose of instructing his son on making his way in the world. Horatio
Alger's classic *Ragged Dick*, published in 1868, reinforced the message to boys

that sleep restriction was an ingredient in success. Nonfiction success manuals, which also aimed primarily at young male readers, decried dormant potential and lionized entrepreneurs like Horace Greeley, whose ascent in the newspaper business depended on dividing the day into twenty hours of work and four of sleep. As early as 1891, Edison was being held up as a paragon of industry in a moralistic piece appearing in the *Reformed Church Messenger*. In a fictionalized conversation, a bored boy complains of having nothing to do, only to receive a sharp scolding from his aunt. She advises her lazy nephew that "Mister Edison, the great inventor, limits his hours of sleep to four or five daily, because he has so much to occupy his time." The chastened youth dutifully agrees to start working himself to exhaustion. In 1900, *Youth's Companion* described how as a student the great inventor Nikola Tesla won a job at Edison's laboratory in Paris by surviving a two-week probationary period in which he worked constantly, sleeping less than four hours a day to prove that he fit the Edisonian mold. Four decades later, Francis Miller's *Thomas A. Edison: An Inspiring Story for Boys* gave its subject a hagiographical treatment that highlighted a regular schedule of twenty-hour workdays, multiday sleepless stretches, and catnapping in the workplace. The juvenile motivational text featured a photo of Edison with a group of workers identified as his Insomnia Squad.[11]

Adult audiences had an array of full-length biographical studies to ponder. All purveyed essentially the same adoration of the restless genius. In 1894, William Dickson, a veteran of the Edison crew at the Menlo Park and Orange facilities, and his wife, Antonia, produced the first major insider's account. Unsurprisingly, sleep deprivation featured prominently in this volume. One anecdote, presented as benign evidence of the inventor's seriousness of purpose, concerned an early troubleshooting effort involving his stock printers:

> Edison immured himself on the top floor of the factory, together with a handful of scientific devotees, and conveyed to his followers the pleasing information that there he proposed to have them remain until such time as the printer was in smooth working order. "Now, you fellows," said the determined inventor, "I've locked the door and you'll have to stay here until this job is completed." And they did stay. Sixty hours of physical and mental work ensued, unbroken by sleep and scarcely by food, at the end of which time the difficulty was discovered and rectified.

The Dicksons took indefinite imprisonment of employees not as a display of authoritarianism in the form of peremptory sleep denial but rather simply as proof of the great man's "extraordinary powers of physical endurance." They assured readers that Edison's "severe and protracted labors owe their sustained brilliancy to no artificial stimulus" and stated flatly that he never resorted to cocaine.[12]

The Dicksons took pains to celebrate the boss as one of the boys, a regular fellow whose "kindly humor and unostentatiousness were calculated to call forth the best qualities in those around him." This characterization extended even to Edison's informal sleeping practices. Consider this sketch of the late-night scene at the Menlo Park lab:

> Men [were] lying in attitudes more suggestive of ease than elegance, taking what sleep they could on tables, benches, and floor; others plying their labors with tense brows and bloodshot eyes, while the master was calmly slumbering amid the general turmoil, his unkempt head supported by a stick of wood, round which an overcoat was carelessly flung. Thirty men were usually at work in this room, sometimes for forty and sixty hours at a time. These abnormal tests of endurance were generally enlivened by choice selections on the organ. . . . Jokes scintillated, yarns were spun.

Pranks and horseplay were other integral parts of a dense shop culture. In one instance, a worker set the clocks ahead several hours while Edison was napping. When he arose and believed it was four A.M., he told the crew to quit for the night. Upon discovering that he had been duped, the Wizard of Menlo Park "indulged in a hearty and unresentful guffaw." Overall, the Dicksons presented Edison as a natural leader who led his gang of sleepless men by example and force of personality.[13]

Subsequent biographical studies filled in the details of this picture of manly wakefulness. In 1908, Francis Jones delivered a breathless account of a "sleepless wonder" conducting endless experimentation sessions. At Menlo Park, Edison "was accustomed to his chief assistants working with him for two and three days at a stretch without rest." The author described the cot that the inventor kept in his lab for naps and marveled at his efficiency in falling asleep instantly. "He has the ability to accommodate himself to circumstance," Jones concluded, "and if he had to sleep on a fence or a telegraph wire, he would probably secure a very refreshing rest and awake fully recuperated." Jones was sure that Edison's exertions had not undermined his health, asserting that "he looks twenty years younger than his age, and he can still work twenty or thirty hours at a stretch without feeling unduly fatigued." Overall, this biography characterized its subject as a superman capable of the most prodigious feats of overwork.[14]

The most fervent expression of hero worship came in a two-volume popular biography published in 1910 by Frank Dyer, general counsel for the Edison Laboratory, and Thomas Martin, a prominent electrical engineer. Dyer and Martin gathered numerous close observations from Edison's colleagues. Francis Upton provided an admiring assessment: "He could work continuously as long as he wished, and had sleep at his command. His sleep was always instant, profound, and restful." Samuel Insull (who later became a senior executive at GE) recalled the indefatigable leader interviewing him as a job applicant at around four in the morning. But leaving little to chance, Edison himself prepared extensive notes to guide the authors. Dyer and Martin reported their subject's recollection of napping on a pile of iron pipes in the cold, dank cellar of his New York City power station, with an overcoat as the only bed linen. This tale, like others that featured Edison sleeping on floors and lab benches, served to fill out the legendary image. These stories of this sort made the hero a hardy pioneer, roughing it with manly disregard for the discommodations of the workplace and of civilization. The authors dutifully quoted Edison's own account of the treatment accorded a new employee, a refugee from Wall Street, during the early years in Newark:

> The second night he was there he could not stand the long hours and fell asleep on the sofa. One of the boys took a bottle of bromine and opened it under the sofa. It floated up and produced a violent effect on the mucous membrane. The broker was taken with such a fit of coughing he burst a blood-vessel. . . . But the broker lived, and left the next day.

This episode of horseplay suggested that his subordinates freely bought into the master's commitment to protracted wakefulness and had made it so much a part of their collective identity that they disciplined themselves. Immediately following that story, however, Dyer and Martin made clear that there was more than workers' camaraderie involved. Here again, they relayed Edison's recollections of his methods: "Each man was allowed from four to six hours' sleep. We had a man who kept tally, and when the time came for one to sleep, he was notified." Undeterred by contradictory evidence, Dyer and Martin uncritically celebrated the high jinks and merriment surrounding Edison's hardy and energetic gang. In that vein, they described the use of a noise-making device to jolt awake workers who snored too loudly and revisited the convivial festivities of the midnight dinners that broke up all-night work sessions. This authorized work illuminated a rough-hewn masculinism prevailing in Edisonian shop culture.[15]

Over the course of his career, Edison's stance gradually shifted with regard to feeding the public's curiosity regarding his life and labor and their meanings. To a great extent, he became less the observed and more the observer. The famous man began to emphasize his strong opinions about the expendability of sleep. Engaging in what biographer Randall Stross called "pontificating on demand," Edison sometimes came out as stridently judgmental in his denunciations of more than a minimal resort to slumber. Moreover, he pressed for making his own behavior the societal norm, just as he had sought to naturalize his biologically unnatural method of working at night. Countering worshipful biographers who presented him as an exceptional phenomenon, Edison maintained that anyone could emulate his productive wakefulness. The aging magician found a comfortable niche in a Progressive Era obsessed with the pursuit of efficiency—technical, societal, and personal.[16]

Edison's judgments were sweeping. Sleep was needlessly lost time, a self-imposed hindrance to productivity. In 1895, the *Congregationalist* magazine reported that "Mr. Edison claims that people do not need several hours of continuous sleep, and that a few minutes, or an hour, on unconscious rest now and then is all that is required. He says that the habit of sleep was formed before the era of artificial light when people had no other way of spending the hours of darkness." Ten years later, Edison declared that his fellow Americans slept and ate too much and worked too little and that reversing these tendencies would work wonders. Bolton Hall's 1911 book on sleep issues reconfirmed and publicized Edison's beliefs that most people wasted too much time dozing and that his long-observed practice of four hours' rest a day was sufficient for others as well. Hall disclosed that one reason for his subject's firm conviction on this matter was that experiments on his own factory workers had convinced both him and them that they slept too much and could make do with less. A 1913 piece in *Hearst's Magazine* gave Edison a platform to issue a warning: "I have no doubt whatever that eight hours of sleep is harmful. An invalid, or a semi-invalid, may require eight hours, but no well man does." On this occasion, he went on to insist that the body could repair itself fully with only five hours' rest.[17]

In 1914, the thirty-fifth anniversary of the invention of the incandescent light provided another occasion to hold forth. Edison castigated sleep as "an absurdity, a bad habit" and damaging to one's health if indulged in for seven or more hours a day. He contended that "humanity can adjust itself to almost any circumstance" and announced that he and eight associates had recently spent more than a month working 145 to 150 hours a week. Framing the question as one of progress toward fulfillment of human potential, he predicted a radically different future: "Everything which decreases the sum total of man's sleep increases the sum total of man's capabilities. There really is no reason why men should go to bed at all, and the man of the future will spend far less time in bed." As a step toward minimizing this anachronistic habit, Edison proposed that all Americans sleep one hour less per day. Because of their provocative nature and the esteemed status of their source, provocative comments of this sort attracted considerable attention, usually solicitous or at least respectful (but sometimes quite skeptical), throughout the early twentieth century. In 1918, efficiency expert Edward Purinton extolled the indefatigable seventy-year-old who was still putting in seventeen-hour days. "Edison has learned how to work, how to relax, how to sleep . . . , how to regulate his whole mental-physical-social-industrial-moral machinery so as to produce three or four times as much work as the ordinary man can turn out," Purinton effused. If nothing else, Edison sowed further doubts about the value of unconscious rest.[18]

In the last decade of his life, Edison finally faded as a leading American celebrity. Nonetheless, even in semiretirement he remained a champion of sleeplessness who continued to criticize reasonable rest as a wanton habit. In 1925, he boasted that he had suffered no extended illness in the last fifty years because he did not "drug his system with too much sleep." In 1930, Henry Ford, who built a replica of the Menlo Park lab at his Dearborn Village historical site, contributed to the legend with his lavish praise in a book devoted to their friendship. Upon his death in 1931, the obituary in the *New York Times* drew on biographer Francis Jones's characterization of the man as a "sleepless wonder." Long after passing from the scene and indeed up to the present, the great inventor has remained the standard of wakeful industry.[19]

In 1927, Charles Lindbergh supplanted Thomas Edison as the foremost embodiment of manly sleeplessness in America. Although the outcomes of his activity were often quite dramatic, the midwestern inventor had always presented an image of plodding persistence in his pursuit of practical objectives. In contrast, the dashing Lindbergh linked sleep deprivation to daredevil adventure. Unquestionably, his achievement was a sensational one—an unprecedented transoceanic flight of thirty-six hundred miles in a craft barely fifty feet long, with neither crew nor communications equipment nor even a thermos of coffee to assist him. The flight posed the most elemental challenge of wakefulness: falling asleep meant almost certain death. The Lone Eagle's romantic style of heroism, very much in tune with the ebullient spirit of the twenties, captured and held the public imagination long after he landed at Le Bourget airfield in Paris. His solo flight across the Atlantic made Lucky Lindy the object of international adulation. In this country, he became the recipient of numerous prizes, medals, proclamations, and other official awards; the honoree at countless banquets, parades, and other celebratory mass events; and the subject of songs, poems, editorials, and other florid expressions of admiration. Perhaps as remarkably, his subsequent adventures made him a leading celebrity for a decade after his pioneering flight.[20]

When Lindbergh took off from Roosevelt Field on Long Island on the morning of May 20, 1927, he launched the biggest news story in American history. Sleeplessness immediately became an integral part of the storyline. While the flyer was still aloft, Floyd Bennett, who had flown over the North Pole, told the *New York Times* that the crucial question was going to be Lindbergh's ability to remain awake, not the weather or the functioning of the airplane. Bennett believed that such a strong, energetic young man would pass this test. In the same edition of May 21, Harry Knight, one of the pilot's backers, confidently predicted that Lindbergh's resilient constitution, ample long-distance experience, and rigorous self-discipline had "made him nearly impervious to ordinary physical fatigue." The newspaper that day added further to the drama of the event by reporting that Lindbergh had slept for only an hour or two prior to departure.[21]

The pilot's seemingly easy victory over the lethal risk of unconsciousness while spanning an expanse of open ocean figured prominently in the journalistic outpouring following his safe arrival in France late on May 21. The day after the historic landing, the *Times* gave over its first four pages to coverage of the flight of the *Spirit of St. Louis*. An editorial reminded readers that "all his faculties, his strength, his skill would count for nothing if he lost consciousness in the vigil or could not endure the ordeal." The fresh new hero himself did not see the experience as an ordeal, however. At the airfield, he told Henry Wales, a reporter from the *Chicago Tribune*, "I had no trouble keeping awake." The awe-struck journalist did not challenge this assertion, even though he described Lindbergh as groggy upon landing. At his first press conference, held at 2:30 A.M. of the twenty-second, that is, less than five hours after his arrival and before getting any sleep, Lindbergh stated, "I didn't really get what you might call downright sleepy, but I think I sort of nodded several times. In fact, I could have flown half that distance again." In an exclusive report to the *Times* appearing the next day, Lindbergh stated that he was "not sleepy at all" while flying overnight and that he was tired but not exhausted at the conclusion of his journey. Another article in that edition suggested that the aviator might have inherited his wakeful tendencies from his father, a longtime Minnesota congressman who had often been seen entering the Capitol in the predawn hours. However, that piece was juxtaposed to another entitled "Trained to Fight Sleep," which claimed that preflight practice sessions involving staying up for as long as forty-nine hours, not just genetics, had enabled young Lindbergh to maintain control of his aircraft.[22]

Besides enjoying the adulation of the newspapers, Lindbergh won praise from many other sources for his conquest of sleep. In ceremonies at the Washington Monument on June 11, President Calvin Coolidge lauded the pilot's energy and alertness. *Time* hailed Lindbergh's freshness at the end of his flight and later named him its Man of the Year. Despite his own genuine modesty and lack of interest in capitalizing on his fame to gain personal enrichment, Lindbergh did contribute to the frenzy of hero worship, from a desire to promote aviation. Two months after his flight, he produced an autobiography in which sleep deprivation before, during, and after his transatlantic adventure received no notice at all. The plain implication was that this topic did not merit any discussion. Instead, consistent with his self-effacing manner, Lindbergh hailed the nonstop efforts of the manufacturers of his plane earlier that year, when "it was not unusual for the men to work twenty-four hours without rest." In his world, men with important work under way naturally pressed forward without stopping. The protagonist's extraordinary stamina did, however, receive attention in a lengthy appendix to his volume written by Fitzhugh Green. A poetry contest that drew several thousand entries resulted in a volume full of superlatives for the modern Viking hero. One ode dramatized the battle to maintain consciousness: "Will the wearied body yield/To fatal lullaby of wind and sea?/Ah, no! He rouses him and mounts again/To heights from whence the mocking waves are still./Thus passed the crisis."[23]

Before the year was over, Dale Van Every and Morris Tracy put out a biography that shed additional light on the hero's habits. Van Every and Tracy portrayed a man of boundless energy, too busy to sleep. Lindbergh's demanding schedule as an airmail pilot had seasoned him for long solo trips undertaken after little rest. They also found that the quiet and seemingly withdrawn young man was a lively fellow among his colleagues, up late in the pilots' dormitory amusing or tormenting them with practical jokes, a staple of masculine mischief making. In this account, during the months leading up to the transoceanic trip, Lindbergh systematically tested the limits of both his wakefulness and the alertness that would be necessary to carry out his mission. Thus prepared, the flyer had no need to use caffeine or other stimulants. Van Every and Tracy expressed the glowing consensus of American opinion that Lindbergh represented "the epitome of what every man of today could wish himself to be."[24]

After a decade of immense popularity as a national hero, Charles Lindbergh's reputation crashed in the late 1930s. He fled to England in 1935 to escape relentless media scrutiny and to recover from the traumatic kidnapping and murder of his son. Beyond an isolationism that he shared with many Americans prior to the bombing of Pearl Harbor, he also engaged in a disastrous flirtation with the fascist regime in Germany. In a widely publicized ceremony, he accepted the Service Cross of the Order of the German Eagle with Star from the Nazi leadership in 1938. When the United States and Germany became world war adversaries, the revered aviator plunged into disgrace. In the postwar era, Lindbergh, who had returned to his native country in 1939, undertook a long campaign to restore his reputation, mainly by assisting the air force.[25]

A key component of Lindbergh's efforts to rehabilitate his image was his retelling of the story of his epic flight. Published in 1953, *The Spirit of St. Louis* was a best seller that won the Pulitzer Prize and returned its author to a place of honor in American culture. The book also became the basis for a big Hollywood movie. *The Spirit of St. Louis* offered a revisionist account of the sleep loss involved in the transatlantic adventure. Gone was the dismissive attitude of the superhuman hero unbothered by extended alertness while operating a small aircraft alone. The 1953 interpretation presented instead a more human actor, locked in a life-or-death battle to stay conscious. In his desperate struggle to escape disrepute, Lindbergh seemingly spared no dramatic detail of his ordeal. Resetting the circumstances of his departure, he now revealed that an untimely interruption had thwarted his attempt to get a couple hours' sleep prior to takeoff. He began to feel sleepy around the fourth hour of the thirty-three-hour flight. Drowsiness mixed with dread of the greater strain to come: experience as an airmail pilot had taught him "what torture the desire for sleep can be." Before the trip was even one-quarter over, still in daylight over eastern Canada, Lindbergh had already fallen into a precarious state: "Sleep is winning. My whole body argues dully that nothing, nothing life can attain, is quite so desirable as sleep. My mind is losing resolution and control." After nightfall, he resorted to singing, shaking himself, stamping his feet, prying his eyes open with his thumbs, and exposing himself to cold air. At some point in the predawn hours, he found himself "asleep and awake at the same moment, living through a reality that is a dream." By early morning of the second day aloft, he was getting advice from "ghostly presences" in the plane. But at the conclusion of his expanded story, Lindbergh claimed that he felt wide awake when he touched down in Paris after being awake for sixty-three hours. Miraculously enough, the hero, still larger than life, managed to defeat hallucinatory exhaustion and the associated desire to sleep. Lindbergh's cursory explanation was that he kept himself functioning by his ability to concentrate on the danger at hand and the fatal consequences of losing consciousness. The pioneering pilot emerged from this revised narrative as even more of an icon of manly sleeplessness. As the only person present to witness this journey, Lindbergh of course became the authoritative source for subsequent biographical studies of this episode.[26]

Lindbergh never attempted to hold himself up as a role model for the common working man. The Lone Eagle preferred to stand out as a singular figure. But a variety of other modern advisors stepped forward to argue for the expendability of sleep, much as Thomas Edison had done in urging his fellow citizens to rest less and work more. For the most part, these experts based their legitimacy not on their own record of success but on their scientific expertise. Authorities trained in the biomedical and behavioral sciences used their advanced skills largely to interpret the patterns of sleep and work evident among those who had won fame and fortune. Psychologists came to occupy an especially prominent place within the growing ranks of sleeplessness specialists.

Foremost among the emerging authorities was Donald Laird, a professor of psychology at Colgate University. With a jargon-free writing style palatable to a mass audience, Laird carved out a place for himself as a popularizer through an efficient strategy of minimal research and maximal publication. Over the course of a long career, Laird's agenda sprawled across several areas of applied psychology, including leadership, productivity, and employee relations. The topic of sleep deprivation in its relation to practical business behavior recurred in his prolific writings, many coauthored with his wife, Eleanor, from the very beginning of his long career. In 1925, Laird opened his first major book, *Increasing Personal Efficiency*, by damning the existing literature on business success for its ignorance of psychological principles. After dismissing fatigue as primarily an imaginary phenomenon, Laird devoted a chapter of the tome to sleep. In what would become a regular gambit, he invoked a familiar legendary leader: "We find Edison saying that no healthy person requires more than two hours of sleep a day." He went on to note that German philosopher and diplomat Wilhelm von Humboldt slumbered only three hours a day. Laird calculated that 99 percent of cases of sleeplessness were a blessing rather than a curse. In his estimation, "the majority of individuals sleep longer than they need because they do not know how to sleep properly." The applied psychologist proceeded to offer guidance on sleeping techniques, such as establishing habits of evening relaxation and ensuring quiet places to rest. He also promoted naps as an efficiency measure, asserting that a half hour of dormancy after lunch delivered the same restorative value as three or four hours' sleep taken in the early morning. Without providing specific details of the intervention, Laird reported that he was currently experimenting on an individual who had reduced his daily sleep quota from nine hours to six, with plans to reach four hours within a few weeks. Subsequent editions of this popular how-to text gave no follow-up on this experiment. However, the fourth and final edition in 1952 still announced Edison's supposed two-hour standard and retained the emphasis on sleep hygiene.[27]

Laird's views may have been consistent through successive versions of his personal-efficiency guide, but in other writings he swerved about. In 1926, he announced that his investigation of mental work done after one to three sleepless nights had found no significant decline in performance. Then four years later, the psychologist, with collaborator Charles Muller, brought out *Sleep: Why We Need It and How to Get It*. As its subtitle indicated, the authors took a more appreciative view of the necessity of dormancy. Embracing the tradition of moderation and regularity, Laird and Muller invoked Benjamin Franklin's early-to-bed, early-to-rise adage. But the temptation to draw on the authority of great men at every turn remained irresistible, creating a contradictory message. Immediately after declaring that most people needed eight hours' sleep, the authors relayed the elderly Thomas Edison's latest self-report of dozing little more than three hours a day. On the other hand, Charles Lindbergh's airborne feat was attributed not to preflight training in extended wakefulness but rather to his reserves of stamina acquired by regularly sleeping seven to nine hours. Adding further to the confusion, Laird and Muller held that the strenuous manual labor of a lumberjack or longshoreman required a daily allowance of only four hours' sleep, in contrast to the executive's need for double that amount.[28]

In later writings, Laird stressed the quality, not quantity, of sleep, with additional suggestions about behavioral and environmental changes and new ones about the importance of maintaining a calm emotional state. His preoccupation with the habits of the famous continued. In this pursuit, he offered anecdotes about both short and long sleepers to reinforce the point that individual needs varied widely. The catalogue of sleep-cutting tips contained the fact that Founding Father John Jay cut a hole in his window shutter to allow the earliest rays of the sun to awaken him by shining on his face. Overall, the self-help advisor provided no single recipe for success but rather a variety of possible ingredients, with sleep restriction still very much in the mix.[29]

Other would-be authorities continued to advocate sleeping less than eight hours. In 1938, *Sleep! The Secret of Greater Power and Achievement, with 101 Tips from Famous People* by Ray Giles promised that any number of behavioral changes might well yield sleep of sufficiently higher quality to permit wasting less time in bed. The same year, in his guide, *How to Be Strong, Healthy, and Happy*, wealthy barbell manufacturer and magazine publisher Bob Hoffman shared the secrets of a system that promised not merely greater muscularity but a prosperous life. Hoffman worried that too much time in bed led to lethargy. Beyond the obligatory reference to Edison's short-sleep regimen, he suggested that "many great men of the past are reported to have slept only a fraction of the time that average persons spend in 'wooing Morpheus.'" The champion weightlifter declared that he generally slept only six hours, had slept only five for months while preparing for the 1936 Olympics, and had recently thrived during stints of four hours per night. This paragon of masculinity propounded the vague notion of "fast sleeping," which enabled disciplined men to get by on an hour or two less slumber. How one actually accelerated the restorative processes involved in sleeping remained a mystery in Hoffman's formulation, however. All-out mobilization during World War II led management consultants at the Arthur D. Little firm to review favorably the abandoned experiments of futurist R. Buckminster Fuller. Interrupting his architectural and other design work for short naps, Fuller had gotten by for two years on a ration of two hours' slumber a day, while purportedly performing proficiently. Even after dropping this approach because it could not coordinate with his colleagues' schedules, the visionary adopted variants of this plan that gave him only three or four hours' daily rest. However, neither Fuller nor his promoters at the Little firm appear to have convinced anyone to work this way. Shortly thereafter, Dale Carnegie, self-help mentor to millions of middle-class men, celebrated the strenuous work style of eminent Wall Street attorney Samuel Untermyer. In his best seller *How to Stop Worrying and Start Living*, Carnegie attributed the successful lawyer's prodigious productivity to insomnia. Untermyer "read half the night and then got up at five A.M. and started dictating letters. By the time most people were just starting work, his day's work would be almost half done." Carnegie concluded, "We don't know how many hours of sleep each individual requires. We don't even know if we have to sleep at all!" This agnostic stance hardly concealed the suggestion that getting enough sleep was not something for strivers to worry about.[30]

Most experts on self-improvement took men as their primary target audience. For women, the experts assumed that female success meant something altogether different from reaching the corporate executive suite, the medalists' platform at the Olympic Games, or the Oval Office of the White House. A physical appearance attractive to a winning male partner remained the key to feminine success, and proper sleep habits played an important role in attaining that goal. A steady refrain urged American women not to skimp on their beauty rest. As early as 1906, physician Emma Walker, writing in *Ladies' Home Journal*, deployed the term "beauty sleep" in discouraging young women from late-night activities: "As a rule, girls do not realize what a very important element of beauty is the early bed-hour. It is not until they begin to see the lines coming and the dark circles appearing that they wonder if late hours have anything to do with these fingermarks of time." Women's magazines continued to play on fears that excessive wakefulness would undermine good looks. In 1933, *Good Housekeeping* warned that inadequate slumber meant not only the dreaded circles under one's eyes but also lifeless hair. Three years later, *Ladies' Home Journal* added "nervous tension at the side of the mouth" to the list of concerns. Donald Laird's 1937 book *How to Sleep and Rest Better* offered this counsel: "Truly beautiful women also know the secret of relaxation, and their beauty naps . . . do wonders in easing the mental and emotional tension that destroys both youth and beauty." The gender divide regarding sleep and success could not have been much wider.[31]

After World War II, triumphalism bred moderation. Extreme sleep deprivation seemed an unnecessary sacrifice—a vestige of a bygone age—to much of the nation's increasingly complacent corporate leadership, insulated from international competition by the wartime devastation of their rivals and often enjoying cozy oligopolies in the domestic marketplace. In one chapter of *The Organization Man*, "The 'Well-Rounded' Man," William Whyte in 1956 captured the transformation in attitudes: "Overwork may have been necessary once . . . , but business now sees that the full man is the model. What it needs is not the hard driver but the man who is so rested, so at peace . . . that he is able to handle human relations with poise and understanding." The same year, the *New York Times Magazine*, always a reliable register of the values and practices of those at the commanding heights, announced that the exclusive and exclusively male New York Athletic Club was setting aside a darkened nap room with fourteen beds for its members. Shortly thereafter, *Business Week* encouraged its readers to get "plenty of sleep." Adding further to the reorientation but also shedding light on the persistence of unhealthful habits, the mass-circulation health magazine of the American Medical Association in 1957 printed an attack on "the suicidal cult of 'manliness'" by Lemuel McGee, a corporate medical director. McGee's article presented a series of vignettes of sleep loss:

A business man fills a day with conferences, passes up lunch. Accompanied by two younger associates he takes passage on a plane at dusk, works out of his brief case during half the night, dozes a few hours, and then dashes from appointment to appointment on a tight schedule during the following day.

A salesman matches his customer drink for drink during the evening, announces at two o'clock in the morning, "It's just the shank of the evening; I know where there's a wonderful floor show." At a convention he feels that he must point to the number of nights he has not been to bed. A comfortable chair and another highball is enough for him, he is constrained to point out. Sleep is a waste of time.

The good provider sends his family to the shore for the summer, adds to his working day working evenings in the office, repaints the game room at home during the middle of the night, and Friday drives all night to join the family.

McGee saw these men not as role models of industry and self-discipline but as self-abusers headed for heart attacks. The founder of General Electric, who expected to find this sort of scurrilous attitude espoused only by union troublemakers, would have been shocked and dismayed by this want of manliness.[32]

Reasonableness was but a short-lived interlude. America confronted a mounting challenge to its economic supremacy from the 1970s onward. In response, a resurgent commitment to going all out, in business and in other areas of endeavor, swept across the upper reaches of an insecure society. Global competition intensified the time demands placed on corporate leaders. Reports of phenomenal overwork in Japanese corporate culture, including numerous cases of managers literally working themselves to death, circulated widely. Sleep became again a luxury that those intent on winning the global contest would have to minimize.[33]

Scientific authority bolstered the enthusiastic claims by and about the latest winners in the marketplace. Journalists selectively sampled the growing biomedical and psychological literature for evidence of sleepless success. In his 1979 book, *Sleep Less, Live More*, Everett Mattlin put on a long parade of corporate, political, and military leaders and other "Super-Achievers" who slept little, to be sure. But Mattlin devoted the bulk of his book to recent research findings that refuted the "eight-hour myth" and promoted "sleep efficiency." In the same vein, a 1981 article in *Harper's Bazaar* invoked the work of Ernest Hartmann, a Tufts University sleep psychologist. This piece broadcast Hartmann's judgment that those who slept six hours or less were "more energetic, confident, successful, happier and less introspective." It also noted that "many sleep researchers believe you can train yourself to shorten sleep hours just the way a dieter forces himself to eat less" and that "some researchers maintain that sleep is largely an anachronism." It went on to summarize a University of California study in which participants gradually cut their slumber time from around eight hours to five hours and maintained that level for a year. The old doctrine of righteous self-discipline took on deeper, scientific legitimacy, bolstered especially by psychology, the fundamental science of the modern middle class.[34]

Charismatic executives set the pace for the sleep-deprived Second Gilded Age. The nondescript bureaucratic type that had prevailed in corporate America was replaced by a colorful new breed. At Wal-Mart Corporation, the biggest business firm in the world by the end of the century, the cult of personality enveloping founder Samuel Walton extended to his stamina. The founder's preparations for his legendary weekly staff meetings, held on Saturday at seven A.M., began at two or three A.M. with an exhaustive review of his stores' performance statistics. Company loyalists cherished a tale about the sleepless homespun hero appearing at one of his distribution centers at 2:30 A.M. to surprise the crew on the loading dock with a batch of donuts, an episode recounted in 1982 in management guru Tom Peters's immensely popular *In Search of Excellence*. When Walton took buying teams to New York in the 1970s, the work day began with a meeting at six in the morning and ended after midnight. In later years, top-level managers at headquarters in Arkansas put in ninety or more hours a week, trying to keep up with Walton, who was often in his office by around four A.M. The requirement that managers be available for very long hours translated into a policy not to promote married women, discriminating out of respect for their traditional and apparently inescapable domestic responsibilities. With the extra time he gained by sleeping only four hours nightly from 1982 on, Benjamin Plumb Jr. launched a software company, acquired a fresh wife, and wrote a book advising others how to cut down their dozing.[35]

Women who wanted to compete against men in the business world had to play by their rules, of course. Media powerhouse Oprah Winfrey boasted of getting by on four hours' rest per night. Martha Stewart, another prominent entertainer and entrepreneur, made no secret of her need for only five hours in bed. In a 1996 article in *Redbook* titled "How to Feel Rested on Too Little Sleep," successful author and working mother Tamara Eberlein advised striving women to cope by ingesting caffeine and protein and by using weekends to catch up on forfeited rest. Eberlein reminded her readers that "we've got a society in which the ability to survive on minimal sleep is a badge of dynamism, while lying down brands us as lazy." With men still holding nineteen of every twenty senior corporate management positions at the end of the millennium, ambitious women could help themselves reach the executive tier by demonstrating sleepless stamina. A recent self-help manual aimed primarily at striving managerial and professional women carried the taunting title *Balance Is a Crock, Sleep Is for the Weak*. The female authors' advice to emulate their tough male counterparts included skipping any opportunities to use spare moments on business trips to catch up on lost rest, with the tired reminder that "you can sleep when you're dead."[36]

No one embodied the highly masculine executive style of the late twentieth and early twenty-first centuries more than real-estate and gaming entrepreneur Donald Trump. From his first appearance on the national scene in the 1980s, this flamboyant self-promoter cultivated an image of superhuman energy and drive. His series of popular books publicized an ability to function at the highest level despite little sleep. His first best seller, *Trump: The Art of the Deal*, began by announcing a regular practice of arising "very early" to launch a daily whirlwind of dynamic deal-making that "never stops." At this point, the celebrity capitalist admitted to sleeping about six hours a night. That amount of time out of action later became excessive for the quickening pace of the new millennium. In *Trump: Think Like a Billionaire*, released in 2004, the author claimed that he slept from one A.M. to five A.M. and that this plan gave him a decided advantage over competitors. Trump advised aspiring billionaires, "Don't sleep any more than you have to. . . . No matter how brilliant you are, there's not enough time in the day. You may be wondering: Why do you need a competitive edge? You don't if you're happy to be an also-ran in life." Snoozers, in Trump's unvarnished estimation, were simply losers. In *Trump: How to Get Rich*, also published in 2004, he assured his audience that he was "still making deals around the clock." Trump stressed the need to work harder than one's employees and reiterated his practice of starting his work day at five A.M. One indication that the popular author and television host was getting his message across appeared in an entry on the website *The Business Student* in 2007. Student Jason Lamarche grasped Trump's attitude that sleep was "for the weak" and inferred that his twenty-hour-per-day wakefulness generated a powerful image of omniscience. Lamarche vowed to try this winning approach. In his latest autobiographical work of career counseling, *Think Big and Kick Ass in Business and Life*, Trump has seized on one of the buzzwords of the moment. After declaring that "passion is more important than brains or talent," the entrepreneur again moved easily from his own behavior to a general prescription: "I'm so passionate about my work that I only sleep three or four hours every night. I can't wait to get up in the morning and go to work because I love my work so much. If you love what you are doing, you are probably not going to sleep more than three or four hours." Sleep deprivation thus returned as a hallmark of a strongly masculine style of dominance, one that aimed not only to pursue passion but to "crush the opponent." Wakefulness served to intimidate potential prey of the relentless competitor.[37]

Professional football, America's civic religion by century's end, played out a hypermasculinity of old-fashioned physical violence. (Unlike Donald Trump, on occasion football players actually did crush their opponents.) Head coaches who dominated in the National Football League attracted considerable attention, often becoming exemplars of leadership. Albeit in a less salient role than that of star players, coaching icons helped make football a significant (though not unquestioned) force in identity formation for Ameri-

can males. A growing number of winning coaches considered sleep deprivation essential to their winning ways. The prototype for the overworking team
leader was George Halas, who built and ran the Chicago Bears while serving
as coach and then principal owner from more than sixty years until his death
in 1983. George Allen, one of Halas's former assistants, took his obsessive
style to further extremes during his tenure as head coach of the Los Angeles
Rams in the 1960s and the Washington Redskins in the 1970s. Besides regularly putting in workdays of sixteen hours or more, Allen began the practice,
subsequently widely emulated, of sleeping in his office night after night. He
expected a similar dedication from his subordinates. According to former
player Deacon Jones, the coach told his teams, "Leisure time is the five or six
hours you sleep each night." Allen set a standard others felt compelled to try
to meet. One subsequent Washington leader, Joe Gibbs, also became known
for taking his scant rest on an office couch. When Gibbs returned for a second stint with the team in 2004, he reverted to that system and inflicted it on
his assistants. Redskins staff had work sessions Monday through Thursday
that lasted until three or four in the morning, followed by two or three hours
of sleep. Gibbs's subordinates were free to go home and have dinner with
their families on Friday nights. More than enough obsessive underlings as-
pired to reach the top rung of the coaching ladder to perpetuate this system.[38]

A few NFL coaches used their time in the media spotlight to hold forth
on their self-disciplined devotion to overwork. Capitalizing on his triumph
in the 2003 Super Bowl, Tampa Bay Buccaneers coach Jon Gruden immediately published *Do You Love Football? Winning with Heart, Passion and Not
Much Sleep*. On the second page of this volume, Gruden proclaimed, "I'm
up at 3:17 A.M. most days." He went on to detail a driven devotion to work
during twenty to twenty-one wakeful hours every day. Justin Peters's 2006
examination of the abstemious behavior of several NFL coaches speculated
that more than a strictly functional desire to find a better game plan fueled
such exertions: "For these overachievers, sleep is for the weak. . . . Endurance
is a way for someone like the miniscule Jon Gruden to prove his masculinity.
Maybe he can't bench-press 500 pounds, but Gruden can go without sleep for
a week." As he prepared for his first season handling the Green Bay Packers
in 2006, Mike McCarthy explained his socialization: "I've done the sleep-in-
the-office routine two or three nights a week. I did that in 1999 when I was
here as the quarterbacks coach, and that's kind of the way I was brought up
in coaching. You outwork everybody." After declaring himself "not a believer
in sleeping in the office," McCarthy stated that lately he had been doing it

again. Despite minimal acknowledgment of the damage overwork does to family life, many NFL coaches have persisted in cheating themselves of sleep and letting the world know about their powers of endurance. Presenting their sleep deprivation as a sacrifice and as compensation for a lack of genius makes these luminaries appear to regular working-class males, and to others across American society, as admirable regular fellows.[39]

Even where colorful individuals did not rise to prominence, the business world held an aura of excitement for many Americans in the late twentieth century. Hostile takeovers and other tense battles raging in many industries captured much attention. In particular, Wall Street and the financial sector as a whole gained newfound visibility as an economic force and cultural presence. In 1978, Citibank launched an advertising campaign with the theme "Citi Never Sleeps." The campaign, meant to convey the firm's boundless energy, ran until 1996; it was revived, with a five A.M. announcement by its chief executive officer, in 2008. A 1988 report that attempted to depict chronic sleep deficits as problematic, not exemplary, had to concede its weak position in the national conversation:

Ours is a society with an antisleep bias. We look down on societies like Mexico and the countries of the Mediterranean world where the afternoon siesta is a tradition. On Wall Street, mergers and acquisitions specialists boast of working 18-hour days. Small wonder that cocaine, a hyperstimulant, has become the drug of choice among Wall Street types and fast-track executives. The message: Real men don't sleep, and to be tired is to be a wimp.

Nine years later, the New York Times Magazine shed further light on the uphill battle to reframe sleep deficits in negative terms, even as evidence mounted of their damaging effects. "Visible fatigue is an acceptable pledge of earnestness and ambition," Verlyn Klinkenborg concluded, "and there is a profound reluctance in the business world even to acknowledge the subject of sleep loss."[40]

The dawn of the twenty-first century found movers and shakers continuing to reject the body of solid science critical of inadequate sleep. In the legal profession, associates at big firms knew that running up their billable hours promised the surest path to the coveted objective of partner status. These young employees on multiyear probation still enter into a game that severely disadvantages women. The American Bar Association's Commission on Women in the Profession portrayed the situation prevailing in 2001: "In the view of many supervising attorneys, extended and unpredictable schedules are part of the way of life in the law. If women want to be 'players,' they should be willing to play by the existing rules. . . . From this perspective, the choice resembles one that leading litigators are famous for putting to associates in high stakes cases: 'Would you rather sleep or win?'" In 2011, Will Meyerhofer, a refugee from high-powered business law at a prestigious New York firm who became a psychotherapist, characterized socialization into the legal fraternity in unsparing terms: "The process begins with sleep deprivation—plain, simple sleep deprivation. Not sleeping. Staying up all night and facing sarcasm if you plan to take the following day off. . . . Sleep deprivation is like binge drinking. There's a machismo around staying up all night, night after night—like doing ten shots of tequila." The growing oversupply of legal talent has served to perpetuate the professional culture of deprivation.[41]

In its in-house legal departments, executive suites, and other realms of business leadership, corporate America in the new millennium has clung to the unhealthful masculine code. In 2001, Harvard medical professor Jerome Groopman observed, "In the corporate world, of course, to be able to get by on five hours of sleep or less is a badge of honor, a sign of the Olympian executive who can straddle the time zones, bridging the Nasdaq and the Nikkei." With the accelerating globalization of finance, and of business more generally, the need to deal with foreign markets in the middle of the American night intensified. In 2011, the New York Times announced, "The nest of night owls is growing more crowded. Senior executives at the Pacific Investment Management Company, the giant bond-trading house, awake at 1 A.M. in Southern California, to check . . . for updates from their colleagues in Europe." Meanwhile, in northern California one hallmark of the high-tech creative style is a refusal to sleep. One sociological study found that hard-driven Silicon Valley software engineers "compare themselves to some real or mythic person (male) who works when they are asleep." Aspiring tech innovators happily tolerate the spartan accommodations in crowded "hacker hostels" in San Francisco and Menlo Park in part because they spend so little time trying to sleep. The race for status and riches has continued to fascinate masses of spectators who have eagerly consumed television programs, movies, books, and Internet offerings featuring overworking, undersleeping entrepreneurs. Tens of millions of viewers of the 2010 film The Social Network took in the all-night programming sessions of Mark Zuckerberg and the team that designed Facebook. In Ben Mezrich's The Accidental Billionaires,

Zuckerberg's monomaniacal approach to invention echoed that of Thomas Edison: "Eduardo [Saverin, his partner,] was pretty sure Mark hadn't slept much in the past week. He had been working around the clock, light to dark to light. He looked beyond exhausted, but it didn't matter. At the moment, nothing mattered to Mark. He was in that pure laser mode." This breathless account delivered yet another reminder that taking the world by storm depended less on a moment of inspired genius than on a marathon of grinding concentration.[42]

Throughout American history, prominent men have devised and promoted a number of sleepless work styles, each exhibiting a variety of attributes, most of which have carried masculine markings. Benjamin Franklin made wakefulness a measure of self-control and righteous industry. Thomas Edison made restlessness synonymous with dogged perseverance and brilliant innovation. Charles Lindbergh gave it an association with courageous daring and resolute self-reliance. Donald Trump made sure that his own brand of alertness reflected brash aggressiveness and unblinking vigilance. Taken together, these iconic figures, along with many others, fashioned a tradition of heroic manly sleeplessness that valorized wakefulness.

These luminaries also overlooked the manifold dangers of overextended consciousness. All remained oblivious to the damage inflicted by chronic sleep deprivation. Not even such studious observers of natural phenomena as Franklin and Edison admitted to paying any price in well-being for the neglect of rest. In part, this blithe disregard may have followed from a sense that success simply necessitated overwork and sleeplessness, as well as many other unhealthful behaviors. As psychologist Will Courtenay has observed, "The social practices that undermine men's health are often the instruments men use in the structuring and acquisition of power." Powerful leaders could rationalize engaging in excessive sleeplessness and promote it as beneficial. Working-class men, who faced different prospects for and definitions of success, had reason to doubt the value of such prescriptions. But those who doubted or rejected this approach had to contend with authoritative voices proclaiming sleep optional and sleepers weaklings.[43]

Chapter 2

In a Drowsy State:
The Underregulation of Overwork

It seems almost beyond belief that a man who has been a railroad man for years will absolutely sit down on the track and go to sleep, when he knows that another train is liable to come along and kill him, but they will do it. They would not do that if they were not so pressed for sleep. When a man goes without sleep a certain length of time, he is not responsible for what he does.

—Henry Fuller, 1906

Unless the slumbering flagman failed to protect a train full of passengers, his risky situation represented no public concern. Over the course of the twentieth century, the state did nothing to help ensure necessary sleep for the vast majority of the nation's workers (or for other members of society, for that matter). Instead, the prevailing policy in America has been to acquiesce in, if not to encourage, overwork, at the expense of sleep. Where public authority has limited working time, the interventions have targeted those whose sleeplessness posed a threat to general welfare. From that perspective, in the early part of the twentieth century the most important safeguards were extended to wage-earning women, whose reproductive capabilities served societal interests and supposedly depended on adequate rest. When protections for female workers eroded in the second half of the century, women obtained the right to work all day and all night, like their male counterparts. In recent years, governmental expertise has been primarily committed to studying the harmful effects of sleep deprivation, for the enlightenment of policy makers and society as a whole. Thus far, however, fuller recognition of the risks of insufficient rest has not translated into meaningful large-scale exercise of state power for remedial purposes.

Working time became a significant political issue in the United States in the 1840s. The onset of industrialization both lengthened the work day and intensified the labor process. In the prototypical cotton and woolen mills of New England, time on duty approached eighty hours a week. Almost from the outset, health considerations underlay demands for shorter hours on the job. Initially, reformers' objections were vague in nature and did not directly address lost sleep. However, as overwork, particularly in the expanding manufacturing sector, persisted into the late nineteenth century, the forfeiture of sleep entered into the discourse of labor reform. Progressive reformers came to believe that lost rest warranted state action in order to prevent women from toiling after dark. In particular, the spread of night work after the Civil War prompted a good deal of opposition. Thomas Edison's lights facilitated the adoption of second shifts in textile production and other industrial operations that used many female employees. In 1890, Massachusetts lawmakers responded by barring women and girls from manufacturing work between ten P.M. and six A.M. A few other states followed this precedent, with variations in the hours of prohibited employment. In 1907, Massachusetts tightened its law by forbidding female employment in textile factories after six P.M.[1]

After 1900, Progressivism brought legislative safeguards against workplace injuries and illnesses, child labor, sweatshop conditions, and other ravages of industrialism. But any hopes that adult male workers would gain relief from overwork in general and sleeplessness-induced fatigue in particular disappeared with the U.S. Supreme Court's decision in *Lochner v. New York* in 1905. This landmark case brought before the court an 1895 state statute to protect bakery workers, virtually all of whom were men. The key provision of the law limited bakers' daily working hours to ten and weekly hours to sixty. John Lochner did not challenge a section of the law that prohibited sleeping in the workplace itself, thus ending the practice of trying to doze atop flour sacks. At issue, instead, was the state's role in regulating the duration and rhythm of bakers' labor. Many bakers resided in cramped dormitories upstairs from the cellar production site. Under this system, workers put in up to a hundred hours per week on the job, toiling through the night, and then were essentially on call. Master bakers roused the conveniently available employees as the baking cycle required. Over time, inadequate and frequently interrupted rest undermined the health of bakery laborers. Supporters of the New York law saw it as a public-health measure.[2]

Most members of the Supreme Court did not view it that way. Justice

Rufus Peckham expressed the majority opinion that baking was not an unhealthful occupation and that bakers were free men capable of protecting themselves. Moreover, the court rejected the argument that debilitated employees could menace the consuming public: "We think that a law like this one before us involves neither the safety, the morals nor the welfare of the public, and that the interest of the public is not in the slightest degree affected by such an act." Rather than a public-health issue, this was only a private matter concerning terms of employment, a contractual transaction into which the state had no grounds to intrude. Justice John Harlan's dissent defended the hours law as a health regulation. Harlan quoted German medical authority Ludwig Hirt on the perils of "compelling the baker to perform the greater part of his work at night, thus depriving him of an opportunity to enjoy the necessary rest and sleep, a fact which is highly injurious to his health." Harlan's opinion noted bakers' susceptibility to respiratory disorders and other specific conditions, as well as evidence of their poor overall health. But clearly, Harlan's arguments did not prevail, and in the wake of *Lochner* the vast majority of male workers could not expect the state to protect them from overwork.[3]

Reformers retreated to a more tenable position. The revised strategy had two components. Advocates of legislative change concentrated on safeguarding women and children, each of whom could be construed as especially vulnerable to exploitation and, therefore, as legitimate wards of the state. In addition, Progressives intensified their marshaling of empirical evidence to illuminate for the judiciary the adverse consequences of overwork. The crucial test of this strategic adaptation came in 1908, in the monumental case of *Muller v. Oregon*. Like the bakers' legislation, the controversial Oregon law limited hours to ten per day. However, unlike the New York statute invalidated by *Lochner*, this one applied only to female industrial employees, such as those who toiled at Curt Muller's commercial laundry in Portland. In defense of the challenged statute, attorney Louis Brandeis maintained that more was at stake than the welfare of a fraction of the workforce. In support of this contention, he presented a formidable brief—long celebrated for its seminal use of social science data in legal argumentation—comprising medical findings on overwork gathered from around the world by Josephine Goldmark, a most ingenious and industrious researcher (and, as it happens, his sister-in-law). This body of evidence showed that many physical differences made women too weak to endure extremely long hours in industry. Goldmark's review included a Massachusetts report of female factory workers falling asleep on the job and a French critique of the damage to sleep hygiene wrought by night work, as well as other expert observations on work-induced sleep difficulties. These conditions, in turn, undermined women's capacity to bear healthy children. In the majority opinion upholding the constitutionality of the ten-hour law, Justice David Brewer agreed with Brandeis that Oregon's policy was fundamentally about public health, not freedom to buy and sell labor. From that premise, Brewer declared the court's consensus that "as healthy mothers are essential to vigorous offspring, the physical well-being of woman becomes an object of public interest and care in order to preserve the strength and vigor of the race." By this reasoning, motherhood stood out as a compelling societal concern, not a strictly personal or family one, based on health considerations that encompassed a dangerous lack of sleep.[4]

The *Muller* victory gave renewed energy to the legislative drive against women's overwork. Not all the advocates of such circumscribed reforms accepted either the presumption of female weakness or the notion that men did not need similar safeguards, but the path to partial relief now seemed clear. Sociologist Annie MacLean's 1910 treatise on working women drew on the Goldmark-Brandeis formulation. In her call for more legislation, MacLean translated the brief into economic terms: "The prime function of woman must ever be the perpetuation of the race. If these other [employment] activities render her physically or morally unfit for the discharge of this larger social duty, then woe to the generations that not only permit but encourage such wanton prostitution of function. The woman is worth more to society in dollars and cents as the mother of healthy children than as the swiftest labeler of cans." Reformers worked to build a knowledge base powerful enough to sway legislative and judicial decision makers. The New York State Factory Investigating Commission, created in reaction to the disastrous 1911 Triangle sweatshop fire, delved into nonstandard scheduling, among myriad topics, in an early report to the legislature. Its discussion of night work began with this forceful declaration: "None of the investigations carried on by the Commission has shown conditions more dangerous to health and public welfare than the employment of women at night in the factories of the State." The New York investigators discovered that married women working after sunset at one large upstate factory averaged about four and a half hours of sleep a day under the double load of industrial and household labor. The commission did not leave the meaning of extreme sleep deprivation entirely to the imaginations of legislators: "Experimentation upon animals has shown that in extreme cases death results far more quickly from continuous loss of sleep than from starvation." This indictment also insisted that "injury to health is the greater because sleep lost at night by working women is never fully made up by day."[5]

Lawmakers in many states responded to these revelations and the agitation that accompanied them. Restrictions on daily and weekly hours for working women spread immediately after 1908. In the interval 1909–17, nineteen states put in place their first limits on women's working time, and twenty of the twenty-one that already had laws strengthened them. California Progressives set the pace by establishing eight-hour daily and forty-eight-hour weekly statutory limits in 1911. New York imposed a fifty-four-hour weekly ceiling the following year. In the numerous jurisdictions where maximum weekly hours were fixed at fifty-four or less, the probability of obtaining a reasonable amount of sleep rose substantially.[6]

The *Muller* precedent also encouraged advances in restricting night work. After 1908, New York, Pennsylvania, and a number of other states passed laws keeping women out of the workplace at night. By 1919, twelve states regulated night work. When the New York statute covering industrial employment faced its inevitable test in state court, Goldmark and Brandeis produced a lengthy brief that captured innumerable facets of the meaning of the sleep deprivation endemic among women employed at late hours. The opening passage of this 452-page document made its priorities clear: "The most serious physical injury wrought by night-work is due to the loss of sleep it entails. This is because recuperation from fatigue and exhaustion takes place only in sleep, and takes place fully only in sleep at night. Sleep in the day time is almost inevitably interrupted and less continuous than sleep at night." The New York Court of Appeals found this law to be a constitutional exercise of police powers. In the same vein, the U.S. Supreme Court unanimously upheld a 1917 Empire State statute that blocked women from restaurant employment in large cities after ten P.M. Justice George Sutherland's opinion construed night work as unhealthful, and particularly so for women: "The loss of restful night's sleep can not be fully made up by sleep in the day time, especially in busy cities, subject to the disturbances incident to modern life. The injurious consequences were thought by the legislature to bear more heavily against women than men, and, considering their more delicate organism, there would seem to be good reason for so thinking." The court recognized that legislators had based their action on the authoritative evidence amassed by Josephine Goldmark and the Factory Investigating Commission.[7]

Despite the cold political climate after World War I, which had brought an end to the Progressive Era, reformers pressed for additional measures to reduce women's overwork. In 1919, Florence Kelley of the National Consumers' League illuminated the fatigued state of textile workers in Rhode Island, Pennsylvania, and New Jersey. In Rhode Island, she heard a married immigrant laborer summarize her own predicament and that of many of her coworkers on the night shift: "Too much work, too much baby, too little sleep." Kelley's survey of the sleep habits of married night workers found roughly two thirds getting less than six hours slumber a day. This deficiency drove some to try to sleep on bare factory floors during their lunch break. Kelley ridiculed nocturnal employment in manufacturing as "a confession of incompetent management," while noting that by 1910 fourteen European nations had abolished women's night work. A similar Consumers' League inquiry in Passaic, New Jersey, discovered rampant sleep deprivation among textile operatives. Comparing New Jersey and Rhode Island, investigator Agnes de Lima saw "the same appallingly little sleep, the same break-down in health of the women, the same neglect of their children." Among the hundred women she interviewed, de Lima could not locate a single one sleeping eight hours a day. More than two-thirds had a daily allowance of less than five hours. One informant told this activist that she got "little pieces of sleep." The league pressed for a political approach to the mission of aiding workers such as these. Its staff and volunteers stuck with this issue through the 1920s and 1930s, despite adamant opposition and dwindling resources.[8]

From its establishment in 1920, the Women's Bureau in the Department of Labor championed reforms to assure adequate rest. In 1928, the bureau's Mary Hopkins issued a searching indictment of the still largely unregulated phenomenon of nocturnal employment. Hopkins found one night-shift foreman who admitted that he made his subordinates stand for jobs that could be sedentary because workers given chairs fell asleep at their places. This investigator offered a financial metaphor for the impact of forfeited slumber: "The night worker is constantly overdrawing his physical balance. The deficit of rest and sleep, small at first, gradually assumes disastrous proportions; there is no escape from physical bankruptcy." Inevitably, such a state of "general weakness is the open sesame to all diseases." Hopkins called attention to elevated rates of gastrointestinal disorders, anemia, and tuberculosis, among other conditions. She challenged the oft-cited report of the British Health of Munition Workers Committee for its cavalier disregard of the sleep-wrecking realities of combining outside employment with onerous domestic duties. She suggested that "the strain of the twofold job perhaps has hardly been given its due emphasis by male writers, whose inexperience naturally leads them to minimize the home duties of the woman wage earner." Hopkins also made a critical assessment of the many gaping holes in legislative safeguards in this area. In a companion study, the bureau's Mary Winslow took aim at those, including many feminists, who opposed special protections for women in part because they cut women off from opportunities for advancement. Winslow began with the basic fact that most employed females were laboring in completely unregulated positions. Drawing upon census data, she estimated that hours laws covered little more than one in three gainfully occupied women and that night-work laws reached only one in six. She defended prohibitions on night work by arguing that they effectively kept women out of debilitating rotating-shift schemes. She pointed out that many women did not want opportunities to work at night because of the well-known concomitant sleep difficulties.[9]

The determined efforts of these advocates yielded little. In the 1920s and 1930s, only five more states began to regulate night work, so that working women in almost two-thirds of the states had no such protection as of 1940. Gains over this period in setting maximum hours were similarly meager. Moreover, with regard to both night work and long hours, many laws never covered more than a few occupations. None covered all female employees. None extended to domestic service, still the leading female occupation. Most were riddled with loopholes for "emergencies" and vaguely defined special circumstances. One indication of the minimal nature of some of the patches in this patchwork is a 1923 Minnesota statute regulating employment at late hours by allowing women to be kept on the job overnight for up to twelve hours, provided that they were given four hours during that time to sleep. Enforcement of these laws was also problematic. Several states had no enforcement mechanism whatsoever. Therefore, even after decades of progressive activism, the best way for women of working age to avoid harmful sleep deprivation was to remain outside the paid labor force. However, the protection for women through working-time legislation certainly far surpassed that for men. No state forbade employment of any adult male workers at any hour of the night. (Workers' advocates in a few states did, however, find ways to circumvent the constitutional barricade erected by *Lochner* by creating a health rationale for a handful of highly dangerous or endangering male-dominated occupations.)[10]

The pragmatic shift to defending women and children did not rule out all universalistic initiatives. Day-of-rest laws sought to capitalize upon and modernize the Sabbatarian tradition. No advocate of these respites pretended that the need for sleep could be met on a weekly rather than daily basis, but supporters did appreciate the potential of such legislation to allow additional rest to compensate for deficiencies accumulating during the work week. Beginning with a measure passed in California in 1893, these statutes did not specify Sunday as the mandated day of the week on which many business activities had to be suspended. But like the old statutes promoting observance of the Christian Sabbath, the modern laws tended to focus on closing commercial and recreational establishments that lured people into secular activities. Work in transportation, manufacturing, construction, agriculture, public services, and other realms generally continued unabated. Indeed, after the turn of the century, seven-day schedules proliferated in continuous-processing industries like petroleum and chemicals. As will be discussed in Chapter 3, arduous, hazardous, nonstop operations in steelmaking caused particular alarm in liberal circles. The American Association for Labor Legislation (AALL) attacked the growing menace of the restless week at its 1911 annual meeting and began a campaign for legislative relief. The association claimed that seven-day employment tended to undermine the health of those engaged in it "by depriving them of the opportunity for reasonable rest." The 1912 platforms of the Socialist Party and the Progressive Party called for a weekly day off duty for the nation's workers. Later that year, the AALL began to circulate a model day-of-rest bill to state legislatures. It noted that sixteen nations guaranteed a day free from marketed work and that a handful of states already barred some employees from working seven consecutive days. Of most importance, in 1906 California had adopted a sweeping law granting twenty-four consecutive hours of respite per week for men, women, and children in all occupations. The labor legislation group made clear that it sought to gain leverage from the recent condemnation of the seven-day system by the Federal Council of Churches. Although unnoted at this juncture, in all probability the AALL also knew of mounting discontent in the Jewish community over the common requirement to work between sunset on Friday and sunset on Saturday. Lawmakers in New York quickly responded to this pressure by passing a law mandating at least twenty-four straight hours free from work in manufacturing and mercantile establishments during any seven-day interval. In neighboring Pennsylvania, home to the world's largest center of steel production, no similar change in public policy came forth. However, the 1913 session of the Pennsylvania legislature did prevent the employment of "any horse, mare, mule, ox, or any other animal" of either sex for more than fifteen hours in any twenty-four-hour span and for more than ninety hours in a week. Subsequent legislative sessions in both Pennsylvania and Illinois had day-of-rest proposals "ruthlessly strangled," as AALL secretary John Andrews put it in 1923. On the other hand, Massachusetts and Wisconsin enacted statutes based on the association's bill. All in all, the political project of securing a weekly day of relief accomplished relatively little. Reformers could show that the lack of a day off harmed personal health, religious observance, and family life; but they could not make the case that most unrested workers posed a threat to the general public.[11]

In contrast, the predicament of overworked railroad workers at the turn of the twentieth century very much frightened the American public at large. Many of the all-too-frequent collisions and other mishaps involving passenger trains were of disastrous proportions. Investigators traced a sizable share of these sensational events to errors committed by train operators who were exhausted, drowsy, or fast asleep on the job. The Interstate Commerce Commission (ICC) used its 1903 annual report to Congress to agitate for a law to force rail carriers to expand the block system of automatic signaling, an available technology that removed most of the risk associated with manual signaling by allowing only one train at a time to enter a segment, or block, of track. The old system depended upon flagmen whose limitations included the occasional loss of consciousness and consequent failure to place warning lights behind stopped trains. The commission offered Congress a draft bill to fix this problem.[12]

Close observers of the rail system realized that mandating safer signaling amounted to something less than a comprehensive solution. The April 1904 issue of the *Brotherhood of Locomotive Engineers Monthly Journal* carried an appeal from J. F. Freenor, a member in Wisconsin, who considered it essential to place legal restrictions on working hours. According to Freenor, "You may as well have a drunken or crazy man on an engine as one that is unable to keep awake." He suggested a limit on duty hours in the range of twelve to fifteen a day. Later that year, Edward Moseley, secretary of the ICC, brought the issue to a wider audience with an article in the *American Monthly Review of Reviews*. This was a classic illustration of the Progressive formula for launching reform: a body of empirical evidence of a social problem subjected to careful expert analysis would generate public support for the experts' plan for government intervention. Moseley used recently mandated accident data from carriers to construct a profile of accidents that had resulted in passenger fatalities. He then examined the accidents deemed preventable, finding that installation of state-of-the-art block signals could have averted a sizable share. He impugned the common habit of obtaining low-quality sleep aboard sidetracked trains, citing instances of poorly rested engineers pulling out onto the main track after such an interlude and immediately colliding with an oncoming train. Moseley quoted one Chicago newspaper's mordant commentary on a recent wreck that killed numerous passengers, in which the locomotive engineer had been working over twenty hours at the time of the disaster: "The officials of the company might as well fill their engineers and firemen with whiskey or drug them with opium as to send them out for fifteen and seventeen hours of continuous work." Moseley concluded that the United States needed to emulate effective British innovations instituted by force of law. The British reform package included "rigid rules governing the hours of labor." At the same time, *North American Review* published an article on rail safety by John Esch, a member of the House of Representatives who served on the Committee on Interstate and Foreign Commerce. Esch lamented that "wreck has followed wreck with such regularity, during the last twelve months, as to make the reports of them in the daily press no longer sensational, but rather commonplace." Beyond the general carnage, the congressman observed that in the year ending March 31, 1904, nine sleep-related collisions had taken thirty-eight lives. Esch argued that "no demand of traffic, however urgent, should deprive passengers of the service of alert, wakeful and attentive operatives." He concluded that preventing excessive hours on duty through federal legislation was a necessary corrective step. Adding fuel to the fire, President Theodore Roosevelt's annual message to Congress, sent on December 6, 1904, declared that "the ever-increasing casualty list upon our railroads is a matter of grave public concern, and urgently calls for action by the Congress." Roosevelt requested legislation "in the interest of the public safety limiting the hours of labor for railroad employees." None of these advocates of reform placed any weight on the simple fact that the mass of statistical data accumulated by the ICC showed that over 80 percent of those killed on the rail system were employees, not passengers. For purposes of making national policy, workers were only dangerously sleepy when they imperiled others.[13]

Presidential support for limits on hours increased rail workers' hopes for finding a nationwide solution to overwork. The railroad brotherhoods' long pursuit of reductions in working time through negotiations and state-level legislation had proven an unsatisfactory piecemeal approach. The prospect of standardizing terms of employment and taking this issue out of competition was, of course, highly attractive to unionists. In February 1905, Atlanta engineer Walter Simmons informed his comrades that Georgia law allowed rail crews to work five twenty-hour stints a week, and that violations of this minimal stricture sometimes left operators out on the job for up to thirty hours at a stretch. Simmons believed that chronic overwork took ten to fifteen years off the lives of railroad men. Many others in charge of speeding locomotives wrote to their union newspaper to complain of the unsafe conditions during trips of twenty or more hours and to offer a variety of ideas for ameliorative legislation.[14]

Labor leaders worked with the Interstate Commerce Commission to draft an hours bill for railroad labor, which John Esch introduced in early 1906. This was a modest proposal to curtail the errors made by exhausted train operators. It mainly sought to codify the private arrangements made through collective bargaining and the legislative standards in place in several states. For engineers and other members of train crews, the proposed daily limit on service was sixteen hours. Employees could not resume work until they had had at least eight hours of rest. Hearings before the House Committee on Interstate and Foreign Commerce gave the coalition of unions representing engineers, conductors, firemen, and trainmen the chance to plead its case. Lobbyist Henry Fuller decried the massive casualties among workers and passengers, dismissed the state laws as "dead letters through lack of enforcement," and conceded that union contracts suffered from noncompliance. Fuller presented a number of cases of fatal accidents caused by unconsciousness in exhausted workers. In one instance, a collision occurred when a flagman keeled over after more than thirty hours on duty and thus failed to set a warning signal. Fuller characterized this overworked man as "working directly against nature, and that is a thing we cannot successfully do." Rather than treat such lapses as culpable behavior, Fuller maintained that "when a man goes without sleep a certain length of time, he is not responsible for what he does." Consistent with his organizations' ingrained aversion to radicalism of any sort, the rail brotherhoods' representative rejected as impractical any interest in establishing by law the eight-hour day.[15]

Other witnesses ranged across the spectrum. George Norris, a House member from Nebraska, put into the record a long list of sleep-induced accidents in which train passengers had perished. But Norris also identified flagmen killed when they passed out on the tracks and were run over. One terse entry described the death of a flagman who had worked the last twenty-five hours of his life: "Sat on track, fell asleep and was struck by train." Over-

all, however, like other proponents of reform, Norris stressed the dangers
faced by the traveling public. ICC safety expert W. P. Borland testified that
his agency had learned of 225 accidents over the previous five years involving employees who had worked fifteen or more hours. Railroad officials, on
the other hand, attempted to shift the discussion away from excessive hours.
They argued that this proposal was not only unnecessary in light of their
own safety efforts but also futile, given the prevalence of employee carelessness on the job, refusal to sleep during their free time, or other mistakes in
judgment. Digesting all this material, the commerce committee endorsed the
sixteen-hour cap on hours, with a requirement that anyone working that long
be given at least ten hours off before returning to duty. In addition, the committee's report called for a minimum eight-hour rest for train employees who
had put in ten hours on the job.[16]

   After this initiative stalled in 1906, debate resumed in the next congressional session. Renewed hearings in the House in January 1907 gave the opposition a forum for a more nuanced defense. Rail executives had managed
to muster some employee opposition to the proposed regulations, based on
these workers' apprehensions about overnight stays away from home or even
the possibility of having to move to new communities located within range
of sixteen-hour trips. One executive used the opportunity to cast doubt on
the manly stamina of those seeking federal intervention. As Daniel Willard,
vice president of the Chicago, Burlington and Quincy Railroad, put it, "I have
had charge of a locomotive more than sixty hours at a stretch. I did not object
to it." However, with the issue framed as one of public safety, the opposition
could not rely on masculine posturing and other forms of obstruction alone.
Accordingly, the rail carriers strove to slip in as many loopholes as possible to
maintain flexibility in operations, irrespective of employee exhaustion. The
law that emerged from the legislative mill in March 1907, to take effect in
March 1908, was a compromise that did grant rail employees and passengers a new assurance of safety. The Hours of Service Act retained the central
demand of the reformers, the sixteen-hour ceiling on work hours. Railway
employees who put in sixteen consecutive hours on the job were entitled to
ten hours off duty before being recalled. However, workers who worked sixteen hours within twenty-four with any break during that span of time had to
be given only eight hours off. This meant significantly less than eight hours'
sleep after the inevitable encroachments on one's time in bed caused by commuting, meals, and personal care. The law covered train operators, virtually
all of whom were white men, and excluded service workers, such as dining-

car waiters and sleeping-car porters, virtually all of whom were black men. Congress also imposed a nine-hour limit on the daily hours of telegraphers and dispatchers, whose sleepy errors also put others at risk. Railroad management got a loophole it could exploit in the form of an exemption from hours limits whenever acts of God, accidents, or any unforeseen conditions caused delays in the movement of a train. Despite its shortcomings, the law was greeted with enthusiasm by its overworked beneficiaries.[17]

Merchant seamen pursued a similar route to gain limited protection. Andrew Furuseth, the president of the International Seamen's Union, engaged in an unrelenting campaign on behalf of his overworked members. With the 1912 sinking of the *Titanic* added to the list of maritime disasters, Furuseth redoubled his efforts to obtain federal assistance with a barrage of shipboard grievances, ranging from corporal punishment to cramped sleeping quarters in the forecastle. Robert La Follette, a Republican Progressive senator from Wisconsin, sponsored a series of bills to protect seamen and promoted the bills, in part, as measures for the preservation of oceangoing travelers. Furuseth and other advocates of plans to improve the terms and conditions of sailors' employment also invoked a racist rationale for reform: jobs had to be made tolerable for white men, in order to reverse the Asian influx into maritime transportation. In 1915, Congress passed a wide-ranging bill that delivered a modicum of relief with regard to temporal and spatial aspects of rest. The Seaman's Act limited working hours out of port to eight per day for engine-room men and to twelve per day for other members of the crew. For the latter, the statute left untouched the traditional watch schedule of four hours on duty followed by four hours off, a rhythm that could only ensure sleep fragmentation. The law promised every seaman 120 cubic feet of personal space and his own sleeping berth. It also provided vague guarantees of proper ventilation and heating of crew quarters.[18]

The development of commercial air travel also brought regulatory action on behalf of passengers. Given the widespread fear among potential customers of the very idea of sailing above the clouds in a relatively small and highly vulnerable craft, the aviation industry was not as antagonistic to removing any concerns regarding overly tired pilots and other members of flight crews. In 1937, the U.S. Bureau of Air Commerce limited continuous hours of service in the cockpit to eight in twenty-four. However, if spelled by a second pilot, the first officer could be at the controls for as much as twelve hours out of twenty-four. Any pilot who flew more than eight hours in twenty-four had to receive twenty-four hours off duty before going aloft again. Beyond the cockpit, only flight dispatchers, whose errors most obviously endangered passengers, won limits on their daily working time. Dispatchers could work up to ten hours within twenty-four. Following the prototypical rail workers' restrictions, the rules applying to aviation employees' daily labor were expressed not in calendar days but in uncertain twenty-four-hour blocks, which could well run from dawn to dawn or over other periods that clashed unhealthfully with circadian rhythms and forced workers to sleep at the worst times. Moreover, these rest periods were not fixed and could vary considerably and erratically, further undermining recuperation.[19]

Just as the railway Hours of Service Act had excluded car-service workers, the airline regulations overlooked the cabin crew. Although some air carriers employed male stewards to serve passengers, by the 1930s this occupation was well on its way to becoming a female preserve. To address customers' manifold fears of air sickness and other acute medical problems, a number of airlines hired registered nurses as "stewardesses" and used this policy in their marketing. Provision of health care was not the only criterion by which cabin workers might have claimed a right to protection against overwork. They performed many routine and emergency safety duties. They might also have merited protection as members of the supposedly weaker sex. The several bureaucratic successors to the Bureau of Air Commerce certainly had the authority to institute working-time safeguards for flight attendants. Yet they neglected to do so, despite the readily available public-safety rationale. Instead, for several decades federal officials essentially conceived of cabin workers as carefree hostesses and waitresses, a stereotype made only slightly less implausible by the abandonment of the requirement for nursing expertise. Throughout their marathon campaign for relief, the flight attendants emphasized not their own well-being but that of their passengers. As recently as 1991, for example, Cheryle Leon, president of the Association of Professional Flight Attendants, gave Congress this perspective: "In our view, 200 cases of 200 fatigued flight attendants potentially affecting the safety of thousands of their passengers is a serious safety problem." Of course, flight attendants' responsibilities only grew in the era of terrorist hijackings. After many years of pressure by their unions, attendants finally won limits on their working hours in 1994.[20]

The early aviation regulations did, however, move beyond those pertaining to trains and ships in one important way. Taking cognizance of the phenomenon of cumulative fatigue, the 1937 federal rules also held pilots to thirty hours of working time in seven days, with a requirement of at least one period of twenty-four consecutive hours of rest during that week. Pilots and other members of the cockpit team were limited to one hundred hours service a month and one thousand hours a year.[21]

Taken as a whole, the body of legal regulations prohibiting work beyond daily, weekly, monthly, or yearly limits never became more than a scrawny one. The half century between the Spanish-American War and World War II witnessed only piecemeal reforms. All these measures were formally limited in scope by occupation, place, or gender. Moreover, all were tacitly hamstrung by inadequate enforcement and an underlying lack of societal and political will.

For the vast majority of American workers whose sleeplessness endangered no more than themselves and perhaps a few of their immediate coworkers, the state took a different stance. The predominant public policy in the twentieth century was not to set clear-cut limits beyond which employees were forbidden to work. Instead, a series of private deals and political decisions established a consistently weak and deeply ambivalent policy. The main tool of policy has been premium pay for work performed beyond some daily or weekly threshold. Even at a glance, it is apparent that the choice of this instrument guaranteed tension by giving employers a disincentive to impose overwork but at the same time luring employees to push themselves too far. The purpose of my analysis of this dilemma is not to review the entire well-known history of overtime-pay legislation, but rather to capture those moments at which there was a real possibility of addressing the predicament of the sleep-deprived worker.[22]

Almost from the first conflicts over working time, mixed messages abounded regarding the time-money tradeoff. In 1832, the New England Association of Farmers, Mechanics, and Other Working Men demanded the ten-hour day, but only for those not receiving bonus pay after ten hours. By the early twentieth century, organized labor in general and affiliates of the economistic American Federation of Labor in particular had made it abundantly clear that premium pay, usually at the rate of time and a half, was all it took to make a bargain that extended working hours, often indefinitely. Public policy largely took its cues from these private trends, reflecting and reinforcing the tendency to waffle on the question of excessive hours. Passage of the Adamson Act in 1916 marked a major step in the development a federal policy based on premium pay rather than hard limits on working time. To avert a strike in an industry deemed essential to the national economy, this statute granted railroad employees a basic work day of eight hours and mandated time-and-a-half overtime compensation, without placing any lid on working time beyond that imposed by the Hours of Service Act. Shortly thereafter, when World War I drew federal authorities much further into setting national wage-and-hour standards, this precedent served as a template for other groups of workers seeking reduced hours.[23]

In the 1930s, the context for rethinking work hours changed dramatically. To the accepted fungibility of time and money was now added the overriding fact of economic collapse. The unfortunate masses of unemployed and underemployed had plenty of time to sleep during the Great Depression. They also had more pressing fears, like averting the state of homelessness that left so many sleeping outdoors. Accordingly, the immediate objective of Franklin Roosevelt and other New Deal leaders with regard to working time was to distribute more widely the scarce opportunities for employment. In 1933 and 1934, the National Recovery Administration established several hundred industry-specific codes regulating working time and other aspects of employment relations. Although intended primarily to promote work-sharing, limits on hours—commonly eight hours per day and forty hours per week—served to promote adequate rest. More directly addressing sleep-related health concerns, fourteen codes outlawed the graveyard shift for women workers and four more did so for all workers. This brief experiment in comprehensive economic planning ended when the Supreme Court declared it unconstitutional in mid-1935.[24]

In the late 1930s, renewed efforts to curtail hours, now linked to a drive to set a minimum wage, again left prevention of sleep loss at the margins of the reform agenda. The Roosevelt administration's original wage-and-hour bill allowed for creation of special financial disincentives not only for overtime but also for night work. One prominent figure in the legislative debate wanted to go further in that direction. Secretary of Labor Frances Perkins, whose political perspective had been forged during the Progressive Era, boldly called for putting an end to most work on the biologically unnatural graveyard shift—for all workers. In congressional testimony on June 4, 1937, Perkins asserted that it was "not unduly limiting the productivity of machinery to prohibit night work except in those industries which are necessarily continuous." American Federation of Labor president William Green backed the softer alternative of mandating a differential in pay for employees on late shifts, even though his organization four years earlier had taken the position that "night work should be eliminated wherever practicable" for both men and women on health grounds. The House of Representatives combined these ideas, while maintaining the accustomed gendered order in the work-place. In August 1937, the House passed a labor standards bill that required time-and-a-half pay for all work done between midnight and six A.M., except in continuous-process operations, and banned employment of women and children during that time interval. However, in the dismal circumstances of a protracted depression, it is no wonder that the final version of the Fair Labor Standards Act (FLSA) of 1938 dropped both those provisions. Instead of re-stricting night work in any way, the law phased in only an obligation for em-ployers to pay a 50 percent penalty in compensating work performed beyond a weekly threshold of forty hours. Exemption of many industries and occupa-tions meant that this stimulus to share the work applied to many fewer than half the nation's employees. Ultimately, the FLSA put the last nail in the coffin of the Progressive drive to recognize excessive hours as deleterious to health, in part because of sleep deprivation and degradation. Politically, lost sleep was a nonissue.[25]

World War II exacerbated overwork. All-out economic mobilization transformed both employment relations and the workforce. Overtime pay and bonuses for accepting second- and third-shift assignments proliferated in booming industries like aircraft manufacturing and shipbuilding. To make the disadvantages of the later shifts more palatable by sharing them broadly, many firms instituted rotational systems that predisposed strongly to poor sleep. The most common arrangement by far was a weekly rotation. In early 1942, Surgeon General Thomas Parran warned the business community that such upheavals in workers' routines unhealthfully disrupted recuperative sleep. Parran recommended changing shifts no more frequently than once every two to three months to allow physiological adaptation to differing con-ditions. Parran also urged employers to allow employees one day of rest a week and to refrain from putting women with domestic responsibilities on the night turn. The nation's top health official offered this guidance in the in-terests of sustaining productivity; his proposals took the form of appeals only to management self-interest and to patriotism.[26]

Parran was by no means the only critic of rotating shifts. Nathaniel Kleit-man, a professor of physiology at the University of Chicago and the father of modern American sleep science, volunteered his expertise to the war ef-fort. With twenty years of original research on sleep and sleeplessness behind him, Kleitman was one of a mere handful of academic investigators seri-ously committed to understanding unconscious rest and the only scientist to make sleep his primary research interest. Like Parran, he opposed frequent changes in working hours. One of Kleitman's major findings, reported in his seminal 1939 work, *Sleep and Wakefulness*, was the importance of "following a definite routine with respect to daytime and evening activity and the time of going to bed." The physiologist advised not only individual firms but the business community in general. The February 1942 issue of *American Business* conveyed his advice to avoid rotation wherever possible and not to change workers' shifts more than once in several months. Kleitman also made constructive proposals for less unsettling nonstandard schedules. He delineated an innovative three-shift plan that improved over the common pattern of eight-hour shifts starting at seven A.M., three P.M., and eleven P.M. Under Kleitman's alternative, workers went to work at noon, eight P.M., and four A.M. This arrangement forced no one to sleep at the worst time of the day, the afternoon. It forced no one to alter normal sleeping time by more than four or five hours. Kleitman also prepared a four-shift variation on this scheme that minimized damage to sleep. The U.S. Department of Labor, which had retained the Chicago physiologist as a consultant, embraced his three-shift proposition, naming its blocks of time the Red, White, and Blue shifts. Federal labor officials actively promoted the system, as did Kleitman himself. In a presentation to the Industrial Hygiene Foundation in late 1942, he described the impact of rapid shift rotation on the worker in a way that presciently captured the essence of what would later be defined as shift work sleep disorder: "It [rapid rotation] causes him to be sleepy at a time when he should be wide awake and wakeful when he should be sleeping." Probably the greatest influence of Kleitman's intervention was to convince employers to adopt permanent shift assignments, whatever their varied starting and ending points may have been.[27]

The war changed the composition of the labor force, however briefly, in ways that had potent policy ramifications in the area of work hours. Women flooded into defense jobs in a host of occupations that had always been reserved for men. The shortage of male labor, together with the imperative to produce around the clock, forced the suspension of state laws that barred women from night work and that set maximum hours for them. The U.S. Women's Bureau and other advocates fought to minimize these reversals. In June 1942, the bureau warned of the toll inflicted by nocturnal work, considering it "inevitable that household duties during the day plus work at night will cause chronic fatigue." The agency considered deployment of women on night duty appropriate only as a last resort and recommended daily exercise, bonus pay, and at least seven hours' sleep a day. At the same time, it conceded the futility of sleeping well during the day and, therefore, supported shift rotation. In the bureau's view, if conducted at a slow pace, rotation allowed women employees to "repair the results of lack of sleep during the night-work period."[28]

The Women's Bureau signaled a willingness to be flexible but not to desert its constituency. Examining the great experiment under way, bureau investigators brought to light the extraordinary burdens shouldered by female wage earners in important war industries. Ethel Erickson's study of the steel industry, where weekly rotation was long established, found women struggling to adjust to a sleep-wrecking regime. Research into the cramped and noisy conditions in which many industrial recruits had to sleep led the bureau to propose minimal housing standards to ensure a quiet, dark, and relatively uncrowded environment for resting. On the legislative front, the bureau and its allies blocked attempts to weaken permanently or repeal hours limits.[29]

Temporary relaxation of safeguards contributed to a long-term erosion of protections for women. As Sue Cobble's careful analysis has shown, gender-specific labor laws came under increasing attack after the Second World War. Defenders of restrictions on night work did not go quietly, however, even though more feminists came to see the protections as outmoded and discriminatory. (Because by the mid-twentieth century the vast majority of all workers' weekly time on the job was well below sixty hours, i.e., down to a level that left over one hundred hours per week for sleeping and other activities besides work as employees, the primary focus in this period necessarily falls on night work.) Labor feminists and other remaining supporters argued that special provisions remained necessary because working women did the bulk of time-consuming household labor. In 1946, Anna Baetjer, a professor of public health at Johns Hopkins who had examined women workers as a military consultant during the war, presented an incisive critique of the social, not biological, challenges to women laboring at late hours. According to Baetjer, the source of the problem lay in "the household and personal responsibilities which fall on women to a far greater degree than on men." Her study changed the terms of the debate, effectively retiring the old Goldmark-Brandeis brief. The Women's Bureau welcomed her revelations as it struggled to resist the mounting pressure to weaken or abolish state protections. "The explanation [for fatigue]," the bureau argued in a 1949 defense of restrictions on female employment at night, "is not to be found in their lower physical stamina, but in their greater practical difficulty in getting daytime sleep." Some advocates of protection for women also continued to hold out hope that firm limits on night work and maximum hours would someday extend to male workers, thus removing the charge of preferential treatment.[30]

In a sense, the 1963 debate within the President's Commission on the Status of Women was the last stand of the advocates of humane working time, with its corollary of reasonable rest. Most members of the commission's Committee on Protective Labor Legislation grudgingly accepted night work for women, with only the qualifying suggestion that third-shift assignments be at the employee's option. Moreover, the group's report made no mention of the sleep-disruptive aspects of this issue. In the same vein, the labor-legislation experts abandoned absolute limits on working hours in favor of the weaker premium-pay formulation of the FLSA. Whereas the committee endorsed extension of stronger maximum-hours regulations to working men, the full commission refused to go that far. In contrast, on night work, the commission was more inclusive but unwilling to support strong government intervention: "Nightwork, especially on the graveyard shift, is undesirable for most people, and should be discouraged for both men and women. Overly rigid prohibitions, however, may work to the disadvantage of women in some circumstances. Strict regulations to prevent abuse are therefore normally preferable to prohibitions." The death knell for protective statutes came in 1969 when the Equal Employment Opportunity Commission ruled that labor laws that impeded women's opportunities were discriminatory violations of Title VII of the Civil Rights Act of 1964. America's female workers thus gained a dubious new form of gender equality in the postwar era—the freedom to work all night, all day, all week. This formal equality came, however, without any concomitant informal equality in the sharing of work at home.[31]

In the final quarter of the twentieth century, the state began to reassess the health effects of overwork and sleep deprivation. Scientific discoveries in Europe and the rise of big science under federal auspices in America after World War II opened the way for rigorous inquiries into workers' sleeplessness. The increasing scale and novel manifestations of the old predicament also helped to place sleep deprivation on the national agenda. A prosperous consumer society demanded access to goods and services at all times, forcing the wider adoption of nonstandard schedules. By the 1970s, about one-sixth of the workforce was on a nonstandard shift. Moreover, a substantial proportion of Americans, mainly in the middle class, fell into needless overwork because of the enticements of what Juliet Schor termed "the insidious cycle of work-and-spend." At the same time, blue-collar and pink-collar workers raised their expectations beyond subsistence and security, in pursuit of an enhanced quality of life that encompassed adequate, restful sleep. But even as most Americans no longer accepted regular bouts of daytime drowsiness and nighttime insomnia, work-induced sleep difficulties were apparently becoming more prevalent.[32]

Although working time was a dead political issue by the end of the 1960s, dangerous conditions on the job were certainly not. In 1970, Congress passed the Occupational Safety and Health Act, which held out to workers the promise of freedom from major workplace risks of injury and illness. That is to say, the nation declared its commitment to safeguarding all workers, not just those whose injuries and illnesses threatened the public at large. The act established the National Institute for Occupational Safety and Health (NIOSH), within the structure of the National Institutes of Health, as the repository of federal expertise in the field of occupational biomedical science. As the authoritative advisor to the Occupational Safety and Health Administration (OSHA), NIOSH had a mandate not only to bring to light unrecognized hazards but also to make the scientific case for new standards concerning exposure to those hazards. In its wide-ranging efforts to fulfill that mission, the institute soon came to the work-related sleep disorders.[33]

By the 1970s, a sizable body of research findings on the sleep-related afflictions of shift workers was already available to American officials charged with controlling occupational health hazards. Beginning in the late 1940s, Scandinavian investigators uncovered elevated rates of gastrointestinal and mental illnesses among shift workers. Expressing the consensus of an expert panel of the Permanent International Committee on Industrial Medicine, pioneering Norwegian researcher Eyvind Thiis-Evensen reported that "a very great number of shift workers sleep badly. This is their most usual complaint." Subsequent studies elsewhere across Europe confirmed this pattern, suggested an increased risk of cardiovascular disorders, and called attention to the inferior work performance of employees disabled by somnolence. In 1965, an interdisciplinary team at the University of Michigan, largely funded by the National Institute of Mental Health, produced a lengthy overview of the diverse effects of shift operations. Summarizing the state of global knowledge at that juncture, one member of the team, social psychologist Floyd Mann, concluded that "the social, psychological, and physical costs of working shifts are not unimportant." Hence, by the time NIOSH entered the field, there was a substantial amount of information and expertise at hand in the scientific world. In fact, by calling attention to a "functional syndrome," the Michigan study had helped to point the way to identification of shift work sleep disorder as a legitimate disease in its own right. The individual suffering with that syndrome "most commonly reports that he is tired all the time and has difficulty getting up in the morning or getting to work; he reports that this sleep pattern is disturbed in that he has trouble either getting to sleep or staying asleep." Thus, a federal agency was venturing into territory that was already partially, if roughly, charted.[34]

Beginning in the mid-1970s, NIOSH strove to raise awareness of the ill effects of sleep deprivation in the workforce. In 1975, the institute held a symposium, "Shift Work and Health," in Cincinnati to explore a topic that lay well outside the accustomed realm of discrete chemical, biological, and physical agents of occupational disease. Nonetheless, NIOSH representatives advised participants that their ultimate objective was not the acquisition of scientific knowledge but rather the shaping of regulatory action. Peter Rentos indicated in his opening remarks that the event aimed to "place us well on the road to providing criteria essential to the establishment of standards that are both effective and realistic." Despite their cautious refrain regarding the unsettled nature of this field, the conferees could agree that the leading problem associated with shift work was sleep disturbance. Paul Mott, the principal investigator in the Michigan project, put forward the radical idea that "we should encourage more worker participation in the design of their shift patterns." Short of the embrace of workplace democracy that this provocative idea implied, Mott also noted interest in the potential of individual adjustments through flextime scheduling. Attempting to extend the frontiers of inquiry, prominent Swedish researchers Torbjorn Akerstedt and Jan Forsberg encouraged an encompassing view of the damage wrought by shift work, one that went beyond conventional disease entities to a fuller consideration of workers' human well-being. This holistic perspective won a measure of support from discussants: "Some of us felt that 'well-being' was a pretty good concept though difficult to define, especially when it often happens that people say things like . . . 'We don't care if he's sleepy or if he's not functioning well as long as he doesn't injure himself on the job.'" However edifying the more evolved European perspective may have been, public-health authorities in America had a mandate only to prevent disease and injury, not to maximize worker well-being.[35]

Subsequent work within these constraints yielded insights nonetheless. NIOSH made a survey of shift work practices, which estimated their increasing prevalence and explored their many variations. It underwrote an evaluation of groups of nurses and food-processing workers that underscored the axiom that shift rotation aggravated sleep disorders. A 1979 conference co-sponsored by the institute and the Office of Naval Research brought together a multitude of international experts to offer alternatives to the prevailing schemes now recognized as problematic. The discussion at this event went so far as to broach the possibility of incorporating naps into work schedules.[36]

NIOSH's regulatory partner did nothing to translate the accumulated body of knowledge into protection for workers. To be sure, this would have been quite a leap for OSHA, which was oriented toward setting exposure limits on individual toxic chemicals and other well-defined, discrete agents. Yet through proposals like the Generic Carcinogen Standard and employees' right to know about the hazards they faced, the agency, especially when Eula Bingham oversaw it during the Carter administration, was moving boldly toward setting more expansive and ambitious regulations. With the advent of Ronald Reagan's presidency in 1981, any window of opportunity for safe-guarding somnolent members of the workforce closed.[37]

The retreat from any decisive intervention notwithstanding, the federal government could not quite ignore sleep-deprived employees. Questions regarding the ways their behavior might endanger society at large dragged public officials back to this problem. The Three Mile Island incident (which commenced at about four A.M.), the *Exxon Valdez* disaster (which began at about midnight), and other heavily publicized events kept Washington inter-mittently involved. The Association of Professional Sleep Societies invoked not only the Three Mile Island episode but also the 1986 *Challenger* space shuttle explosion and other catastrophes to justify its recommendations for government countermeasures. But investigators in the legislative and execu-tive branches of government learned that shift workers' fatigue tended to occur in technologically and organizationally complex settings, in which a multiplicity of factors combined to produce disasters or near-disasters. These complexities helped assure political inaction. Following the common pattern of dynamics without change, Congress collected and analyzed masses of in-formation. In 1988, it created the National Commission on Sleep Disorders Research. The commission's report, appearing in 1993 and 1994, illuminated numerous workplace aspects of a multifaceted crisis and encouraged further examination of shift work sleep disorder and other conditions afflicting the workforce. Most remarkably, given that its mandate was to assess research needs and capabilities, the commission's working group on epidemiology recommended that the government review working-time regulations in the transportation sector. In 1991, the Office of Technology Assessment advised federal lawmakers on the impact of nonstandard schedules. The technology office set out several options for congressional action. One alternative was to "direct the Occupational Safety and Health Administration to determine whether the issuing of standards related to hours of work and scheduling is warranted." Congress did not pursue this course, in part because of an awareness that OSHA had become much less committed to setting and enforcing standards, operating instead largely in a consulting and educational capacity. This nonregulatory method reflected the generally conservative political climate of the 1980s and 1990s.[38]

One small but tragic event prompted corrective legislation in one state in the late twentieth century. On March 4, 1984, Libby Zion, a healthy eighteen-year-old woman, entered New York Hospital in Manhattan, a training site for Cornell University Medical College, for treatment of flu-like symptoms. Within hours, she was dead. Although a number of factors contributed to this fatality, one important cause was the fatigued condition of the medical interns and residents caring for this patient. At that time, the hospital was typical in its lack of any policy on working hours for postgraduate medical trainees. The intern directly in charge of this case worked about a hundred hours a week and was on call every third night. Zion's father Sidney, a lawyer and journalist, launched a furious crusade for remedial action. Although a grand jury in 1986 refused to indict the physicians involved for negligent homicide, it did recommend legal limitations on interns' and residents' time on duty. This proposition led to the creation of an expert panel, chaired by medical professor Bertrand Bell. The following year the Bell Committee proposed restricting weekly hours to eighty, with no stint of more than twenty-four hours, and a guarantee of at least twenty-four consecutive hours off each week. Amid mounting criticism of the man-of-steel culture of postgraduate medical education, many within the profession acknowledged the necessity for some reform. In February 1989, an editorial in the *Journal of the American Medical Association* acknowledged that "the public is outraged that life-and-death decisions are made by residents working thirty-six-hour shifts and 100-hour weeks." The editorial embraced the central working-time proposals of the Bell panel: "Eighty hours per week—the equivalent of two full-time jobs—is enough! The mandated day off per week should also help." A few months later, the New York legislature amended the state health code to reflect the Bell Committee plan, capping weekly hours at eighty and shift hours at twenty-four and mandating a weekly respite of at least twenty-four consecutive hours.[39]

Even though their primary objective was the more politically attractive one of patient safety, not worker well-being, the New York rules did not show the way for authorities in other states or in Washington. To be sure, they received considerable scrutiny in medical academia, leading to corroboration of the manifold dangers associated with chronic sleep deprivation in hospital medical staff. But sobering realizations were undercut by widely expressed fears that a golden age of rigorous training had sadly concluded, succeeded by a decadent era of irresponsible clockwatching. Those anxieties fueled continuing controversy and may have helped divert attention from the decision of the European Union in 2000 to require that its members phase in an average weekly limit of forty-eight working hours for medical trainees. This move aimed to bring the working time of doctors in training into line with that of the European workforce as a whole.[40]

After more than a decade of waiting for legislative relief, the Committee of Interns and Residents, an affiliate of the Service Employees International Union, and other allies in 2001 petitioned the Occupational Safety and Health Administration to set a standard that reduced hours. Although this petition was rejected, it probably helped to catalyze a voluntarist response. In 2002, the Accreditation Council for Graduate Medical Education decided that its constituent medical schools had to bring their student-employee hours down to eighty per week, when averaged over a four-week period, and down to twenty-four per shift. In 2010, the accreditation body revisited this matter, keeping the eighty-hour limit but restricting first-year (but not other) residents to shifts of sixteen hours. The deficiencies in self-imposed regulations, along with persistent widespread violations of them, led the Committee of Interns and Residents and other interested parties to file another petition to OSHA seeking stricter protection. Like the request submitted almost a decade earlier, this petition concentrated on the adverse effects of overwork and sleep loss on medical workers themselves, not on the risks to their patients.[41]

In contrast, the recent drive by other health-care workers for protection maintained the traditional emphasis on second-party victimization. Beginning in the 1990s, organizations representing registered nurses and, to a lesser extent, other providers of health services pressed state legislatures for relief from mandatory overtime as a matter primarily of patient safety. The nurses' wave of activism won them some statutory immunity from forced overtime in five states in 2001–2, with several others following suit over the course of the decade. As of late 2012, seventeen states have placed some restrictions on mandatory overtime for nurses. The momentum generated by these advances prodded a few jurisdictions to consider reining in mandatory overtime for the entire wage-earning population. Thus far, only Maine has enacted protective legislation along those lines, albeit with more than a few exemptions. In 2001, that state enacted a ceiling of eighty hours of mandatory overtime per two-week period for the majority of its workforce. Although the law in Maine offers only a very modest amount of protection against sleep-denying levels of overwork, its coverage does reflect a striking disregard for the longstanding requirement that sleeplessness place someone beside the worker herself or himself in jeopardy. At the national level, Congress held two brief sets of hearings in 2001 and 2002 that gave nurses' leaders a chance to reiterate their dissatisfaction with exhausting marathons such as sixteen-hour double shifts. Federal legislators were not at all prepared to enact the nurses' demand for a ban on forced overtime.[42]

The minimalist public policy regarding workers' sleep deprivation that has predominated over the past century is of a piece with American public-health policy in general over more than that period. From yellow fever to AIDS, government has forcefully intervened only when widespread fear of a serious infection gripped society as a whole. Consider the classic case of the hapless immigrant Mary Mallon, "Typhoid Mary," a cook in early twentieth-century New York who had the misfortune to be carrying a communicable bacillus. Mallon endured two long terms of imprisonment to protect the community from infection. Conversely, noninfectious conditions have elicited little or no commitment of the police power or other resources of the state. Until very recently, chronic noncontagious conditions that endangered no second parties, like the major cardiovascular disorders and cancers, have warranted little or no preventive action. Of course, most work-related illnesses are not infectious and, therefore, have not prompted state action.[43]

Within the confines set by this narrow perspective, the challenge facing advocates of protection was to take advantage of the elasticity of such socially and politically constructed concepts as "public welfare" and "public safety" in order to carve out protected refuges for a fraction of the working population. For most of the twentieth century, shrewd framing of the plight of women workers as a valid societal concern brought a measure of protection to a sizable minority of employed females. Only a few intrepid agitators went into the political arena to assert the right of all workers to an adequate amount of rest. Despite the futility of their efforts thus far, they have managed at least to make work-induced sleeplessness visible and thus have contributed to making it into a legitimate political issue.

Chapter 3

The Long Turn:
Steelworkers and Shift Rotation

I often grieved when I saw the men lined up at the Steel Plant gates
waiting for relatives to bring their meals for another twelve hours. What a
shame! Work a horse twenty-four hours and you go behind the bars.
—Alfred Kiefer, 1920

Making steel in America at the turn of the twentieth century depended on a
system of long working hours that guaranteed sleep deprivation for the men
and boys who toiled under it. Some departments in the mills ran twenty-four
hours a day, 365 days a year. A severe imbalance of power between labor and
capital turned the technological necessity of continuous operations into an
inhumane grind that exploited masses of immigrant laborers and large numbers of native workers as well. Those in control of the industry demanded
from hundreds of thousands of employees a twelve-hour day and a seven-
day week. A scheme of weekly shift rotation compounded the burden of the
eighty-four-hour week. To make the reversal from day work to night, workers every other weekend put in a twenty-four-hour double shift, known as
the long turn. Few, if any, workers could escape the sleep-denying implications of this schedule. The uncomfortable places in which most steelworkers had to try to recuperate exacerbated sleep shortfalls and low-quality rest.
This brutal regime produced shift work sleep disorder, on-the-job injuries,
and other unwelcome effects.

Attempts to alleviate these onerous terms of employment arose throughout the early twentieth century. Middle-class and upper-class Progressive
reformers waged a series of withering publicity campaigns in the hope that
public outcry would produce enough moral suasion to bring about a volun-

tary reduction in steelworkers' hours by management. Progressives also agitated for corrective legislation restricting hours. At the same time, collective self-assertion by employees culminated in a whirlwind organizing campaign and a titanic strike in 1919. None of these remedial efforts brought immediate relief. But in 1923, the accumulation of public embarrassments, the prospect of unrelenting agitation on the issue, and belated recognition of the economic irrationality of excessive working time finally combined to put an end to the eighty-four-hour week and, with it, the infamous institution of the long turn. The rotational plan survived the reforms of the early 1920s, however, and, in fact, has continued up to the present.

This chapter opens up previously unexcavated aspects of the plight of laborers in industrializing mass production. It revisits a familiar struggle over working time with the aim of deepening our understanding of it by focusing on the previously neglected dimension of lost and unrefreshing sleep. This emphasis serves to highlight the especially pernicious role played by biologically jolting rotational schedules. Along with manufacturers of cement, glass, paper, aluminum, soap, and numerous other products, iron and steel firms relied heavily on this dehumanizing method of arranging work time in order to operate continuously. The distinctive pattern of long and unnatural hours in this industry reflected in part a subculture of virile toughness that pervaded the mills. Management manipulated employees' fears of appearing weak, leading some workers to accept unrealistic standards of overwork and sleep deprivation. However, many mill laborers came to recognize the pernicious effects of insufficient sleep and rejected the hegemonic view. These dissidents tried to preserve their health by engaging in various forms of resistance to overwork.[1]

This case of belated reform also captures the persistence and efficacy, albeit limited, of the conscientious new middle class as a mediating force in class relations. In this instance a few college-educated women and men, especially the pivotal figure John Fitch, found varied ways to pursue their humanitarian objectives. A handful of Progressive stalwarts were stubbornly unwilling to abandon this cause despite numerous setbacks.

By the end of the nineteenth century, a series of technological advances had left American steelworkers at a severe disadvantage in their relations with their employers. Making iron had been a small-batch cooking process in which skilled workers enjoyed control of most stages of production. When the superiority of less brittle, more workable steel became evident for use in railroad rails and numerous other applications, the skilled elite who puddled and rolled iron became an endangered breed. The Bessemer process of refining iron into steel and, later, the advent of open-hearth technology pushed iron to the margins and ended the era of workers' control. Traditional skills suffered a deep devaluation or disappeared altogether. A host of unskilled and semiskilled jobs emerged to use machinery and hand tools to move or shape raw materials, half-finished metal objects, waste, and finished products. There was seldom a shortage of laborers, most newly arrived immigrants from central and eastern Europe, ready to take arduous and low-paying jobs that appeared to offer a better opportunity than subsistence agriculture and other unpromising pursuits in the old country. For the hardy young men recruited into the mills, very many of whom risked taking a fatal bath in molten metal every day on the job, the hazard of short and fragmented sleep did not immediately loom large.[2]

Keen interest in further technological innovation impelled the leading steelmaker, Andrew Carnegie, to crush the Amalgamated Association of Iron and Steel Workers, whose work rules obstructed changes in production methods and otherwise undercut efficiency. One of the largest affiliates of the American Federation of Labor, this craft union represented the only real countervailing power in the industry. In 1892, defeat of the Amalgamated Association in a crucial confrontation at his massive manufacturing complex at Homestead, Pennsylvania, outside Pittsburgh, gave Carnegie the freedom to dictate the terms and conditions of employment to his increasingly deskilled and demoralized workforce.[3]

Beyond eradication of the workers' union, organizational changes on the employers' side also compounded the growing disparity in leverage in the employment relationship. Making steel was a complex, capital-intensive affair. The drive to build larger corporate structures to administer existing operations and to direct further investment was inexorable. Workers walked into ever-larger workplaces, establishments that were often but one of many facilities owned by a regional or national firm. Hard competition in the late nineteenth century resulted in numerous mergers and acquisitions, as the weaker players fell prey to the stronger. The spectacular culmination of the industry's consolidation was the formation of the United States Steel Corporation in 1901. The House of Morgan purchased the assets of the already-dominant Carnegie Steel Company and integrated them with those of more than two hundred other companies to create the world's largest corporation, the first American business firm worth more than a billion dollars. At birth, the mammoth manufacturer had approximately a quarter million employees and would add to its roster after 1901. U.S. Steel's scale fueled further growth. In the first ten years after its founding, the corporation's productive capacity almost doubled. Although this behemoth dominated numerous specialized markets from barbed wire to bridge beams, it did not end all competition in steelmaking, by any means. Instead, an oligopoly existed, with Bethlehem, Republic, Colorado Fuel and Iron, and other sizable companies also thriving. But in labor policy as in other central concerns, U.S. Steel set the tone with a demanding approach to exploiting its unorganized employees. Throughout the nation's mills at the turn of the twentieth century, employers' economic wealth, managerial control, political influence, and cultural authority placed their workers in a decidedly inferior position in any conflict of interest.[4]

These transformations had dire implications for working time. The primary bone of contention was the length of the normal day's stint. Before 1892, some plants had functioned on an eight-hour basis. In 1886, Carnegie himself approved this policy: "Works that run day and night should be operated with three sets of men, each working eight hours. The steel-rail mills in this country are generally so run." At the Edgar Thomson Works outside Pittsburgh, superintendent Bill Jones embraced shorter hours as a boon to productivity, declaring that "the men can work harder constantly for eight hours, having sixteen hours to rest." But in a turn of events both foreshadowing the fatal encounter in nearby Homestead five years later and announcing abrupt abandonment of his enlightened position on hours, new owner Andrew Carnegie in 1887 locked out the Thomson employees, brought in large numbers of replacements, and imposed the twelve-hour system. (Further evidence that the great entrepreneur's reversal reflected less rethinking than simple hypocrisy comes from his grand statement in 1886 that "the time approaches, I hope, when it will be impossible, in this country, to work men twelve hours a day continuously.") After recurrent battles and skirmishes over daily hours, the Homestead showdown settled this longstanding controversy. Beginning in 1892, many workers who had customarily put in eight or ten hours a day were forced to accept extended shifts or quit making steel. Within the Carnegie enterprise, the twelve-hour day became standard in major operating divisions, such as blast furnaces, coke ovens, Bessemer converters, and open-hearth departments. With the dominant company setting the pace, the twelve-hour day soon became virtually universal in core operations across the industry as a whole. Jones and Laughlin, for example, discarded the union in 1897 and immediately lengthened hours. A decade later, all manual employees at that firm pulled twelve-hour shifts. A survey covering seventeen thousand steelworkers in Allegheny County, Pennsylvania, in 1907 found only 120 working eight hours. Excluding sheet and tin operatives, three in four American steelworkers put in a twelve-hour day at the end of the first decade of the twentieth century.[5]

For a sizable share of the steelworkers, the twelve-hour routine also entailed an eighty-four-hour week. Seven-day schedules had long been associated with blast-furnace labor and a few other activities in which shutting down the heat source would damage equipment. On the other hand, other metal-producing workers commonly enjoyed Sunday as a day of rest. Not even slaves smelting iron in antebellum Virginia had to work on the Christian Sabbath. In its early years, the Amalgamated Association of Iron and Steel Workers succeeded in confining seven-day scheduling within narrow bounds. However, after 1892, more crews continued without a day's respite even where nonstop work was not a technical necessity. Expensive facilities and equipment were deemed too dear an investment to sit idle; more productive machinery generated stockpiles of half-finished products that had to keep moving toward completion. More than a quarter of Bethlehem Steel's force stayed on the job twelve or more hours a day, seven days a week, as of 1910. At the Pueblo, Colorado, complex of Colorado Fuel and Iron, about a third of the employees worked Sunday as well as every other day of the week. For the industry as a whole at the end of the first decade of the twentieth century, roughly a quarter of production and maintenance employees toiled every day. This sort of schedule was reportedly a major factor in the exodus of the Irish from the mills after 1900. Their positions were easily filled by Slavic immigrants, many of whom preferred another day's earnings over a chance to recover from the previous six days' exertions. Although sleep is a daily, not weekly, need, employees pressed into service every day obviously lost the chance for restorative catch-up slumber on their day off.[6]

Voluntary steps to provide a weekly day of rest did occur. U.S. Steel leaders in 1907 declared their intention to abolish seven-day schedules. Three years later, the company revised its scheduling so as to give all employees a free day every week, though management at the mill level knew they could ignore the policy when market conditions warranted it. Big Steel also promptly reinforced its mixed message on this score in 1911 by isolating and encouraging the departure of William Dickson, a senior vice president and member of the board of directors who had been an outspoken opponent of Sunday work. Dickson found himself ostracized despite his strategy of advocating for a rest day as an aid to workers' efficiency, not as a moral issue. When World War I brought both an abundance of war orders and a tight labor market, the biggest steelmaker reverted to its restless ways. Not all of U.S. Steel's competitors saw fit to follow suit in making any pretense of granting a weekly reprieve. In New York, where legislation requiring a weekly day of rest from work went into effect in 1913, Lackawanna Steel outside Buffalo dodged its legal obligations. The company apparently suffered no punitive consequences for its adamancy.[7]

In Pennsylvania, Sunday work disregarded the strictures of an ancient public policy of Sabbatarianism. The commonwealth had long forbidden employment as a desecration of the Christian Sabbath. In 1779, the legislature called for fines or imprisonment "if any person shall do any kind of work of his or her ordinary calling or follow or do any worldly employment or business whatsoever on the Lord's day." The few exceptions were for such services as delivery of necessities like milk and food, not for the manufacture of iron and steel. Nonetheless, the steel industry held enough power to flout the law. The cowed clergy mounted no real opposition to this blatant infraction. Amid the 1910 strike at Bethlehem Steel, where the seven-day week was among the leading grievances, the Federal Council of Churches could not induce local clergymen to oppose a policy that cut into attendance at their Sunday services.[8]

Beyond the weekly grind lay the annual one. Laborers on blast furnaces were expected to report 365 days a year. Many other mill workers in the nonunion era got only Christmas and Independence Day as holidays. Benefits in the form of paid time off—vacations, sick leave, or personal leave of any kind—were inconceivable at this time. Inevitably, all but the most extraordinarily hardy and lucky men had to take a day or more off, owing to sickness, exhaustion, or other common complications of human life. Most absences were direct or indirect outcomes of this draconian system. Managers generally solved the staffing problem by drafting one of the absentee's coworkers into a double shift to cover for the missing individual. In 1904, the U.S. Bureau of Labor revealed that in steel mills "there is more or less irregular overtime work done by children. The night force may be short a few boys when it begins work, and boys who have just finished day work are often kept a part of the night to take the places of the absent ones." A 1913 federal study of nine plants determined that the typical production worker put in six extra hours a week. None of these establishments gave any premium pay for overtime. This investigation noted that working two consecutive full turns had become a common enough practice to merit its own designation, "doubling back."

This study also underscored the point that for those who worked twelve-hour shifts, an assignment to "double back" was actually an assignment to triple back: there was neither a break between the end of the first shift and the beginning of the second, nor one between the end of the second shift and the beginning of the employee's regular twelve-hour turn on the following day.[9]

The same productivist logic of nonstop utilization of capital resources led to the further expansion of night work, long customary in some departments. In many plants, the night turn ran thirteen or fourteen hours, with a compensatory reduction of one or two hours on the day turn. When Bennie Capozza started work at age thirteen in the nail department in Monessen, Pennsylvania, in 1917, he put in thirteen hours starting at six P.M. The rationale for this difference was that the night shift led to such bad sleep and such diminished quality of life that a week on that shift constituted a lost week in any case. In contrast, a shorter day shift offered a promise of a more leisurely, less exhausted evening. As one western Pennsylvania worker explained his acceptance of a fourteen-hour stint, "When you're on night turn, you're supposed to be dead anyway." This beleaguered man dreamed of the eight-hour day but did not expect to get it either by direct action or legislative enactment because "unionism is dead and legislators are company men."[10]

The capstone of the system of continuous operation was the most sleep-disruptive of all: workers' shifts rotated between days and nights. The frequency of alternation proved to be exceedingly daunting. Hypothetically, rotation could have taken place every month or even less frequently. Hypothetically, workers could have had permanent shift assignments and never rotated at all. Instead, by far the most common arrangement was to flip shifts every week. The only other widely used schedule involved biweekly changes. Like many other regressive changes in the terms of employment, this type of schedule predated the Homestead debacle but became more prevalent in its aftermath. In 1894, a laborer in that community who was afraid to provide his name described in *McClure's Magazine* the pattern that he and the majority of his four thousand coworkers followed—a week of twelve-hour days from six to six, then a week of nights from six to six.[11]

The procedure for making the change from days to nights was especially difficult. Hypothetically, mill management could have accomplished this change by bringing in relief crews to give subordinates who were about to invert their routines a day or more off. In 1912, a committee examining labor relations at U.S. Steel concluded that it was "feasible and practicable to eliminate the long turn." Instead, superintendents continued to demand that day-shift employees report for work early Sunday morning and re-main on duty for twenty-four hours, making the notorious long turn. After twelve hours off on Monday, the employee returned, most often at six P.M., to continue a week of night work. As of 1911, in Allegheny County, Penn-sylvania—where factories in Pittsburgh, Braddock, and other communities produced almost one-sixth of the world's steel—about half the mill workers took the long turn. Rather than going to church on Sunday morning, these workers and countless thousands of their counterparts elsewhere picked up two dinner pails and headed off to their workplaces. When Italian immigrant Eduardo Furio began cleaning up scrap at Pittsburgh Steel in Monessen, his job involved making the long turn every other weekend. This fourteen-year-old boy—who put in thirteen-hour nights and eleven-hour days, seven days a week—went into the plant at seven Sunday morning and emerged at seven the following morning. In 1914, reformer Florence Kelley deplored not only the employment of children on such terms but also the failure of inspectors to pursue their duties at night and on weekends. The realist novel *Out of This Furnace* offered this glimpse into the rigors of the long shift as experienced by a blast-furnace hand: "The second twelve hours were like nothing else in life. Exhaustion slowly numbed his body, mercifully fogged his mind; he ceased to be a human being. . . . At three o'clock in the morning of a long turn a man could die without knowing it." Reflecting on the inability of U.S. Steel leadership to eliminate such impositions as the long turn and the long-hours ordeal as a whole, Louis Brandeis lamented that the company seemed "un-able to form a conception of human needs and human suffering."[12]

One of those human needs, of course, was sleep. As Brandeis implied, employers refused to engage in any substantive discussion of the adequacy of their employees' rest time. Sleep deprivation in the ranks of the mill work-ers remained a nonissue throughout this period to those at the commanding heights of corporate hierarchies. The steelmakers chose to talk around the topic. One gambit consisted of self-serving accounts of their own stamina. In 1886, Andrew Carnegie enlightened the public about the numerous "prob-lems which tax the minds of business men during the dark hours of the night, when their employees are asleep." In 1907, William Field, superintendent of U.S. Steel's plant in South Chicago, boasted that he had put in twenty-four hours in his very first day on the job as a laborer and that he had recently put in seventy-two sleepless hours while troubleshooting a problem in his rail mill. Field claimed that he never went to bed during the week it took him to resolve that problem, catching only occasional naps in a chair. Investigator

John Fitch's 1912 survey of attitudes at the executive level of Big Steel turned up one president of a subsidiary who insisted that he and his colleagues all worked more than twelve hours a day, another who pointed to a vice president who had benefited from many years of long hours on the shop floor, and yet another top manager who contended that "a man is a lot better [off] working those extra four hours than he is loafing." Big Steel chairman Elbert Gary did not hesitate to put forward as exemplary his own long-held habit of toiling long hours. According to one of Gary's admiring biographers, "He could not comprehend why any other man should be unwilling to work as long and as hard as he had." The assertions of these leaders both reframed the issue in public discourse and challenged their subordinates to emulate their uncomplaining attitude.[13]

Industry officials and their apologists also indirectly dealt with the sleeplessness question by acclaiming the hardy masculinity of mill workers and managers alike, implying a lack of need for much sleep. Historian Edward Slavishak insightfully observed that "the Pittsburgh Chamber of Commerce used imagery of tireless workers to present Pittsburgh as a place in which workers had nothing to complain about." An issue of an Illinois Steel newsletter in 1920 offered employees at all levels of the organization, as well as some readers outside it, a bit of blithe poetic guidance that celebrated toil without contemplating sleep deprivation and its toll:

> Work!
> Thank God for the pride of it,
> For the beautiful, conquering tide of it,
> Sweeping the life in its furious flood,
> Thrilling the arteries, cleansing the blood,
> Mastering stupor and dull despair,
> Moving the dreamer to do and dare.
> Oh, what is so good as the urge of it,
> And what is so glad as the surge of it,
> And what is so strong as the summons deep
> Rousing the torpid soul from sleep?

At the same time, former steelworker Whiting Williams stated that "most of the executives now in charge of steel mills have worked up through these hours. They think if they can stand it successfully, everybody else ought to. They are rather proud also to admit that 'Steel is a he-man's game anyhow.

Let those who cannot stand it stay out!'" Williams, an Oberlin College graduate who left a management position to explore briefly the world of manual
labor and who would go on to a long career as a labor-relations consultant,
hastened to puncture this he-man image: "I found no laborer who had ever
known a boss who did not himself go to sleep sometime on the turn, usually
every night for an hour or so." Whereas Williams's comments lay buried in
private correspondence, Clayton Patterson's fulminations appeared in a tract
published in 1921. Patterson left no doubt as to the supposedly untroubled
situation of mill labor: "The steel worker of America is a man's man, a he-
man in every sense of the word and asks favors of no man or men. He is a
square shouldered, thick necked, hairy chested, big muscled human being
that fights and conquers with his own hands the burning heat of the furnace,
the molten metal, the churning machinery, and makes it his slave. The steel
mill is no place for the weakling." Moreover, with many immigrant employees
desperate to save enough money to go back home, management representatives could always publicize instances of employees expressing support for
long hours, seemingly heedless of the consequent sleep loss. Former U.S.
Steel executive William Dickson reacted facetiously to one of Judge Elbert
Gary's assertions that workers preferred the twelve-hour day:

> And tell those poor romantic fools,
> That if these new eight-hour rules,
> Are forced on us, we'll up and strike.
> We can't abide our homes; we'd like
> To live in a stockade; and then
> The judge could, every night, at ten
> Tuck those in bed, who had a right
> To this brief rest; kiss them good night.

Dickson stood apart as a lonely dissident. His colleagues in executive circles
held to a sanguine view of a rugged and striving workforce whose sleep troubles remained invisible, obscured by the celebration of virile mastery of the
challenges and opportunities of hard work.[14]

Inadequate unconscious rest could not, however, remain completely un-
noticed, despite employers' diversionary tactics. As reformers at the turn of
the twentieth century began to examine the singularly onerous temporal
terms of employment in this major industry, widespread sleep deprivation
gradually came to light. One recurrent revelation was the simple shortfall

of sleep. Of course, the long turn represented a raw exercise in sleep denial. One of Charles Walker's open-hearth coworkers, identified only as Fred, offered this vignette of the need to catch up after the biweekly sleepless night forced by this managerial scheduling choice: "Once after a twenty-four-hour shift, I fell asleep in the bathtub, and woke up to find the water cold." Besides the obvious impossibilities posed by the weekly shift reversals, some workers found that their basic routine of long hours left them without enough sleep time. A fourteen-hour night shift, commuting, eating, basic personal care, and various unavoidable domestic and other chores sometimes left men with too little time for recovery. One immigrant laborer estimated that he got as little as three hours slumber when working nights. Charles Walker discovered that many of his coworkers slept only about five hours a day during their weeks on the late turn. Other workers got six hours but found that inadequate. Nobody familiar with steelworkers' lives would assume that every hour spent in bed was an hour fast asleep, as noise and light cut down the amount of unconscious time.[15]

Probably worse than the sheer insufficiency of time for sleeping were the frequent interruptions and other annoyances that rendered sleep less than restful. Very few steelworkers lived alone. The vast majority had to cope with being awakened by the noise made by their cohabitants, especially during the day. Off-duty employees, particularly on the night turn, contended with crying babies, squabbling children, drunken roommates, and other sources of daytime commotion in their households. Based on her immersive research into domestic life in Homestead, Margaret Byington perceptively characterized the rest experienced by men on the night shift as "broken sleep." In Thomas Bell's realist novel, an exhausted laborer tried to sleep during the day in August: "[Djuro] Kracha sprawled on a bed that grew sticky with his sweat, gasped for air and in wakeful sleep kept confusing the buzzing of flies with sounds from the mill. . . . [His baby] Anna, suffering from prickly heat, whimpered endlessly in the kitchen. More stupefied than rested, it was almost with a sense of relief that he heard [his wife] Elena start up the stairs to call him, to tell him it was time to go to work." In 1920, Homestead rail straightener Mike Gessner worked thirteen-hour nights and then returned to a residence filled with six children under the age of eleven, who talked, played, and slammed doors. Resigned to this state of affairs, Gessner allowed that "you can't expect little children to be quiet." Daytime sleeping was inevitably shattered for a sizable share of the steel workforce.[16]

Low pay and a shortage of affordable housing forced many workers to share a bed. (This was an arrangement discrete from the hotbed system, in which workers on different shifts took turns using the same sleeping space and managed to dodge one another, except when one party became bedridden with illness or injury.) Reformer F. Elizabeth Crowell called attention to a number of instances of beds with multiple occupants in her 1908 tour of Pittsburgh's South Side. She deplored use of "a space under a staircase that had been walled off and that was entered from a kitchen. Into this 'hole in the wall' a bed had been squeezed by some hook or crook, and there two boarders stowed their bodies at night." The influx of African Americans into Pittsburgh during World War I combined with discrimination to produce a very acute housing shortage. Fewer than half of black migrants had a bed to themselves. In fact, some workers had to combine simultaneous and sequential (i.e., hotbed) sharing, so that four men used one bed. Bedsharing entailed not only close-range exposure to snoring and coughing but also encounters with restless leg syndrome and additional disturbances.[17]

All forms of residential buildings could be overloaded, further imperiling the daily quest for recuperation. From the 1880s on, the growth of the Sparrows Point complex near Baltimore confined African Americans into a densely settled ghetto. This neighborhood was made up of single-family homes crammed with workers, their families, and large numbers of boarders, averaging about a dozen inhabitants per small house. When black workers poured into Allegheny County during the world war, they crowded into all manner of discommodations. Places of questionable merit for purposes of sleeping for these new arrivals included railroad boxcars, basements, attics, sheds, churches, boathouses, warehouses, and other makeshift refuges. In Gary, Indiana, U.S. Steel built four-room wood-frame houses for employees at its mammoth plant shortly after the turn of the century and found up to sixty people wedged into the space of about 700 square feet. Elsewhere, tenements and other multifamily residences were frequently jammed. By 1890, the South Side of Pittsburgh had eighty-four residents per acre. Many buildings originally constructed to accommodate one family were subdivided to hold two or more. Margaret Byington saw three houses in Homestead that had been splintered into a total of sixty-three tiny rooms, containing over a hundred steelworker families. Cramped "backhouse" additions opening on alleys were tacked onto the rears of tenements. Byington's analysis of the living situation of 239 Slavic immigrant families, mostly Slovaks, found that half resorted to having one or more persons sleeping in the kitchen. In 1911, a Lackawanna, New York, worker was observed sleeping in a pantry underneath a hanging dressed pig. As employment swelled at Tennessee Coal and Iron in Birmingham, Alabama, most steelworker homes had someone sleeping in every room.[18]

Just as dwellings and individual beds were overfilled, sleeping rooms were packed with occupants. Very few unskilled and semiskilled mill operatives could afford a private bedroom. A major federal report on immigrant industrial labor published in 1911 showed that, on average, the foreign-born steelworker shared his sleeping room with two other persons. The highest rate of bedroom overcrowding occurred among Rumanian natives, who slept four to a room. In Youngstown, Ohio, and Granite City, Illinois, almost two-thirds of foreign-born steelworkers shared their bedrooms with at least two roommates, and more than a third shared with three or more other men. In Granite City, the Immigration Commission took note of a case of sixteen Bulgarian laborers occupying a three-room cottage of barely 200 square feet, with all rooms used for sleeping. Across all immigrant groups, the federal investigators learned that a quarter of all households had four or more inhabitants per designated sleeping room. A house-to-house canvass of one Chicago steelworkers' neighborhood in 1911 conservatively estimated that about three-quarters of sleeping rooms were overcrowded. In 1912, steel management nemesis John Fitch told the House of Representatives that he had visited "houses where the beds stood in the bedrooms about as thick as they could be and leave space to walk between them." Fitch also called attention to the wretched condition of the furnishings: "The beds are usually without linen, frequently nothing but an old mattress with a few quilts in a heap on top. I have been in some few places where there was linen, usually unwashed for quite a period of time." He also pointed out that the hotbed system of constant use made it difficult to clean any bedding. Margaret Byington's testimony before the congressional panel amplified on Fitch's revelations. She told the House committee that "where the single men were lodging in large numbers, you had to crawl over the beds." Peter Roberts's 1914 exposé of the living conditions of Pittsburgh immigrant wage earners was accompanied by an evocative photograph by Lewis Hine that carried the caption "Four beds in a Room; Two in a Bed." Roberts learned that some workers slept on the floor. The poor ventilation in many of these spaces, particularly in rooms below ground level and those created by makeshift partitioning of or additions to a structure, reduced further the possibilities for gaining fully restful sleep. The probability that not all inhabitants of a given room had either the same work schedule or the same need for sleep increased the chances for disturbances to the slumber of bedmates and roommates. Thus, the sheer number of sleepers per room was perhaps the parameter of residential congestion that most diminished the quantity and quality of sleep obtained by steel men.[19]

Although overcrowding prevailed in all sorts of living situations, the worst concentrations generally occurred where either a family in a small apartment took in boarders or a landlord ran a larger commercial lodging house. For the most part, the renters in these circumstances were underpaid immigrant bachelor laborers who had no alternative but to squeeze into places inhospitable to good sleeping. The burden of providing room and board or just lodging fell heavily on immigrant women, who often had their own children for whom to care. These women endured an exhausting grind of cooking, cleaning, rousing tenants, and countless other chores. In Pittsburgh in 1900, Slavic rental properties in single-family houses or apartments averaged more than three boarders, and the typical Italian operator put up more than four men. In Johnstown, Pennsylvania, at that time, most east-central European families had boarders cutting into their privacy, typically with several laborers from Cambria Steel packed into a modest house. Byington discovered a Bulgarian boarding boss and his wife and two children who shared their Homestead abode with twenty boarders. This involved fitting twenty-four people into two rooms—a kitchen measuring approximately twelve feet by twenty feet and a bedroom of the same size. During Homestead's frigid winters, families and their lodgers all commonly slept in the kitchen, the only warm place in the building. The federal Immigration Commission found Macedonians, Serbs, and other newcomers sharing cheap iron beds, sometimes not furnished with sheets, in the boardinghouses in one steel community. The commission concluded that a sizable share of all immigrant steel families took in lodgers or boarders, on average adding about five more members to the household.[20]

The environment surrounding workers' domiciles made matters worse. Wooden shanties, shacks, and other flimsy structures were not insulated against outside noises or extremes of heat and cold. Usually, the only way to obtain any cooling ventilation in hot weather was to open a window, letting in the ambient noise pollution. Workers' neighborhoods often fell within earshot of the mill itself, so that the frequent percussions, explosions, locomotive whistles, and other sounds of the workplace carried into the home. The South Chicago immigrant mill workers' neighborhood adjacent to the sprawling Illinois Steel Works, for instance, echoed with "the sound of gigantic processes," according to social scientists Sophonisba Breckinridge and

Edith Abbott. As historian S. J. Kleinberg summarized it, "The iron and steel mills made bad neighbors." The noises of streetcar traffic, children playing in streets and courtyards, and a host of other activities also resounded, particularly in urban centers like Chicago, Cleveland, and Pittsburgh. Members of the working class in low-wage occupations enjoyed few, if any, of the comforts of a community setting that protected one from obstacles to sound sleep.[21]

Steelworkers maneuvered to avoid or minimize sleep deprivation. The primary coping strategy was simply to seize all opportunities to obtain unconscious rest. The strenuous nature of so much mill labor produced exhaustion that facilitated dozing off after a long and demanding shift. Men fell fast asleep on streetcars while commuting home. Steve Kika recalled his weariness after twelve hours making tin plate: "When I got home in the evening all I would do is go to sleep. I couldn't even pick up a piece of bread, my fingers were so racked up." Those who tried to read after supper tended to nod off after only a short time. Elizabeth Crowell's exploration of Pittsburgh in 1908 yielded these scenes: "I saw men who had been working on the night shift lying like fallen logs, huddled together in small, dark, stuffy rooms, sleeping the sleep of exhaustion that follows in the wake of heavy physical labor." Rather than only attempt to recover from their exertions, some workers took anticipatory action. Whiting Williams rested up on the Saturday night before a long turn: "I . . . try to be a sort of slumber camel, and store up sleep for the long desert trip ahead." On the alternate Sunday free from labor, many passed up the rare free day for recreation or socializing to catch up on lost sleep instead. Some who managed to venture out to church lost consciousness during the services.[22]

The pattern of overwork and collapse reduced life for many proletarians to a monotonous cycle of working, eating, and sleeping. One former Homestead employee explained why he quit: "It's a dog's life. Now, those men work twelve hours, and sleep and eat out ten more. You can see a man don't have much time for anything else. You can't see your friends, or do anything but work." John Fitch reported that "many a steel worker has said to me with grim bitterness, 'Home is just the place I eat and sleep. I live in the mills.'" According to Whiting Williams, "Night-turn week you do nothing but work and eat and sleep—and not too much of the last two, either." The sleep purchased in this manner came at a high cost. The loss of family companionship was deeply hurtful. One worker in Johnstown lamented that when his young daughter died, he felt that he had never known the child. It was a miserable irony of steelworkers' existence—congested living without intimacy. Many workers were reduced to little more than breadwinners.[23]

The rhythm of many steel-making operations afforded some workers regular opportunities to take a nap in the mill. Operators dozed in the cabs of their dinky engines during the slack time between trips hauling loads around the plant. Members of blast-furnace gangs and other workers who had to wait for charges of raw materials to be smelted into iron or refined into steel took advantage of down time. One pillar of management's defense of the twelve-hour day was the claim that employees worked only intermittently. Percival Roberts Jr., a member of the board of directors of U.S. Steel, told a congressional panel that blast-furnace men had three hours per shift during which they were free to sleep. However, Roberts hazarded no estimate as to how much time mill employees actually spent asleep at work. Those functioning under the system of eighty-four-hour weeks with weekly rotation welcomed any chance to grab a nap on the job.[24]

Not surprisingly, sleeping on duty occurred most frequently when on the schedules that collided most jarringly with circadian rhythms. Some managers imposed the dreaded double shift, which for twelve-hour employees usually meant a triple shift, on those operatives whose jobs were known to allow time for on-site sleeping, particularly after dark. In general, the night shift provided the most favorable conditions for unchallenged slumber at work. The diary of one open-hearth laborer contained an entry regarding a shift in 1919 on which at four A.M. "sleeping [was] pretty general, including boss." Likewise, on Whiting Williams's crew shoveling out furnace debris, the supervisor set no standard of extraordinary wakefulness: "A large portion of the after-midnight portion, our boss sat with his head in his hands and slept while we kept on working. . . . At five everybody sat down and smoked and dozed." When Williams moved on to a job in the Chicago area, he found the same managerial permissiveness. His foreman went as far as to announce at the start of a turn that everyone would be able to sleep for at least an hour. However, he found that noise made it impossible for him to capitalize on this benefit. Looking back on his experience as a whole, Williams concluded that most foremen slept on night duty. "Every night," he recalled, "at a certain time the word would go around, 'Boss asleep; I work one hour, you go sleep.'" On the long turn, workers made every effort to get in as many naps as possible, especially in the later stages of the marathon.[25]

Sleeping in the mill could be a risky cat-and-mouse game. Not all immediate supervisors were complicit in the illicit practice. One U.S. Steel maintenance worker in Gary tried to sleep whenever possible on the fourteen-hour night turn but understood that getting caught would bring a reprimand. John Wolota's father, a Ukrainian immigrant who went to work in the wire mill in Monessen in 1906, received a disciplinary suspension for falling asleep during shifts of sixteen to eighteen hours. During his time at Lackawanna Steel, Alfred Kiefer suffered a layoff for falling asleep after twenty-one hours on the job. Managers at that facility also punished men caught dozing on the long turn by putting grease in their noses, throwing water on them, and kicking them. Some workers struggled to stay awake out of fear of being fired for losing consciousness. Sleepers also left themselves vulnerable to the horseplay of their fellows. After watching a practical joke played on an exhausted napper, one Homestead worker expressed the unsympathetic view that "a man caught sleeping is a fair mark for any joke." When one of Charles Walker's coworkers overturned the plank on which a machine operator was dozing, the witnesses were amused and the startled victim could only cuss out the prankster. As sociologist Paul Willis put it, "Difficult, uncomfortable or dangerous conditions . . . are understood more through the toughness required to survive them than through the nature of the imposition which asks them to be faced in the first place." Sleeping in a steel mill was a practice that tested the bounds of proper employee performance and manly behavior. In the context of the tough shop-floor culture of the industrializing era, any display of weakness left one open to sanctions, formal or informal.[26]

For many workers, alcohol served as the catalyst for securing more sleep at home. This was especially the case for those stuck in a crowded bachelor boarding house or other noisy residence. The many impediments to getting decent rest, even if exhausted, help explain the mill workers' entrenched habit of stopping at a drinking establishment every day after work. In 1916, Lackawanna, New York, with a population of sixteen thousand, had 138 saloons, including nineteen right outside the Lackawanna Steel plant gates. In southwestern Pennsylvania in 1919, Whiting Williams took part in the ritual then called the "whiskey-beer," along with many of his coworkers, who packed into a saloon near the mill after every shift. According to Williams, "Fully one-half take a 'large small' glass of whiskey followed by a big beer. They down it quickly and walk away straight for the door without the slightest joviality. But all say one or two of these 'shots' helps them get a good day's sleep." Williams believed that the mill laborers drank for "the purpose of making sure that they would get a better day's sleep through all the day-time noises of the children, the streetcars and so on." The use of this depressant also offset the stimulating effects of the coffee that many workers relied upon to get through their shift.[27]

The toll of sleeplessness on the well-being of men in this industry went largely unrecognized by experts in medicine and other human services. Steel management had no interest in identifying any negative effects of its working-time policies. The union that might have addressed this matter was only a marginal presence after the 1890s, a faint shadow. Nonetheless, the accumulation of cases of fatigue-related injuries did attract attention after the turn of the century. In a 1907 article titled "Making Steel and Killing Men," journalist William Hard doubted that exhausted workers at U.S. Steel's South Chicago site heeded warning signs posted along the 130 miles of railroad tracks within this huge complex. Crystal Eastman's thorough assessment of occupational accidents in Allegheny County, Pennsylvania, appearing in 1910 as part of the Pittsburgh Survey, captured a pair of fatal incidents involving young workers:

> Two boys were killed in the Homestead works while they were asleep. Both accidents happened at 1:30 in the morning. One boy was a "pull-up," fifteen years old, who had worked eight hours out of a thirteen-hour night turn. He had a few minutes to rest, and went back of the furnace to lie down in a wheelbarrow. He fell asleep and was struck and killed by the extending arm of a ladle which the crane man was bringing back to the pit. The other was an eighteen-year-old "hook on" who, after seven hours of his working night had passed, climbed into a buggy and went to sleep. The crane man, not knowing this, lowered an iron bucket on the buggy and killed him.

Eastman also discovered one injury, in all probability the tip of the iceberg, attributable to the long turn. A man whose job was to smash up masses of scrap iron failed to dodge one of the chunks of metal sent flying in the process. This worker lost one leg below the knee. "Perhaps," Eastman insinuated, "his twenty-four-hour shift the day before had something to do with his lack of agility." She maintained that long hours reduced alertness, an essential factor in accident avoidance where environmental hazard controls (such as isolation of dangerous equipment or erection of structural barriers) were not in place. John Fitch concurred with Eastman's position, arguing that "inquiry should be made as to whether [an accident victim] had been continuously on duty one hour or twenty-four." His 1912 report publicized an injury incurred by a maintenance worker after forty-eight hours on the job at an Indiana rolling mill. This man's foreman had refused his request for a chance to rest after thirty-six hours on duty. Whiting Williams believed that long hours and especially the long turn fostered a pervasive sense of resignation to frequent accidents. "It is apparently figured all the time that there are going to be mishaps in steel," he inferred, "that you are going to have spills, this mess or that." This comment suggested the wider demoralizing effects of running a business with a worn-down, sleep-denied workforce.[28]

Beyond the anecdotal evidence, astute contemporary observers detected an elevated rate of workplace injuries associated with excessive hours under nonstandard schedules. A 1913 report to the Senate by the Bureau of Labor of the Department of Commerce and Labor used plant-level data from 1905 through 1910 to conclude that accidents happened more frequently on Sundays and during night shifts and long turns. This study revealed that most injuries stemmed from four hazards, the avoidance of which involved alertness and agility—falling and flying objects, falls, explosions and spills of molten metal, and movements of cranes. Sleep-deprived workers lacked the quick reactions needed to dive out of harm's way, as well as the alertness to anticipate and avert danger. The federal investigators learned that night-shift injuries peaked during the early hours on duty, not in the later stages when fatigue might be expected to have grown more intense and cause more mishaps. The investigators successfully solved the paradox: poorly rested night-shift employees arrived at work in a vulnerable injury-prone haze. Managers themselves conceded that one of the reasons for this surprising phenomenon was that "men on the night turn do not secure the same amount and the same quality of restful sleep that those may have who are on the day turn; that consequently they come to the mills for the night turn in a less satisfactory physical condition than the men reporting in the morning, and that this more or less definite lowering of the physical tone would tend during the period when they were getting into the swing of the work to bring about a greater number of accidents." In the same vein, historian S. J. Kleinberg's careful analysis of mortality data from Pittsburgh for the period 1870–1900 indicted long working hours and limited rest time as contributors to the high death rate from traumatic injury among men of working age.[29]

Authorities gained less awareness of the more subtle effects of chronic sleep deprivation. After all, biomedical science did not describe shift work sleep disorder as a discrete disease entity until several decades later. A major study by the U.S. Public Health Service in the mid-1920s detected elevated rates of cardiovascular difficulties among steelworkers but did not connect that pattern to overwork and sleep deprivation. Poor laborers looked on health care as a luxury, preventing medical practitioners from becoming conversant with the full range of their maladies. Steel management held adamantly to its oblivious attitude. In addition, the industry's influence may have extended to manufacturing ignorance through intimidation. Clair Hill, an embittered former steelworker, contended that only fear of employer reprisals induced men to say that they were able to adjust to night work. However, some afflicted workers and the reformers who immersed themselves in their world identified the cardinal symptoms of the work-related ailment that has come to be known as shift work sleep disorder. Indeed, deep and often oppressive drowsiness stood out as emblematic of the plight of steel labor in the long-hours era. The routine spectacle of the parade of weary men dragging themselves to and from the mill struck visitors forcefully and made their somnolence common knowledge to all who cared to notice. Mary Heaton Vorse watched the scene at shift change at a Pittsburgh mill one evening in 1919: "The men going to work walk with their heads down. They lurch as if heavy with sleep." Although like other early witnesses Vorse offered a partial characterization of a disease, her observation captured something essential about this condition as lived experience.[30]

Workers' own understandings of the causes of shift work sleep disorder began with recognition of the hardships of working at night and sleeping during the day. Eduardo Furio maintained that "even if you sleep all day, you work nights you was more sleepy going to work than when you were coming home." Charles Walker's coworker Nick blamed his fourteen-hour nights at the mill for his almost unrelenting sleepiness. "Sometime," Nick told Walker, "maybe one day a month—I feel all right, good, no sleepy." When in 1920 Mary Senior conducted a daytime interview with a night-shift worker in North Braddock, Pennsylvania, she was struck by the fact that the man was constantly yawning. These lay analyses grasped one key etiologic factor in this disorder as well as some of its most obvious signs and symptoms.[31]

Other victims or sympathizers placed most of the blame for this sleep disorder on the rotating schedule, with its exorbitant long turn. John Fitch summarized the rapidly rotating worker's predicament: "A man can't get used to sleeping in the daytime until the week is half over, and then he never gets fully rested, so it is a fagged, sleepy set of men who go to work on Monday mornings. It takes them half that week to recover from the last week's unnatural living." Margaret Byington knew well the effect of this wrenching process: "This alternation of shifts interferes with that regularity of meals and of sleep which physicians tell us is essential to health. When a man sleeps in the daytime alternate weeks, it means continual change and adjustment. . . . The irregularity in hours . . . adds in the long run to the fatigue of the work." These dissidents made clear that they accepted no blithe assumption that workers should somehow be infinitely flexible, adapting to whatever working time demands their employers made. Although they certainly did not label it as such, these steelworkers and their supporters saw this physiological whip-sawing as an early form of flexploitation.[32]

A few lay observers and health-care providers believed that steelworkers' troubled sleep made them more susceptible to certain diseases. "Who can doubt," asked John Fitch, "that toward the end of a twelve-hour shift a man's vital energy is subnormal, and his power of resistance to disease is materially lowered? If this is true, it must be trebly so at the end of the twenty-four-hour shift." In particular, some traced the well-known high prevalence of tuberculosis and pneumonia to overcrowded living and sleeping conditions. One South Chicago physician maintained that overwork and inadequate rest accounted for the excessive levels of alcoholism among steelworkers.[33]

In one steelmaking center in Ohio, sleeping conditions received much of the blame for an outbreak of trachoma. In 1914, Joseph Schereschewsky of the U.S. Public Health Service traced the elevated rates of this eye infection among recent immigrants employed at Youngstown Sheet and Tube Company to lodging arrangements under which as many as twelve workers slept in a room. Schereschewsky observed that the common practice of combining bed-sharing with hotbed rotation meant that four men used the same berth every day. He also expressed dismay at the filthy, contaminated bedding that offered a means of transmitting the chlamydia trachomatis bacterium. Schereschewsky concluded that "the crowded insanitary condition of the lodging houses . . . amply accounts for the spread of the disease."[34]

Many harbored concerns regarding nonspecific deleterious consequences of the intertwined phenomena of overwork and poor sleep. Long and unnatural hours seemed to be associated with premature aging and reduced longevity. One of Fitch's articles carried the provocative title "Old Age at Forty," conveying the widely held belief that overwork broke men down and shortened their careers. One Homestead worker felt that he was becoming too old for his job at age thirty-six. Short of career-ending breakdown, other nebulous states of deterioration were attributed to the interrelated evils of long hours and bad sleep. Critics pointed to chronic fatigue (caused in large measure by insufficient sleep but not always manifesting itself as sleepiness) as a condition stemming from employment in steel. The Bureau of Labor investigation found a consensus of employers and employees alike that "men who work at night are more much more apt to be tired and out of condition when they come to work." The federal officials attributed this state of weariness in part to poor daytime sleep. A chorus of rank-and-file voices agreed. Open-hearth worker George Root denounced his long and ever-changing hours: "A man can't sleep more than three or four hours in the day time and he is tired all the time—chronically tired." With chronic fatigue syndrome not yet legitimated and neurasthenia reserved as a diagnostic category for the enervated well-to-do, there were no scientifically validated labels to affix to this run-down state of health, which overlapped with the similarly not-yet-defined shift work sleep disorder.[35]

These ambiguities did little or nothing to impede activists' ameliorative efforts on the mill workers' behalf. With dogged certitude, a cohort of reformers took up the steel employees' cause at the beginning of the twentieth century and agitated on their behalf for a quarter century. Although scattered critical commentary by muckraking journalists had appeared since the 1890s, the full-scale assault on sleep-destructive terms of employment and living conditions commenced with the Pittsburgh Survey of 1907–8. This monumental investigation of industrial working-class life fell within the pattern of Progressive social empiricism. Devoted to the ideal that knowledge of social ills would generate progress in resolving them and that professional experts like themselves were uniquely qualified to produce authoritative knowledge, a team of investigators descended on Allegheny County to drag into the harsh light of day the neglected human problems spawned by industrialization, urbanization, and immigration. The Russell Sage Foundation funded the venture and appointed Paul Kellogg, editor of *Charities and the Commons*, which became the *Survey* in 1909, to lead it. Kellogg assembled a sizable and formidable team of dedicated reformers to carry out the survey, including Florence Kelley, John Commons, Crystal Eastman, and Lewis Hine. After Kellogg's magazine provided a forum for interim reports on the discoveries in southwestern Pennsylvania, the project produced six volumes of reports from 1909 to 1914. Almost all these publications directly or indirectly contributed to a growing awareness of the unrested predicament of mill labor. Margaret Byington's *Homestead: Households of a Mill Town* and, of course, John Fitch's *The Steel Workers*, both appearing in 1910, focused most intently on this topic and offered the most forceful indictment of the unhealthful situation.[36]

Much stronger on diagnosis than prescription, the Pittsburgh Survey tended to avoid making recommendations for government intervention. It was, after all, a survey—a descriptive exercise in social accounting. Despite the generalizability of the Pittsburgh findings to other industrial centers across the nation, the local scope of the inquiry, combined with the traditional division of social policy–making chores under federalism, precluded any appeal to Washington for transformative action on working time. Recommendations for corrective legislation at the state level were almost as futile at this time in conservative Pennsylvania. In any case, in the wake of the decision in *Lochner v. New York*, there were no prospects for state legislation limiting the total hours or night hours of adult male workers. The ability of the steel firms flagrantly to disregard Pennsylvania's Sabbatarian regulations was still unchallengeable as well. The surveyors did press for both strengthening of municipal housing codes and enforcement of existing regulations to curb overcrowding and unsanitary residential conditions.[37]

Moral suasion as a force to impel private action was the main hope of the Pittsburgh researchers. Revelations of awful working and living conditions would cause industrialists sufficient embarrassment to induce them to remedy major abuses. In John Fitch's formulation, as presented in *The Steel Workers* and elsewhere, the advantages of enlightened management went beyond the virtue of pure benevolence. Fitch suggested that constructive action by management might remove the threat that mistreated workers would eventually rise up in revolt. At the same time, he also promoted private collective action, offering qualified support for unions as bargaining agents.[38]

After the conclusion of his work on the Pittsburgh Survey, John Fitch made the interminable hours in steel his personal crusade. One of John Commons's many protégés at the University of Wisconsin, Fitch followed his mentor's approach of diligent research to mediate class relations. His persistence assured that the overwork question did not disappear from public view. In 1911, he made an extensive tour of inspection of steel communities from Colorado to New York. Finding the same overwork and other inequities he had encountered in Pennsylvania, he wrote a series of articles for the *Survey*. Fitch then enlisted U.S. Steel stockholder Charles Cabot in an effort to get investors to redirect company policy from within. Cabot underwrote the distribution of a polemical pamphlet, *Hours of Labor in the Steel Industry*, to fifteen thousand of the firm's shareholders in 1912. That campaign of corporate subversion went nowhere. At the same time, Fitch agitated for state day-of-rest legislation. He also testified in congressional hearings, contributing to an initiative to require the eight-hour day on work done under federal contracts. Unlike with his agitation for state-level reforms, this restriction on federal contractors did become law in 1912.[39]

Unsolicited advice and unfavorable publicity yielded only modest private reforms. U.S. Steel and its associates in the American Iron and Steel Institute began to promise elimination of the seven-day week shortly after unpleasant evidence of extremely long hours reached the media. After 1910, the biggest steelmaker and some of its competitors did briefly institute a weekly day off work. This move proved short-lived, however, as soon as war orders began to roll in. The exigencies of the wartime labor market, together with federal pressure, forced employers to pay premium wages after eight hours on duty, perversely encouraging sacrifice of more rest time. Meanwhile, the twelve-hour day and the rotational plan remained essentially untouched by corporate paternalism.[40]

The end of the world war did not bring the expected reduction in working time. In 1919, perhaps half of U.S. Steel's force was still working twelve-hour shifts. For the industry as a whole, average hours were longer in 1919 than they had been in 1910. This regressive trend set steel apart as a notorious laggard during a decade when millions of American workers reduced their time on the job, often to eight hours. Renewed determination to deal with this frustrating issue gripped the masses of mill workers in the immediate postwar interval. Launched in the fall of 1918, an infectious organizing drive swept across the industry. A loose consortium of two dozen unions ran the campaign through the National Committee for Organizing Iron and Steel Workers. The committee's staff of more than a hundred organizers found that pervasive pent-up anger and budding hopes for industrial democracy compensated for its clumsy ad hoc structure, its lack of funding, and the abiding ethnic and racial animosities among the workers. The two top-priority items on the insurgent agenda were the right to union representation and shorter hours. As the unionization drive reached a rolling boil, one of Charles Walker's workmates enviously remarked on the conversion of steel operations in Britain, France, Italy, and Germany to the eight-hour system. A meeting of the Amalgamated Association of Iron, Steel and Tin Workers and its twenty-three partners on July 20, 1919, drew up a list of twelve demands. The short list included the eight-hour day, one day of rest a week, double time pay for overtime and for work on Sundays and holidays, and abolition of the twenty-four-hour long turn. The composition of this set of demands left no doubt as to the centrality of working time to the workers' cause. The steel companies refused to negotiate. The organizing committee held a referendum, which found 98 percent of the rank and file in favor of a strike. When Whiting Williams asked his coworkers why they were willing to take this big risk, he learned that "in practically no case was ever any reason given except the twelve hour day and seven day week." Federal mediation failed. A work stoppage became unavoidable. On September 18, the National Committee called an industry-wide strike, declaring that "now is the time to insist upon our rights as human beings."[41]

As threatened, a sizable share of steel employees left their jobs on September 22, 1919. At the peak of the strike in late September, approximately half the production and maintenance workforce of about half a million withheld its labor. At the outset, an Amalgamated Association local in Wheeling, West Virginia, announced that its members were "very jubilant at the prospects of eliminating the much-hated and despised twelve-hour day." But any sense of jubilation among the protesters would be short-lived. Their well-prepared and powerful adversaries unleashed a devastating counterattack. Private weapons at the employers' disposal included a veritable army of security personnel; a sizable complement of loyal managers, skilled native-born workers, and other nonstriking employees; tens of thousands of imported strikebreakers, many of whom were African Americans; and newspapers and other cultural institutions willing to frame the contest as one between communistic barbarism and democratic civilization. Public resources available to protect corporate interests, often at the expense of basic civil liberties, included local and state police and a pliable judiciary. The pro-labor Wilson administration did nothing of real value to aid the strikers' cause. However, Senate hearings during the strike did bring to light numerous abuses and forms of exploitation, including some related to sleep loss. The hearings yielded a committee report on November 3 that condemned the twelve-hour day as "unwise and un-American" and recommended a guaranteed weekly day of rest. This report did nothing to soften the steelmakers' stance. Based on careful preparations, many firms circumvented union picket lines by having strikebreakers live inside the mill, sleeping in makeshift accommodations. Companies in Youngstown, Ohio, housed over a thousand at their facilities in November. Striker John Harbert recalled that in Homestead "a lot of people . . . slept in the mill . . . for quite a good while." The half-organized strikers, few of whom had savings or other assets to fall back on in this emergency, were simply overmatched in this battle with some of the most powerful capitalists in the world. Solidarity faded as production increased throughout the fall and into the winter. On January 8, 1920, the National Committee conceded defeat, having won no concessions at all on working time or any other grievance.[42]

Its unequivocal outcome notwithstanding, the strike served to advance the process of hours reform. Early in the dispute, the Interchurch World Movement of North America, a liberal Protestant offshoot of the Federal Council of Churches, tried to mediate a settlement. Although in the short term this intervention proved fruitless, it did involve a searching inquiry into the plight of labor in steelmaking. The report on this investigation appeared in July 1920 and received ample publicity, both in religious circles and in the mainstream media. The report's authors made no secret of their aim of redirecting the conversation away from the supposed subversive radicalism of the immigrant strikers and back toward substantive issues such as hours. The group's extensive fact-finding had confirmed that about half the industry's workers still took twelve-hour shifts and that half of those employees were on duty every day of the week. By their calculations, correcting Elbert Gary's misrepresentations, fully a hundred thousand men at U.S. Steel had the twelve-hour schedule. The church investigators dismissed management's rationale for the long stint: "The only reasons for the twelve-hour day, furnished by the companies, were found to be without adequate basis in fact." The report characterized the recent organizing drive as a genuine mass movement of the aggrieved, not a Bolshevik conspiracy. The Protestant group condemned the long turn as "inhuman" and noted that in some plants the transitional turn lasted thirty-six hours. These Progressives called on the steel masters to abolish the twelve-hour day and the seven-day week. This carefully documented, morally authoritative brief for reform returned the steelworkers' plight to public attention as an important matter of unfinished business. The extensive press coverage of the Interchurch World Movement report focused intently on its revelations and reminders regarding working time.[43]

A more systematic economic and technical critique arose to complement the moral objections. At its annual meeting in December 1920, the industrial engineers of the Taylor Society, in a joint session with their colleagues in electrical and mechanical engineering, heard an address by economist Horace Drury on the eight-hour system. Drury discussed his recent field research at almost all of the approximately twenty American steelmaking facilities operating on that basis. The author of *Scientific Management* lamented the ways the long-hours regime promoted furtive and flagrant napping and worried about "the lax moral tone which must pervade an industry where sleeping is tolerated." Embracing the intensification of labor that was the hallmark of scientific management, he contended for shorter shifts staffed by wide-awake employees: "From the standpoint of those forward-looking individuals who would study the efficiency of processes and men in the steel industry, with the idea of building constantly a better organization, it would seem that the very first thing to do would be to get the men away from the twelve-hour day. Who would deny but that in the long run a brighter future is bound to lie before an industry which has learned that work is work, and has decided that long dull hours, and half-asleep workmen will no longer do?"

Drury pointed to the experience of other continuous-process industries in reducing hours. Paper manufacturers had advised him that "tired men do not make good workmen." He estimated that converting from two shifts a day to three would only minimally increase labor costs and, in turn, product prices. One of the discussants of Drury's paper, Whiting Williams, who had followed his brief adventure on the labor gang with a management appointment at Hydraulic Pressed Steel, elaborated on the widespread sleeping on duty that he had seen and done. Williams told the engineers that the steel industry was "paying a very great price for the long turn in terms of a lowered quality of their personnel." When the Taylor Society published Drury's presentation in its journal, the editors introduced it by stating that England, France, Germany, Italy, Sweden, Spain, and Belgium had abandoned the twelve-hour day and that no other major industry in America remained so dependent on this schedule.[44]

Portraying the steel industry as backward and a holdout against progress was a naturally attractive trope for Progressives. In early 1921, the relentless Fitch fired another salvo, "The Long Day," appearing in his favored venue, the *Survey*. Fitch presented the twelve-hour day as a stale custom, a vestige of the 1860s when the now-outmoded Bessemer process marked an innovation. Fitch refuted the latest reiteration of management's assertions that schedules of excessive hours were being phased out. He and a team of three other investigators interviewed 365 workers in several major steel centers and found three-fourths still working twelve hours. Fitch admitted that this was an unrepresentative sample but argued that it demonstrated the falseness of management's assurances that the long day was now virtually absent from its operations. An illustration accompanying his piece reminded readers of the patent unreasonability of this archaic system by depicting a long turn in which an employee toiled from seven A.M. on Sunday until seven A.M. on Monday. The same issue of Kellogg's magazine carried S. Adele Shaw's review of many domestic and foreign firms' profitable conversion to the eight-hour plan. Shaw stressed the practical expertise being deployed to tackle this challenge: "Industrial engineers have been at work in steel plants, demonstrating the relation between the shorter shift and efficiency; industrial relations experts have testified as to the effect of the mental attitude of steel-workers on production; economists have established the relation between the long turn and waste; mechanical engineers are taking up the matter of engineering revision with the idea of showing how changes in equipment may cut labor costs in steel; and workers themselves have pointed out waste effort in certain of the tasks to which they have been assigned." Two days after the publication of these critiques, Elbert Gary announced that his company had finally decided to abolish both the long turn and the seven-day week in all its plants.[45]

The twelve-hour shift remained, and the assault against it continued. Damaging blows came from sources that were much harder for industrialists to dismiss than the predictable Progressives. President Warren Harding, a most conservative Republican, began to urge the steelmakers to do away with the exceptionally long day. Meanwhile, with funding from the Cabot Fund, the Federated American Engineering Societies reviewed the situation. Late in 1922, its Committee on Work-Periods in Continuous-Industry brought in a lengthy assessment from an economic and technical perspective. President Harding's foreword for the volume emphatically portrayed long hours as archaic: "The old order of the twelve-hour day must give way to a better and wiser form of organization of the productive forces of the nation, so that proper family life and citizenship may be enjoyed suitably by all of our people." The bulk of this report consisted of a survey of the varied industries in manufacturing, transportation, services, and other sectors, presented by Horace Drury. Drury reiterated his contention that iron and steel could switch to a three-shift approach with little, if any, increase in labor costs. In the other major section of the text, engineer Bradley Stoughton dealt exclusively with iron and steel, where about half the nation's three hundred thousand or so twelve-hour employees worked. Stoughton maintained that ongoing mechanization was eliminating labor while increasing productivity, and this both facilitated compromise on employee earnings for a shorter day and reduced any management fears of a labor shortage to cover a third shift. He pointed to the continued profitability of plants that had made the adjustment to shorter hours. He reported that managers at mills functioning on the eight-hour plan appreciated the fact that their workers were more alert and careful. This sleep-related consideration was bound to impress steelmakers. Workers' compensation legislation, now in place in all the major steel-producing states, meant that blaming employee negligence would no longer spare employers the costs of job injuries. More important, the advance of continuous-process technologies, while destroying old craft skills, had elevated new skills of troubleshooting and timely intervention to prevent or limit mishaps that entailed interruption of the flow of production, lower product quality, or damage to expensive equipment and facilities. Sleepy workers lacked the attentiveness essential to proper exercise of these new diagnostic and problem-solving skills, and the dollars-and-cents consequences were becoming apparent.[46]

The White House continued to press the recalcitrant employers. Secretary of Commerce Herbert Hoover, a recent president of the Federated American Engineering Societies, was the driving force within the Harding administration. Hoover's confidence that private trade associations could resolve problems with only encouragement from federal authorities led him to concentrate on the American Iron and Steel Institute and its leader, Elbert Gary. When steel executives met with Harding and his team to discuss this matter over dinner on May 18, 1922, Secretary Hoover made the case for reform. His presentation set off what he called an "acrid debate," followed by more evasions and delays by the manufacturers. Finally, in mid-1923 Gary and his colleagues grudgingly agreed to discontinue the twelve-hour day and then quickly implemented this change. Besides the obvious factors of presidential influence and public outcry, which contemporary commentators and some historical interpretations have emphasized, it is worth noting that more than acquiescence to external pressures against their own self-interest animated the industrialists. By 1923, foreign and domestic experience had at least strongly suggested the economic feasibility of shorter hours. Moreover, scientific-management experts had marshaled compelling evidence that reduced working time would increase efficiency and productivity. In the same vein, for more than a decade, steel executive William Dickson (who had moved on to Midvale Steel and Ordnance) attacked long hours primarily on economic, not moral, grounds. Workers became the beneficiaries of reform in large part because their employers had become more cognizant of the losses they incurred from having an exhausted, drowsy workforce. In complex capital-intensive activities like making and working steel in the 1920s, management was increasingly aware that inattentive sleep-deprived employees posed a danger to profitability.[47]

The end of the twelve-hour day and the twenty-four-hour long turn across the industry unquestionably improved substantially the chances for steelworkers to obtain more sleep. The situation improved most dramatically for those who went from working twelve hours a day to working eight. For many, however, the reduction was only to ten. Average weekly hours for blast-furnace employees fell from seventy-two in 1922 to sixty in 1924, and hours in open-hearth departments made similar declines. Employees in steel-working operations, such as those making bars and plates, won even shorter hours. By the end of the 1920s, about 60 percent of the force at U.S. Steel's Duquesne Works had an eight-hour day; but some there still put in shifts of ten and a half hours and had frequent overtime. Overall, though hours in iron and steel were still long compared to other manufacturing industries, the amount of time available for rest was sufficient after 1923. With the breakthroughs in contractual negotiations by industrial unions from 1937 on, mill workers finally achieved a standard day of eight hours and a standard week of five days.[48]

The derangement of free time continued to present a serious drawback, however. Most unfortunately, the weekly or biweekly rotational schemes remained in place. Indeed, their elimination or modification was not a strike demand in 1919. Rapid rotation did not become a major object of protest by social or industrial engineers in the final push for reform in the 1920s, though it had figured significantly in the litany of tribulations found by John Fitch and other early explorers. This aspect of class relations apparently never became contested after 1936 when the Steel Workers Organizing Committee emerged as the voice for mill employees on working time and as the committee and its successor, the United Steelworkers of America, reached contractual settlements with most firms in the industry. Instead, it appears that the union quietly accepted rotation as a matter of equity, of equal sharing of the misfortune of fragmented daytime sleeping and diminished social life. Those embracing this misguided sense of fairness failed to take into account the growing scientific evidence of the disruptive effects of too-frequent changes in sleeping time, evidence that had become considerable by the 1940s. By that time, the expansion of corporate labor-relations bureaucracies was exacerbating the predicament by devising more complex designs. In the late 1940s at the Duquesne Works, men on some furnace crews could go twenty weeks without repeating their assigned hours of the day and week. Certainly, in the mid-century heyday of organized labor in this oligopolistic industry, union leaders might have pressed for permanent shift assignments, to be made on the basis of seniority. The only way the rotational schedules in steel seem to have accorded with human capabilities for handling anticircadian instability was in their use of forward rotation in three-shift plans, that is, having workers proceed from day shift to evening and then to graveyard. Rotational schemes have remained a fixture in steel employment up to the present despite their undeniable physiological toll.[49]

In summary, steelworkers and their non-working-class allies won an important victory in 1923 with the abolition of the twelve-hour day, an advance that took with it the odious long turn. Without question, reducing the work week substantially, sometimes by more than twenty hours, constituted a historic breakthrough. This belated reform meant, in a sense, the end of the dark ages in a basic industry. However, the victory was still quite a limited one. The persistence and implicit ratification of highly unnatural forms of rotational scheduling left workers with low-quality sleep and the ramifications thereof.[50]

Chapter 4

Asleep and Awake at the Same Time: Pullman Porters on Call

Twenty-one hours out of twenty-four the porter was expected to pay strict attention to the performance of his many duties, and he was still held responsible for anything wrong that might happen during the three hours given for rest. In other words, he was to be asleep and awake at the same time.

—Ashley Totten, 1949

During hearings held by the U.S. Commission on Industrial Relations in 1915, commission chair Frank Walsh asked railway sleeping-car porter G. H. Sylvester about opportunities to sleep on his overnight run on the Twentieth Century Limited from New York to Chicago. Sylvester was responsible for preparing the berths for a carload of passengers and for meeting their many needs related to getting a full, comfortable night's rest. But he had no such expectations for himself or his coworkers. Sylvester's employer, the Pullman Company, which held a virtual monopoly on the sleep services business on the nation's railroads, chose not to staff its cars in a way that assured porters a reasonable amount of sleep. Sylvester told Walsh that he had to be on duty continuously from the mid-afternoon departure from New York until arrival the following mid-morning in Chicago and that he had a similar schedule for the return trip the next day. The twenty-year Pullman veteran put it succinctly: "You ain't supposed to get any sleep." Porters on the Twentieth Century Limited had no choice but to try to deliver attentive personal service to passengers despite a severe lack of sleep.[1]

Like their counterparts in the steel mills, porters in the late nineteenth and early twentieth centuries endured extremely long hours on the job and unnatural schedules. But one distinguishing characteristic of their situation, compared with work in steel and many other occupations, was the tendency for very frequent departures from what was barely a regular schedule. Another difference was management's expectation that porters try to sleep in public places, mainly in the men's lounges and restrooms of the sleeping cars. This mix of impositions and uncertainties virtually guaranteed injurious denial of rest. To a much greater extent than either steelworkers or long-haul truckers, African American sleeping-car employees and their union leaders came to share and express a keen awareness of the health risks posed by inadequate and disrupted rest. This awareness arose before the fields of sleep science and sleep medicine existed as established areas of expert inquiry. By close observation of their predicament, the Pullman porters, like some other groups of workers with no training in the biomedical sciences, detected patterns of illness prevalent in their occupation that stemmed wholly or partly from sleeplessness. Porters called attention to respiratory infections, heart disease, mental health ailments, and what we would now consider shift work sleep disorder. Moreover, they recognized job stress as an important contributor to sleep-related disorders. This body of lay knowledge accords well with current state-of-the-art scientific findings.[2]

The porters' primary aim was not to add to society's fund of knowledge but rather to exert a measure of control over this threat. The first step, many of them came to believe, was to build a union. Dissatisfaction with unhealthful terms and conditions of employment became one of the driving forces in the founding and early development of the Brotherhood of Sleeping Car Porters (BSCP). This motivation has thus far received relatively little notice from the union's historians. The BSCP not only raised the issue of sleeplessness but also framed it as one of sleep denial. The union's forceful advocacy made clear that, more than any other factor, managers' decisions caused the porters to suffer deficient and unrestful sleep. Mounting a searching critique that helped undermine the Pullman Company's image of benevolent paternalism, the BSCP succeeded in establishing rest as a legitimate health concern. Placing an emphasis on management's role captured the essential conflict of interests at stake and thus set the stage for recurrent struggles over rest time. Although it could not eradicate sleep irregularities and shortfalls, the black brotherhood did make important gains in this area.[3]

As transportation workers, the Pullman porters were situated in a sector of the workforce where sleep degradation had always been acute and endemic. Traditional forms of exploitation in maritime work did much to set the tone. Long before the twentieth century, ocean-going vessels sailed at full speed at all times, with merchant seamen juggling the demands of performing necessary chores all night. The watch system that prevailed during the colonial era, with its complex pattern of short stints of work and rest, constituted the first system of rotating shifts. In this wicked (and fortunately, not prototypical) plan, the mariner's working-time commitment switched back and forth between two schedules on a daily basis, and neither schedule granted more than four consecutive hours off duty. Foreshadowing one railway porters' complaint, at the turn of the eighteenth century sailor Edward Barlow expressed dismay that workers at sea were sent up on dangerous tasks atop masts while "half awake and half asleep." Cramped, noisy, and unsanitary shipboard sleeping spaces also set low standards of comfort. Crews on inland steamboats fared little better. To be sure, vessels put ashore for the night on some highly dangerous river passages. But then roustabouts, many of whom were African Americans, often labored by torchlight hewing timber to replenish the fuel supply. As late as the 1910s, workers loading and unloading ships not infrequently toiled for forty-eight hours or more at a stretch. Perhaps the first widespread use of cocaine by any group of Americans occurred among black longshoremen in New Orleans during the Gilded Age, as a method of coping with extraordinary overwork. Nineteenth-century stagecoach drivers and couriers hauling mail on the Pony Express ran with minimal sleep for extended periods. The transport system as a whole had an altogether miserable heritage of overwork and sleep deprivation.[4]

Employment relations at the Pullman Company developed within the more specific context of the rail industry in the United States. Railroad corporations, perhaps more than any other force, created the time discipline crucial to industrializing American capitalism from the mid-nineteenth century onward. During the formative years of industrialism, the ever-expanding rail system spread an obsession with clock-based management into more recesses of American society than did manufacturing enterprises. The railways led the campaign for nationwide standardization of time in the 1880s. Pullman sleeping-car workers, therefore, toiled in an industry long preoccupied with thoroughgoing control and exploitation of employees' time. It was also an industry in which nonstop operations under unconventional work schedules left train crews sorely deprived of rest. Well before the agitation that culminated in the federal Hours of Service Act, engineers criticized the long and erratically distributed hours that led to treacherous somnolence on the job.[5]

The railroads practiced occupational segregation by race and gender.

Women occupied extremely marginal roles at all times except during world wars. Men of color held a few of the coveted skilled jobs in the earliest days of railroading. But, as Eric Arnesen has demonstrated, after the turn of the twentieth century, ever fewer opportunities remained for black firemen and other train operators. Increasingly, African Americans got only the most menial service work—as waiters in dining cars, as red caps hauling bags in stations, and as porters and maids on sleeping cars.[6]

From its founding in 1867, Pullman hired only African American porters for its sleeping cars. Maid jobs were reserved exclusively for black women, until the firm took on a small number of women of Chinese ancestry on the Pacific coast in the 1920s. Of course, by employing men and women of color in car-service jobs, Pullman aimed to obtain cheap and docile labor. This practice also gave customers a comforting sense of superiority, an integral part of the joy of patronizing a luxury hotel on wheels. George Pullman considered former slaves particularly appropriate candidates for jobs involving innumerable forms of personal service—making beds, shining shoes, fetching drinks in the middle of the night, polishing spittoons, and so on. Growing acceptance of the germ theory of disease added to the porters' multitude of cleaning tasks as their employer issued detailed instructions regarding proper procedures for sweeping, mopping, brushing, and spraying disinfectants. Solicitude for passengers' fears of infection by black vectors also produced a more elaborate set of requirements regarding handling of drinking glasses and other contaminable objects. A half century after it began recruiting freedmen, the company still preferred southern blacks who had experience as house servants or steamboat porters over the growing supply of migrants to the northern rail hubs in which its business was concentrated. Despite the transparency of its strategy of racial segregation and subordination, Pullman offered a comparatively attractive employment alternative for many African Americans. The company employed over ten thousand porters and approximately two hundred maids in 1926. With sizable numbers of black employees also laboring in its manufacturing and maintenance facilities (where the color bar also kept them from skilled and managerial jobs), Pullman was the nation's largest private employer of African Americans in the 1920s.[7]

Racial employment practices fit comfortably within an overarching policy of paternalism. From the construction of Pullman, Illinois, as a model community near Chicago in the late nineteenth century through the development of monetized benefits such as pensions in the early twentieth century, the company stood out as a paragon of welfare capitalism. But within the Pullman family structure, historian William Harris considered blacks "stepchildren at best." African American employees could not climb above the lowest rungs of the job ladder. Yet the firm's leaders believed that they were performing a benefaction by hiring, training, and supervising large numbers of African Americans, who should be grateful for secure positions with a reputable employer.[8]

Prior to unionization, porters endured extraordinarily long hours on duty, compared with the average American wage earner. When George Pullman first employed newly emancipated slaves, he took advantage of individuals who had worked under a system providing scant if any restrictions on the time they were required to work. Accordingly, as with other servants in the late nineteenth century, there were initially no specified limits on sleeping-car workers' hours. Because neither Congress nor the Interstate Commerce Commission considered their work essential to the safety of the traveling public, the Hours of Service Act of 1907 did not cover them. Porters and maids received a fixed monthly salary with no provision for overtime compensation. During Pullman's first half century of operations, service workers put in approximately four hundred hours per month. Such excessively long time on duty, in and of itself, constituted a risk to the employees' health.[9]

During World War I, the U.S. Railroad Administration set a meaningless limit on the service obligation on Pullman cars. Whereas the members of operating crews received government-mandated overtime pay after eight hours on duty, an incentive for management to restrict working time, the porters' stint took the form of miles traveled. Railroad Administration Director General William McAdoo defended the exclusion from eight-hour protection by referring to the peculiar rest benefits that Pullman employees supposedly received. McAdoo made eleven thousand miles per month the basic term of service. Mileage above that level entitled employees to overtime pay, not compensatory time off. Computing workload on a mileage basis left workers unpaid for the substantial amount of preparatory and boarding time served while a train was not moving. The eleven-thousand-mile standard had no practical effect: porters and maids remained at their tasks for up to four hundred hours a month.[10]

Such lengthy working time entailed considerable denial of sleep. Particularly demanding were longer runs on which management scheduled little rest time. G. H. Sylvester's experience on the Twentieth Century Limited was not exceptional in its disregard for the need to sleep on the first night on the rails.

On the five-day, four-night Chicago-to-Oakland run, C. F. Anderson spent the entire first night on duty. Anderson received five hours off on the second and third nights, but no rest allowance on the final night prior to arrival. He maintained that "it frequently happens that we are on duty forty-eight or even sixty hours without rest, and yet we are expected to look fresh and be just as attentive as if we had taken our regular rest, as our all-wise Creator intended." According to Anderson, "Porters have actually fainted and fallen in their cars while enroute, because of the awful strain on the constitution, occasioned by long hours of continuous service without sleep or rest, and insufficient nourishment." Pullman expected porters to rest up on their own time both in advance of their assignment and at its conclusion.[11]

The ready availability of car-service employees for extended hours allowed the company to engage freely in "doubling back" or "doubling out" its employees. In a practice similar to that used in the steel industry, Pullman management, without prior notice, often ordered a porter finishing his scheduled run to immediately make another trip. In some instances, the second trip was followed by a third, or more. The experience of a porter who used the pseudonym A. Sagittarius resembled that of a human pinball, careening around the eastern United States in 1913. Sagittarius's normal schedule called for six consecutive overnight round-trips between New York and Buffalo, followed by two relief days, during which he was supposed to reduce his accumulated sleep deficit. But after completing his twelve-day stint, Pullman sent Sagittarius on this itinerary, spanning an additional eleven days on the road: New York City to West Point, New York; to Washington, D.C.; back to West Point; to Syracuse; to Boston; back to New York City; to Cleveland; to Buffalo; and finally home to New York, only after defying an order to take another car to Boston. After twenty-three days of uninterrupted service, the porter was completely exhausted and "quite sick." Similarly, on one occasion in 1903, C. F. Anderson accumulated enough extra assignments following a Chicago-Oakland round-trip to spend thirty-one consecutive days on the road. Doubling back often entailed irregular working time, which further diminished the quality of sleep by disrupting the porter's daily routine. The practice epitomized this firm's cavalier disregard for porters' well-being.[12]

Pullman's early policy regarding onboard sleep regressed after the turn of the century. Rules set in 1874 granted porters a rest period from ten P.M. to three A.M. But this regulation had loopholes for station stops and did not excuse car-service employees from such nighttime chores as answering passengers' calls for assistance or tending the wood stoves then used to heat cars.

In 1901, Pullman conductor Herbert Holderness marveled at the many, varied tasks performed by the porter and, "above all, the ability to keep wide
awake when he is a living corpse from want of sleep." Holderness estimated
that these men got four or fewer hours sleep per night, not the supposed five.
Nonetheless, in 1903, management cut the nominal sleep allowance by ten
minutes. Eleven years later, the company dropped any pretense of guaranteed
rest time, leaving the matter to the discretion of local officials. For a brief
interval during World War I, porters again enjoyed a right to a specific rest
allowance, albeit only three hours, on orders of the U.S. Railroad Administration. After the war, control over rest time reverted to Pullman management.
The company's governing consideration was that some employee be awake
and vigilant at all times to guard against thieves and other villains. This usually meant a division of responsibility between the porter and the conductor.
During the porter's share of the night watch, he was required to sit on a stool
in the aisle at the end of his car to protect the customers, their belongings,
and the company's property. Even though these stools were so unsteady and
uncomfortable as to merit the nickname "broncos," some porters managed to
catch naps on them. A study of several hundred porters in the 1920s discovered widespread sleep denial, with only 23 percent of those surveyed sleeping
more than three hours per day and 16 percent getting no regular sleep on the
rails. From these findings and other information on opportunities to sleep, it
appears that while on the job in the early twentieth century porters averaged
less than half the normal eight hours of sleep needed by most adults.[13]

Failure to perform one's job—whether rested or sleep-deprived—carried
serious consequences. By the turn of the century, Pullman had a formal system of progressive discipline for dealing with those caught sleeping while
on duty or in proscribed places. Offenders received warnings or, more often,
suspensions that could range from five to thirty days. Undercover inspectors
("spotters") and dissatisfied passengers reported the unconscious transgres-
sors. Company disciplinary proceedings usually resulted in ten- or fifteen-
day suspensions for falling asleep on the job and leaving a car unguarded.
Repeated violations could lead to discharge. Incurring a disciplinary sanction
meant that an employee lost any chance for a sizable annual cash bonus for
good behavior. In 1904, C. F. Anderson protested against strict enforcement
of the rule against sleeping on duty: "Since the Pullman Company seems to
think it the porter's duty to live up to every rule and regulation prescribed for
his guidance, no matter what the circumstances, we feel it is the duty of the
company to be considerate enough to make only such rules as it is possible for

us to live up to without a too serious violation of the laws of health." Managers could, however, exercise paternal indulgence. Robert Lincoln, chairman of Pullman's board of directors and the Great Emancipator's son, assured the Commission on Industrial Relations that the prohibition of sleeping during working time went largely unenforced but left unexplained the disjuncture between policy and practice. General Manager L. S. Hungerford contended that the company carefully distinguished between those who surreptitiously retired to an empty drawing room or berth with a pillow and blanket and those who nodded out while trying to maintain their posts. Hungerford told the federal commissioners that porters who unintentionally fell asleep during the day at their work stations lay in no danger of punishment, but acknowledged that this was a grey area: "There are no instructions that they can go to sleep, but we do know they go to sleep." Under this variant of paternalism, management could assess which employees were doing their best to avoid losing consciousness but could not put enough porters and maids on the cars to ensure that all employees got a reasonable amount of sleep.[14]

In the 1920s, Pullman set up a new system for determining car-service employees' terms of employment. After the world war, the company saw union organizing among porters and maids as a mounting threat. Railroad operating crews had long enjoyed union rights. Pullman conductors had recently formed the Order of Sleeping Car Conductors and successfully bargained with the firm. Some porters had taken steps toward self-organization during the war by joining the Railway Men's International Benevolent Industrial Association, an umbrella group for black rail employees. More ominous still from the company's perspective was the creation in 1920 of the Pullman Porters and Maids Protective Association. In response, management founded and funded a Plan of Employee Representation. As signs of discontent persisted, Pullman entered into formal negotiations on porters' and maids' conditions in early 1924. Porter negotiators raised three sleep-related issues. First, they requested a three-hour rest period on all overnight runs, that is, a return to the wartime benefit. Second, reflecting the workers' assumption that the best way to get a good night's sleep was to sleep in one's own bed, their representatives pressed for guaranteed relief days, a safeguard against doubling out. Third, they proposed calculating service in hours on duty, not miles traveled, with 240 hours to constitute a full month's work. The agreement reached in March 1924 struck a compromise. Management promised a minimum of four full days off duty at home per month. However, it conceded neither a definite rest period on overnight duty nor any monthly limit on hours worked. Pullman executive F. L. Simmons reported that all involved "expressed their happiness in reaching a mutually satisfactory agreement in such a friendly manner."[15]

Discussion of sleep denial at Pullman changed profoundly in 1925. Dissident porters created a real union, the Brotherhood of Sleeping Car Porters. The brotherhood selected as its chief organizer and leader A. Philip Randolph, a well-known New York socialist agitator. Porters saw Randolph's independence from the Pullman Company, that is, his invulnerability to discharge, as an asset that outweighed his lack of experience working in the cars. Along with a brave crew of activists based in numerous rail hubs, Randolph set out to build a national union of black workers. To this end, he and other BSCP leaders drew upon widespread dissatisfaction with sleep-related matters as a recruiting and mobilizing issue in challenging Pullman and its Plan of Employee Representation. According to Ashley Totten, one of the New York porters who first approached Randolph, "harsh working conditions" constituted the main impetus for organization. Totten portrayed the pre-BSCP sleep-denial predicament as one fraught with long hours and brief, uncertain, and frequently interrupted rests. In his view, the company required porters to be "asleep and awake at the same time." He noted that sleep denial had become so much associated with this type of work that car-service employees were commonly called "sleepy porters," rather than sleeping-car porters. The fledgling union raised fresh objections to the negative effects of overwork and sleep denial and offered a variety of corrective measures.[16]

BSCP founders immediately elevated overwork and its ramifications to prominence. In a wide-ranging attack on Pullman paternalism on the eve of the decision to launch an independent union, Randolph excoriated the company's misplaced priority of promoting porters' musical abilities to entertain passengers. This amounted, in Randolph's astringent assessment, to nothing more than a degrading distraction: "So long as they can keep the porters singing, laughing, and dancing, they will be able to underpay and overwork them." Pullman's sponsorship of a band was tolerable only "providing you have also the fundamental things, namely one's manhood, adequate wages, humane hours of work, etc." A notice in the September 1925 issue of Randolph's magazine, the *Messenger*, urged the unorganized to commit themselves to the newly founded brotherhood "if you are tired of being treated like children instead of men; you think you should work shorter hours; you think your wages should be larger; you are tired of doubling back; you are sick of Company tyranny; you have a backbone instead of a wishbone." In the same issue, Randolph observed that "many a porter is doing duty though he has not slept in a bed for two or three days at a time." Inserted in the middle of Randolph's indictment was a cartoon in which a Pullman supervisor chased a porter down the station platform, demanding that he double back. The scowling porter replied, "I've had no sleep for three nights, am nearly starved, and I have to wash up." The union thus seized on onerous conditions as a core concern from the very outset of its recruitment campaign.[17]

An emphasis on health hazards in general and hours in particular aided the BSCP's attempts to enlist outside support during the initial stage of the drive. Influential Americans, black and white, who lent their moral support to the car-service workers commonly cited the need for improvements in this area. Not long after its editor, Oswald Garrison Villard, embraced the brotherhood and decried the porters' lack of sleep, the *Nation* published an article critical of both inadequate sleep allowances and doubling out. The union publicized a resolution introduced into the House of Representatives in April 1926 by Emanuel Celler. The New York congressman called for an investigation of the porters' grievances, including "conditions and hours of labor . . . such as to menace their health and efficiency, allowing them only three hours of sleep a night on the average run." The *Pittsburgh Courier* ran a front-page article on Celler's initiative. In May 1927, the *Messenger* approvingly reported this appraisal by the Methodist Federation for Social Service: "At present provision for sleep is very inadequate; this is one of the most pressing of the porters' problems." Similar expressions of support poured in from civil-rights organizations, unions, African American fraternal and religious groups, and prominent progressive individuals. Elite allies' gestures helped the union-building project gain momentum at a crucial juncture. Winning public expressions of sympathy also helped to create a sense among the porters that they were engaged in a monumental, righteous battle. Thus reinforced, the pro-union side was better able to withstand the pressure exerted by both Pullman and its many allies in the African American community, particularly in the clergy and the press.[18]

Improving conditions took on added urgency because car-service workers expected to remain in their positions for the duration of their employment at Pullman. Neither porters nor maids had any prospects for advancement. The natural promotional step for porters was to sleeping-car conductor, overseeing porters and taking more responsibility in dealing with passengers. However, by company policy whites held all conductors' positions throughout the first half of the twentieth century. Similarly, in unprejudiced circumstances African American maids might have filled openings for porters or even moved into the supervisory position of conductor. In America in the 1920s, such moves were unthinkable. Collective action to ameliorate conditions and quitting work were the only viable options for aggrieved sleeping-car workers.[19]

To build internal solidarity and external support, the BSCP attempted to reframe the discussion of employment at Pullman. Randolph and his comrades countered management's master frame of fatherly benevolence with assertions of the essential rights of Americans, emphasizing restoration of the porters' (but, obviously, not the maids') diminished manhood. In 1925, Randolph contended that "the Pullman porter has no rights which the Pullman Company is bound to respect. So far as his manhood is concerned, in the eyes of the Company, the porter is not supposed to have any." The underlying task at hand was to make the performance of personal services by black men for white customers a worthy role and not a slavish one. To this end, a 1926 organizing appeal asserted that the ideal unionized porter was "manly, courteous and respectful, but never cringing or servile." The BSCP rebels were not prepared to demand that white passengers treat them respectfully, but they were demanding that their employer acknowledge their manhood by granting them some of the same terms and conditions enjoyed by their white male coworkers.[20]

Union proponents challenged porters to summon the courage to fight for better conditions. In its most provocative moments, the BSCP resorted to a version of victim blaming that taunted prospective recruits to alleviate onerous conditions. Very early in the organizing drive, Randolph declared that "the cause is in ourselves that we are overworked" and that the current situation stemmed from a "sheer downright lack of manhood, of stamina, of guts and spirit on the part of the Pullman porters for the last fifty years." "If we are real, red-blooded he-men," he continued, "we should not whine and cry over our lot, for it is within our own power to change it." Proving one's manhood by organizing and collectively remedying conditions of employment would blunt any potential criticism about physical or moral weakness. In much the same vein, St. Louis activist E. J. Bradley urged his fellow porters to pursue their interests more aggressively: "Our people have been taught how to protect other people . . . , but they have never been taught how to live and how to procure some of the better things of life, which can only be realized through a better salary and a longer rest period." The tactic of using masculinist rhetoric to prod unorganized workers to claim their rightful rest became a mainstay of the BSCP's recruitment drive.[21]

The brotherhood shrewdly took advantage of Pullman's failure to meet its own standards. By the 1920s, the company had an extensive safety program. The union portrayed doubling out and other causes of inadequate rest as safety hazards for porters, who took seriously their responsibility for both the well-being of customers and the protection of their employer's assets. In 1929, one dissident denounced the contradiction in forcing a porter to attend a safety meeting after finishing a twenty-four-hour run and before immediately sending him out for another twenty-four run. Randolph used this report to editorialize on the corporate priority of safeguarding profitability over that of preserving human life. He also announced the initiation of a regular feature in the union newspaper, "Scientific Service and Safety Efficiency." The main theme running through this feature was that higher efficiency depended on safety, which, in turn, depended on well-rested workers. An installment in the series in 1930 argued that "efficient service requires . . . that a porter when off duty take the proper rest and sleep in order that he may be able to perform his work when on duty. Of course, in order to get the necessary sleep, porters need the 240 hour work month; and they will only be able to get this through the Brotherhood." At the same time, Randolph drew a sharp conclusion from porters' sleep-denied plight: "Every time the company doubles a porter, it nullifies its preachments about 'safety first,' for an overworked porter is not only less safe to passengers but to himself. It is a well-recognized principle in psychological physiology that fatigue destroys efficiency and lessens productivity." Even as it took an adversarial stance, the union tried to find common ground with management through a mutual interest in operating efficiency. Combining solicitude for the company's business interests with opposition to overwork and sleep denial, the union wove together working-class militancy and a largely middle-class quest for respectability. This nuanced approach confounded Pullman's attempts to characterize the BSCP as simply anti-company. It also undoubtedly appealed to more conservative porters leery of Randolph's well-known radicalism.[22]

The brotherhood initially demanded a 240-hour month, a substantial reduction from the roughly four-hundred-hour obligation. Insistence on racial equality guided this demand for the same monthly working time that the Order of Sleeping Car Conductors had won for its all-white membership. Activists condemned the prevailing system as an inhuman grind that left porters and maids exhausted. They rebutted the company's claim that their work was intermittent, pointing out that they were never truly off duty when a passenger's call bell could summon them at any moment. The union also dealt with

Pullman's contention that its scheduling policy redounded to the porters' advantage by enabling them to remain on duty to the end of long runs, allowing them to collect tips which passengers were much more likely to dispense at their destination. Based not only on a desire for more reasonable hours but also on exasperation with the obsequiousness that dependence on gratuities promoted, the union demanded increased monthly wages and abolition of the tipping system. Indeed, a sizable share of porters' compensation had always come from gratuities, given at the discretion of individual customers. In its formative organizing phase, the BSCP made a special target of the much-resented degrading custom and linked it to harmful sleep loss.[23]

The BSCP condemned doubling back. Its critique stressed the serious, if ill-defined, health effects of the practice. In 1925, Randolph denounced doubling out as "a hardship . . . [that] wears the porter out. It undermines and wrecks his health." He maintained that after the company wore out a man through repeatedly denying recovery time at home, it callously replaced him. The union held that it was giving voice to the longstanding consensus view among porters that doubling caused "a drain on their health." To be sure, not all objections rested on health considerations. The decision of the Pullman board to grant shareholders an extra dividend in 1926 outraged one union supporter. Black journalist George Schuyler commented that investors had not earned their reward by having been "doubled back without rest" and instead "lived a life of luxury and pleasure."[24]

Initially, the union's proposed solutions suggest both a determination to resolve this grievance and the unsettled state of its agenda. On the eve of the founding of the BSCP, Randolph was receptive to monetary terms that would only discourage this practice: "Doubling back . . . must be abolished or paid for at the rate of time and a half or double time." However, two months later, in his new capacity as general organizer, he declared the brotherhood's unequivocal intention to "abolish the doubling-out evil," which was "undermining the porter's health and preventing him from giving efficient service to the public." The following year, a widely distributed BSCP pamphlet repeated the charge that doubling was "detrimental to the health of the porter" but only vaguely demanded an "adjustment" in the practice. The uncertainty in the union's position perhaps reflected an understanding that a certain share of workers welcomed any additional opportunities to earn money, even those entailing protracted wakefulness. Because maids had less layover time than porters because of doubling, Randolph argued that maids and porters were entitled to home layovers of equal duration and frequency.[25]

The brotherhood sought improvements in the minimal onboard rest periods. Conductors enjoyed relatively generous sleeping allowances of up to six hours per night. In 1926, a Chicago-based porter pressed for parity: "Lack of sleep and exposure kill more porters than anything else. A porter should have at least six hours rest period." The BSCP leadership took a less aggressive position, seeking four hours off on the first night of trips and six on all subsequent nights. The union initially conceded the company's right to subtract rest time from credited hours of service. Randolph recommended a way to make longer rests a reality: "Special provision should be made for the sleep of the porters. This could be arranged through a system of relief porters." Although not even the most militant activist demanded the right to a normal night's rest, one early union supporter in Minneapolis did complain that "we are too far from eight hours sleep, eight hours work and eight hours recreation per day."[26]

Growing discontent over rest allowances awakened the company union, which Pullman continued to promote. In the 1929 round of negotiations, porter representatives again called for restoration of the three-hour respite on overnight shifts. In response, the company gave car-service workers on overnight runs "approximately a three hour rest period where the train schedules of station stops and other operating conditions will, in the judgment of the management, permit." Obviously, this provision did not commit management to assign enough porters and maids to its sleeping cars so that each employee could always sleep for three hours. The revised agreement also made a minimal concession on doubling-out, requiring the company to pay an extra twenty-five cents per hour for any labor performed during designated time off. F. L. Simmons, head of the management bargaining team, declared that this contract had achieved "an ideal set of working conditions."[27]

BSCP activists were unimpressed. Not long after the amended contract took effect, the union's newspaper, the *Black Worker*, reported the dismissal of a porter who refused a third consecutive assignment because he was too exhausted. In this instance, management told the worker that he should have been able to catch naps during the day. Sagittarius observed that the agreement did not prevent doubling that still frequently resulted in stints lasting up to eighty hours, with little or no rest along the way. Sagittarius asserted that doubling led to heart disease by forcing "the reluctant blood through a system depleted for want of proper rest and food." He suggested that those who administered this system "may not be burdened with a high sense of human rights."[28]

In the wake of the 1929 settlement, the brotherhood more intently criticized not just the denial of sleep time but also the inadequacies of the resting places assigned to porters and maids. Because management had done nothing to address this matter, the BSCP had an opening to agitate for reform. At this juncture, it might have chosen to pursue a suggestion offered in 1926 by an aggrieved porter. This unnamed worker objected to being sent off "to the smoking room next to the lavatory, there to relax on a narrow lounge seat provided for passengers with a light shining in his face to rob him of such sleep that he might get." Because this predicament "stop[ped] his blood from circulating," the man had urged Randolph to pressure Pullman to build cars with real berths set aside for the porters. However, in spelling out its position on this issue in 1930, the union only sought some definite place to sleep rather than a guaranteed berth.[29]

A similar tentativeness marked the brotherhood's early stance regarding the well-known and widely resented deficiencies in the sleeping spaces used during layovers. While conductors rested in decent hotels and YMCAs, Pullman's black employees held over in distant cities often faced uncertain and degrading alternatives. These included dank basements in apartment buildings, dubious boardinghouses, cheap hotels, and other quarters likely to be overcrowded and seldom quiet. In Salt Lake City, porters had to make do in a decrepit hotel. The inadequate number of beds available in this condemned building forced workers on layover to resort to the "hot bed" system of resting in shifts. In the Jim Crow South, sleeping-car employees sometimes had to sleep on park benches. The segregationist code also dictated that even after all passengers had left the train, which porters still had to "guard" in the rail yard, the African American workers were forbidden to sleep in any berth except the upper berth at the end of the car, which tended to be noisier and hotter than other vacant spaces. With so many other compelling grievances to address and limited leverage, the fledgling brotherhood did not press Pullman management systematically on the question of sleeping places. The union did, however, criticize the inadequacies of company-provided housing at certain locations. Organizer Roy Lancaster called Pullman's arrangements an insult to any self-respecting employee. Lancaster characterized the layover facilities in Washington, D.C., where "sixty men are required to sleep in one ill-ventilated room," as typical. He urged the unorganized to unite to achieve unspecified improvements. In a few communities, women associated with the union through its Ladies' Auxiliary took the initiative to create better lodging for porters and maids.

In Oakland, organizer Morris "Dad" Moore rented out a few rooms above the saloon where the BSCP maintained its office.[30]

The Brotherhood of Sleeping Car Porters barely survived a steep decline from the late 1920s through the depressed early 1930s. But by the mid-thirties, like American organized labor in general, the organization was resurgent. Of perhaps greater importance, New Deal policy promoted union recognition and collective bargaining rights for porters and maids. Amendments in 1934 brought car-service employees within the scope of the Railway Labor Act and set the stage for the BSCP to win a crucial representation election in June 1935. A month later, after a decade of dodging, the Pullman Company was forced to enter into contract negotiations with the brotherhood. Sleep-related issues figured prominently in the bargaining that played out over the next two years.[31]

The BSCP's opening proposals to Pullman in mid-1935 sought to curtail sleep denial and overwork. Although working time had declined somewhat in the decade since the union first raised this issue, it remained onerous. A 1933 union-commissioned study had found that porters were still working 334 hours a month, or almost eighty hours a week. The union reiterated its position that 240 hours, not eleven thousand miles, should constitute a full month's service. The brotherhood demanded that service workers receive a 50 percent premium in pay for any hours beyond 240. Under this proposal, credited time began when a worker arrived at work, not when the train left the station.[32]

As expected, Pullman strongly opposed the 240-hour proposition. After an impasse on the miles-versus-hours question, in the spring of 1937 federal mediator Robert Cole persuaded the management side to accept time as the basis for calculating service. Pullman negotiators held that 270 hours per month constituted a reasonable standard because porters and maids actually performed work only intermittently and had many opportunities to rest during frequent pauses while on duty. Although Tayloristic techniques of time study and other detailed forms of job analysis had been in use in American business since the turn of the century, the company offered not a shred of quantitative evidence on how car-service workers spent their time. Instead, management negotiators relied on nebulous claims that workers had at their disposal "a very considerable amount of idle time." The company wanted to subtract from credited work hours not only a nighttime rest period but a portion of this "idle time" as well.[33]

Management did not convince mediator Cole. In April 1937, he began to lean on Pullman to accede to the same hours limit that conductors had enjoyed for many years. He recommended no deductions from hours worked other than for a designated rest period. Cole apparently gave no credence to the assertions that car-service workers—burdened with myriad tasks, including mental chores such as anticipating passengers' needs and remembering their station stops—had much true leisure on the job. Only with great reluctance did the company give in to the union's demand in the agreement reached in August 1937. Although this left Pullman employees with almost a sixty-hour workweek, it still represented a big advance in the struggle against overwork.[34]

Settling the question of rest allowances proved to be less than straightforward. With most porters lucky to sleep half the normal eight hours per day, one might have expected the BSCP to push for long rest periods. However, the union sought only a three-hour interval off duty. Randolph explained to his adversaries that sleep taken in railroad cars could never be very restful. Accordingly, the crux of the union's demand was that rest time not be deducted from working time unless Pullman provided a relief worker to cover for the resting worker. On April 21, 1937, California union leader C. L. Dellums told Randolph to hold his ground. "Hours of service," Dellums insisted, "should include all time in which the employee is subject to the jurisdiction [of] or responsible to the company." In his view, the company's proposal to maintain the status quo left the porter with "no protection against his sleeping thirty minutes and being requested to get up for a few minutes, retiring again and then being called after another thirty or forty minutes' rest, which would break up his sleep period in such a way that he would get no value from it whatever."[35]

Management rejected the union demand for onboard rest and went on the offensive. Pullman pursued sleep deductions from work time of up to eight hours per day. Negotiator Champ Carry contended that this position reflected a commitment to seeing that employees received a normal amount of sleep. However, the company indicated that the way for men and women in its service to attain this end would not be by taking a guaranteed full night's sleep but rather by supplementing a short sleep period at night with mandatory unpaid rests during the less busy times of the morning and afternoon. The union considered this plan for haphazard daytime napping an inflammatory provocation. BSCP negotiators well knew that porters and maids had even less probability of obtaining much genuine rest during daylight, amidst the increased noise that accompanied daytime operations. Randolph denounced this as an unhealthful stretch-out system, dangerous to both employees and passengers. With both sides dug in, sleep time was one of the last issues resolved. The employer side clung to its demand for daytime rests; the union remained opposed to deductions, especially during the day. The parties finally came to a compromise. The deal forbade the company from making any deduction for periods of less than two hours. On overnight runs, designated sleep periods were to be determined by the length of the run and remained deductible. On night runs of twelve hours or less, for example, porters received a sleep allowance of three hours or less. On runs of forty to forty-eight hours, up to ten hours' rest deduction was permitted. Maids got nightly rests of up to seven hours, enabling Pullman to extract more working hours from these employees. Notwithstanding its acquiescence in the inequitable treatment of the maids (whose numbers had dwindled to around fifty by the late 1930s), the BSCP had wrung a significant concession from Pullman management in confining deductions to the nighttime hours.[36]

The brotherhood sought to eliminate doubling out on overnight runs by requiring that car-service workers receive some time off following every overnight trip. The union won concessions on layovers, but nothing as generous as it wanted. As recommended by Cole, the 1937 agreement guaranteed a day off after every four one-night round-trips. In addition, the parties accepted the mediator's proposal that workers assigned exclusively to overnight runs got a day off after every second round-trip.[37]

The BSCP made a minor advance in upgrading the sleeping spaces available to its members on the trains. Throughout the negotiations, management sternly opposed making any commitment at all regarding the quality or nature of onboard resting places. Nonetheless, porters gained the right to be assigned to space in the dormitory cars used by other rail crew members, as well as retaining the possibility of taking an upper end sleeping-car berth. However, the contract did sanction continued use of the detested smoking-room sofa, which appears to have remained the primary spot to which supervisors sent porters.[38]

Despite its limitations, this contract represented a landmark in the struggle against overwork and sleep denial. In particular, reducing working time by more than one-quarter in one fell swoop stands out as a notable accomplishment. Moreover, the union had advanced significantly the larger process of recasting the issues of sleep denial and overwork as health risks. They had rejected the fanciful proposition that they somehow got a decent amount of rest while located in the midst of passengers' conversations and while subject to numerous interruptions to provide services. The BSCP had undermined the legitimacy of corporate paternalists who overlooked basic human needs while perpetuating the notion that they knew and represented workers' interests better than the workers could themselves. It is not entirely clear why Pullman ended up giving as much ground as it did on these matters in 1937. Company records disclose no belated recognition that reliance on exhausted employees undercut the high quality of service promised to passengers. Instead, the union's gains appear to have resulted from its ability to convey to its adversaries and to the federal mediator that sleep-related concerns held enough priority with its members to justify a strike. In all probability, Pullman also knew full well that membership in the brotherhood had grown by roughly 50 percent over the course of the negotiations. At this juncture, the BSCP also undoubtedly benefited from the surge of momentum generally enjoyed by the labor movement.[39]

The 1937 agreement unquestionably put the BSCP on a firmer footing in dealing with its adversaries. It did not, however, mark the end of union-building activity. Because the contract contained neither a closed-shop provision nor any other guarantee of union security, the organizing process was far from finished. The brotherhood had to win the allegiance of each individual car-service worker, as well as to retain the loyalty of its members. Overwork and sleep issues were vital to the ongoing process of forging solidarity. Demands to reduce hours and improve sleeping arrangements served to mobilize the rank and file. The union incrementally extended the gains in these areas during the 1940s and 1950s.

Agitation for shorter hours sparked recurrent battles. Especially after the Fair Labor Standards Act of 1938 set the forty-hour week as a national benchmark but exempted railroad employees, working time stood out as an essential piece of unfinished business. With no protective legislation in sight, it was left to the BSCP alone to address the long hours of its members. By 1939, rank-and-file porters were seeking the 180-hour month, the rough equivalent of the forty-hour week. Ten years later, the BSCP won a decrease to 205 hours a month, the equivalent of the forty-seven-hour week, just as other rail unions were attaining forty hours. Only in 1965 did the brotherhood finally reach its goal of the forty-hour week.[40]

Health considerations continued to play a significant part in justifying shorter hours. In 1940, Ladies' Auxiliary president Halena Wilson rallied porters' wives with the reminder that it was "essential to the workers' health that they have shorter hours." Two years later, Spokane porters argued that the eight-hour day served to "protect the health and very life of the worker." They maintained that under the current schedules, "the physical resistance of our brothers is being destroyed and will result in a general physical break-down and loss of manpower." In 1944, a group of Los Angeles porters sought shorter hours because lack of rest lowered their resistance to infections, so that they were "continually fighting colds." After 1950, however, the primary factor in the employment situation was not an overwork-induced shortage of car-service workers but rather a growing surplus of them, because of de-clining business. Commercial aviation and the interstate highway system doomed long-distance passenger rail service. Naturally, the union saw re-duced hours primarily as a way to share more widely the shrinking amount of work. In these dire straits, the health rationale receded but did not disap-pear. Federal mediators who in 1963 recommended the forty-hour week ap-pear to have accepted the BSCP's health argument. Their report to President Kennedy warned that porters' "long hours are not only physically wearing but also interfere with if not prevent a normal home life."[41]

The sleep-allowances clause in the 1937 contract was sufficiently ambigu-ous and inconvenient to management to assure that the union would have to monitor carefully its enforcement. Within a month of the implementa-tion of the agreement, the *Black Worker* began to advise the rank and file on how to assert their new rights to rest. In the same vein, in the Southwest the brotherhood distributed twenty-five hundred copies of a booklet that instructed porters and maids how to compute their working time. In this region, the union set up a Time Sheet Committee to scrutinize the often-complicated arrangements governing rest allowances and to teach rank-and-file members how to identify chiseling. Contract enforcement brought absurdities to light. Union investigators in New York City discovered in 1939 that Pullman scheduled porters for a rest period that ended at 6:00 A.M. on an overnight run that reached its destination at 5:05 A.M. Skirmishing over Pullman administrators' errors, intended or unintended, contributed to the ongoing unionization project of forging a collective identity.[42]

Nothing in the bargaining agreement eliminated the inevitably sleep-denying implications of employees' wide-ranging duties. Management still required car-service workers to be at the beck and call of passengers virtu-ally without restriction, unless a coworker was double-covering for a rest-ing worker. As a result, porters released for their sleep periods often suffered interrupted rest. Well before occupational stress received scientific recogni-tion, rank-and-file members in the New York Division identified as highly stressful the combination of unrelenting demands for service, unreasonable scheduling, and difficulties in recovering pay lost for diminished rest time. These lay observers objected to the "mental hazard" that this situation too commonly represented for conscientious porters.[43]

The union generally tried to limit the scope of time commitments, not the scope of duties. Exactions for nighttime rest continued to stir resentment, given that the company's discretionary powers still allowed it to assign co-workers to cover for those on sleep breaks. Porters argued that a doubled workload fully made up for an equal amount of time off to sleep. Interviews with about 150 of his coworkers led T. Walter Jones to conclude that "the men are absolutely and positively against the application of sleep periods." Jones conveyed the sense of injustice that pervaded the ranks: "A watches B's car for four hours and in turn B watches A's car for four hours[,] making a total of eight hours work that the Pullman Company gets without payment." Sharpening this point, Jones observed that making up for deducted time forced porters to make too many trips per month, a workload so demanding that they then had to miss scheduled runs "for health preservation." But these recuperative respites were not sufficient to maintain family life: "Without an exception 150 men stated that their wives and children complain of lack of companionship, especially the wives[,] for the men are so utterly exhausted that rest and sleep are imperative." To address this perverse consequence of attempts to ameliorate conditions, the 1944 BSCP convention voted to seek the abolition of all sleep deductions. With the issue still unresolved three years later, C. S. Wells, president of the Cleveland Division, underscored Jones's concerns that the system of deductions cut deeply into porters' layover time at home, where they could get better rest and spend time with their families. The union made progress on this front but never succeeded in making sleep periods nondeductible.[44]

After 1937, the spatial aspects of rest presented as many challenges as did the temporal ones. Although lodging at distant terminals remained a catch-as-catch-can proposition for many of its members, the BSCP concentrated instead on improving onboard accommodations. The main targets for reform were the smoking-room couch and its replacement on trains lacking a smoking room, the men's washroom couch. In both these spaces, management forced porters to inhabit a contaminated environment, separated from passengers only by a curtain. Compared with sleeping in a berth surrounded by bedding and other cushioned materials, these couches also exacerbated the safety hazards associated with train accidents. Derailments and collisions sent a number of porters flying into peril. Pullman had to compensate C. E. Bigbee, who lost ten weeks' work in 1935 because of neck and back injuries weeks after "being thrown off couch against the washbasin." In 1944, Jacksonville porters complained that inability to sleep because of smoking-room noise and other disturbing factors left workers sleepless for three or four nights in a row, "causing a hardship on the porters' health." However, full trains meant that setting aside berth space for porters would cut revenue.[45]

Pullman held out against eliminating the smoking-room sofa. The company met union protests with promises that it would try to avoid assignment to that space. However, in 1948 the Los Angeles BSCP branch told the national leadership not to trust soft assurances regarding the "unsanitary, noisy, and degrading" smoking room but instead to get a hard guarantee of its elimination written into the next agreement. Only with the contract that took effect in 1953 did the brotherhood put an end to sleeping in the smoking room. In celebrating its thirtieth anniversary in 1955, the BSCP named abolition of the requirement to sleep on the smoker couch as one of its major accomplishments.[46]

Three decades of union advocacy substantially improved sleeping-car workers' chances to obtain an adequate amount of sleep. The African American union's accomplishments stand out as especially remarkable in view of the racism that hindered advances at every turn. The BSCP fought uphill against embedded cultural assumptions about Africans Americans' proper place in the workforce. In the prevailing racial order, black jobs were supposed to be bad jobs, with inferior terms and conditions only natural. The segregated American labor market made porters' positions coveted ones, so that Pullman had a ready supply of job applicants and contingent "extras" to chill assertiveness. Coordinated bargaining or an inclusive alliance of their industry's craft organizations might well have given the BSCP the leverage it lacked to improve rest time and sleeping conditions. But the lily-white rail brotherhoods, with constitutional color bars, rejected any form of industry-wide solidarity that would have encompassed the sleeping-car workers. The economic institutional setting in which the porters' organization had to function was always hostile.[47]

Similarly, this contest arose in an inhospitable context in terms of biomedical knowledge and other health resources. As previously noted, the fields of sleep science and sleep medicine did not exist. The union lacked the wherewithal to retain any medical expertise of its own. As peripatetic workers of African descent, porters and maids had limited access to high-quality professional services during the era of health-care segregation. Hence, the chances of obtaining any authoritative validation of their sleep-related illnesses and injuries were minimal. Moreover, these workers served an employer who rejected any association between sleep loss and its damaging effects. Instead of investigating its employees' litany of complaints, Pullman management promoted victim blaming. Consider this 1929 Valentine's Day message from the company safety director: "Roses are red/Violets are blue/If you get hurt/I'm through with you." Under these daunting circumstances, it is remarkable that the BSCP made as much progress as it did.[48]

Beyond its concrete gains in limiting working time and improving sleeping arrangements, the organized car-service workers made a valuable contribution merely by bringing to light problems that were widespread within its ranks yet underrecognized in the pre-union era. A salient feature of the BSCP's understanding of health, as expressed in its observations on fatigue and sleeplessness, was its holistic perspective, encompassing both physical and mental well-being. This breadth of vision was achieved, in part, by elevating certain kinds of illnesses and injuries while discounting others. Notwithstanding occasional comments on the cardiovascular and respiratory systems, the union's critique lacked corporeal specificity. Yet it appears that porters suffered not only the traumatic injuries resulting from being hurled off the smoker sofa but also high rates of back problems and respiratory disorders that were, in all probability, to an extent attributable to having to try to rest in drafty, uncomfortable places. The numerous ulcers and injuries from falls incurred by sleeping-car workers may well have been, in part, consequences of chronic sleep denial. Perhaps the quest for respectability led porters and their leaders to downplay particular flesh-and-blood complaints in favor of vaguer concerns about strain, stamina, deterioration, and overall health status. Such attempts to bolster a deracinated, disembodied image of the porter could help to defuse whites' fearful stereotype of the carnal black man. This was a conception of health in which the dangerous African American male body all but disappeared. It was a conception, nonetheless, that raised a fundamental challenge to employer paternalism. The brotherhood demolished the notion that Pullman workers could somehow devote boundless energy and time to service without suffering serious consequences.[49]

The BCSP's sleep-denial critique clearly resonated with porters from the outset of the marathon campaign to build a viable organization. Besides its validity on its own terms, the issue of overwork attracted car-service workers to the brotherhood and helped hold their allegiance through difficult times because it tapped into a larger desire for respect in the workplace. The union helped to channel and to reinforce employees' sense that Pullman's refusal to grant them a reasonable amount of rest constituted not only a hazard to their health but an affront to their human dignity. In this case, the porters also reacted to the especially galling and paradoxical indignity that they devoted countless hours to ensuring comfortable and restorative sleep for others but were denied fulfillment of that very need themselves. Because their sleepiness was not deemed dangerous to any second or third parties, they did not become the beneficiaries of any decisive intervention by powerful public or private institutions or by their well-rested customers. Instead, throughout the campaign to address this inequity, the sleeping-car workers had no alternative but to rely almost exclusively on their own resources, marshaled through the first major national labor union created by people of color in America.[50]

Chapter 5

Six Days on the Road:
Long-Haul Truckers Fighting Drowsiness

We're all kind of proud of the fact that we can push these rigs for hours,
with not much sleep, too much coffee, pullin' eighty head of stinkin' cattle
in a pouring rain, and still not complain about it. I mean we have this
Paul Bunyan—or something like that—image about ourselves.
—unidentified owner-operator, ca. 1975

Unlike almost all other American workers, over-the-road truckers stood a sizable chance of dying as an immediate result of falling asleep during the performance of their job. Hauling freight hundreds or thousands of miles, usually alone, presented unique difficulties in balancing sleep and wakefulness, as well as distinctive consequences for the imbalances between them. Long-haul drivers met safety threats primarily through their own efforts, both individual and collective. To a very limited extent, they also benefited from the intervention of the state. Until quite recently neither public nor private parties have tackled the more subtle health consequences of truckers' inadequate sleep.

Tracing the search for sufficient sleep along the highway reveals that the continuities in the drivers' situation have outweighed the changes since the 1920s. From the first days of intercity trucking through the regulated phase of the industry commencing in the late 1930s to the current deregulated period spanning the past three decades, a large share of the long-haul fraternity has been unrelentingly subjected to essentially the same debilitating chronic sleep deprivation. That is to say, the onset of deregulation did not put an end to a golden age of reasonable working time and sleeping conditions. For too many drivers in this wild industry, there never was such a time.

The men engaged in long-haul trucking have always been a different breed of blue-collar worker. A well-defined occupational subculture has forged a strong sense of identity. At the core of that identity is a rugged version of masculinity. By the 1920s, middle-class women were ensconced behind the wheel of millions of automobiles, exploring fresh freedoms and taking on the chores of family chauffeur. In reaction to this incursion into male territory, the work of loading, operating, and maintaining heavy trucks became a refuge. Expanding female participation in the paid workforce in the second half of the twentieth century did almost nothing to alter gender segregation. Between 1975 and 2000, the share of American truckers who were women increased from 1 percent to 4 percent. Moreover, the vast majority of female drivers took positions in local delivery and other short-haul work. On the stage settings offered by highways, rest areas, and truck stops, men who pilot big rigs have been putting on very public performances of masculine endurance for almost a century. When sociologist Kenneth Ouellet drove a semi in California in the 1970s and 1980s, he was struck by the fact that "a driver does most of his work in front of audiences other than owners, managers, and driver co-workers, and by interacting with these audiences he further develops a sense of himself as a trucker and as a man." Ouellet's fellow haulers asserted the value they placed on manly stamina by deriding as weaklings those who worked only twelve hours a day and anyone who took a break after only four hours in the driver's seat. On the open road, stamina meant strength, a cardinal masculine virtue.[1]

The possibilities for independence have always drawn men to this line of work and shaped truckers' sense of themselves. The freedom to engage in manual labor without direct supervision has long been a rare opportunity in modern economies. In the field of freight transportation, the commonplace role of owner-operator epitomizes the pursuit of independence. Unlike airline pilots and railroad engineers, truck drivers have had relatively easy access to an intermediate status at the margins of the working class, nominally as capitalists but in reality sharing most of the pains of their proletarian brethren. With a reckless style born both of dreams of upward mobility and of desperation amid intense competition, owner-operators have long been celebrated (and celebrated themselves) as freewheeling individualists. As far back as the 1940 film *They Drive by Night*, popular culture portrayed the wildcat trucker as the iconic scrappy underdog. Struggling partners, played by Humphrey Bogart and George Raft, overcome sleepiness and countless other obstacles in this rags-to-riches drama. Tellingly, the film featured numerous invidious comparisons between the ambitious and ingenious independents and their lackadaisical counterparts toiling as mere employees. Disregard for such strictures as legal limits on driving hours has taken a disproportionate toll on hard-pressed owner-operators. In turn, a significant rebel contingent within the long-haul business has undermined the attempts by organized labor and government regulators to fashion reasonable safeguards against overwork and thereby assure a healthful amount of sleep for all truckers.[2]

This chapter examines sleep issues before, during, and after the New Deal era. The federal trucking policy established in the 1930s, like many other pieces of the moderate reform program invented to deal with the Great Depression, survived for almost half a century. Despite its intentions, the Interstate Commerce Commission failed to regulate long-haul working time in such a way as to guard effectively against serious sleep deprivation. The commission and the other agencies with a claim to jurisdiction over the terms and conditions of employment in motor transport adopted a weak, essentially spectatorial, stance, permitting large numbers of dangerously sleepy drivers to roam the highways.[3]

The International Brotherhood of Teamsters, later the International Brotherhood of Teamsters, Chauffeurs, Warehousemen and Helpers (IBT), represented local delivery and hauling workers well before the 1930s but became a force in the long-distance segment of the motor freight industry only in the depression decade. In large measure, the brotherhood prospered because of the supportive policies of the Roosevelt administration and thus became, in a sense, another institutional component of the New Deal order. During the formative years of the 1930s and 1940s, the IBT made improvement of long-haul drivers' sleeping situation a focus of its recruitment campaigns. These initiatives and the larger issues of overwork and sleep deprivation in which they were embedded have attracted relatively little attention from historians. Moreover, we have a paucity of historical knowledge of the overall on-the-job experience of a group of workers that has long been a sizable part of the modern American workforce (and today is the nation's third largest occupation). As historians John Jakle and Keith Sculle recently put it, "Trucks and truckers remain in many ways an invisible realm." This chapter adds to our understanding of that realm by illuminating the peculiar sleep problems common among those who have toiled in trucking's long-haul segment.[4]

Hauling freight over great distances in motor trucks emerged as a significant enterprise only after World War I. Military training gave masses of young working-class men new skills to operate trucks and other motor vehicles. Rising demand for American agricultural products during the war led farmers to invest (and indeed overinvest) in hauling equipment available for use far from the farm. Truck production more than doubled between 1918 and 1925, to more than half a million vehicles a year. The war brought to light the sorry state of the nation's roads, prompting a frenzy of highway construction in the twenties. Federal policy sought not just to extend the total mileage in well-paved thoroughfares but to connect modern roads in order to form a national highway network that reached all cities of more than fifty thousand. By 1935, the federal highway system ran for 226,000 miles. Wartime demands for efficient logistics underscored the inflexibility of the dominant rail system. Expanded production of small and light-weight consumer goods amenable to shipment by truck gave the emerging motor carriers more of a foothold against the entrenched railroads. During the age of Prohibition, bootleggers preferred discrete, flexible, and informal methods of transporting their wares. By the end of the 1920s, more than a quarter million men were engaged in intercity hauling on a for-hire basis.[5]

The Great Depression made hauling freight a long-shot gamble for many more players, who found easy access to an embryonic industry. Countless one-man, one-truck outfits joined the scramble to grab any load. In the depths of the depression, over 80 percent of trucking enterprises had only one vehicle. The hypercompetitive market generated brutal levels of overwork. In 1931, IBT president Daniel Tobin lashed out at newcomers: "Today it seems that every man who makes a failure or loses his job . . . gets a truck on the installment plan and starts to haul over the road at any old price he can get. This individual works twenty-four hours a day if necessary." Tobin, who led the union from 1907 until 1952, branded individual owner-operators the "greatest menace" to his brotherhood. Amplifying this animosity a year later, union organizer J. M. Gillespie denounced both loan sharks who convinced the ignorant to buy trucks and those exploitative managers who were demanding that their employees sleep in their vehicles on extended runs. Independent trucker Bert Glupker delivered farm products all over the Midwest in the early 1930s, resting mainly on the seat of his truck when necessary and spending about one night a week in a bed. Glupker made one four-night round-trip journey between western Michigan and Omaha without any sleep, splashing cold water on his face to maintain consciousness. While the IBT initially confined itself to criticism of deepening exploitation, the long-haul business grew miserable for drivers.[6]

The search for order in trucking was of a piece with the New Deal's larger goal of bringing a measure of stability to America's reeling economy. The National Industrial Recovery Act of June 1933 launched a sweeping corporatist scheme for economic self-regulation to eliminate cut-throat competition and increase consumers' purchasing power. Stakeholders assembled under the auspices of the National Recovery Administration (NRA) to negotiate hundreds of industry-specific codes of fair competition, whose scope encompassed employees' wages, hours, and working conditions. In the vast majority of cases, NRA officials successfully promoted the forty-hour week. Only twenty-four of the first 391 codes set the basic work week at more than forty hours. Weekly hours were capped at forty-eight in fifteen of the twenty-four exceptions.[7]

Truckers had reason to expect the same generous treatment from the NRA. The motor-carrier industry met the threat of regulation by hastily organizing a national trade body, the American Trucking Associations (ATA), the plural designation signaling its role as an umbrella group. The International Brotherhood of Teamsters represented the interests of the nation's truck drivers, both organized and unorganized. In November 1933 hearings on the code drafted by the new trade group, Daniel Tobin pressed for the forty-hour week, with premium pay at the rate of time and a half for work beyond eight hours a day and an absolute limit on daily working time of ten hours. Tobin argued that under the ATA proposal to achieve the forty-eight-hour week only as an average over six six-day weeks, an employer could work a driver sixteen hours a day for three weeks and then lay him off for three weeks. The union leader also called attention to the serious accidents caused by exhausted truckers. The contentious deliberations over this code could not even settle on the definition of working time itself: the addition of the recently invented sleeper berth to some heavy trucks raised the question of whether all time spent on board counted as time worked.[8]

In February 1934, the NRA issued its trucking rules. They accommodated to a great extent the ATA's appeals for flexibility in allocating human resources. Truckers could work 108 hours over a two-week period and 192 hours over four weeks. Compensation for any labor performed beyond forty-eight hours in a week was set at time and a third. The code called for further investigation to resolve the controversial matter of the sleeper berth. But on the key issue of working time, national policy was settled to the employers' advantage. This regulatory exercise set a precedent for treating motor freight as an exceptional case, with inferior safeguards for labor.[9]

Implementation of the NRA code proved to be spotty at best. Many firms never bothered to register with the code authority, much less abide by its regulations. Loopholes in the hours provisions and lack of enforcement machinery made the rules virtually meaningless. In the same vein, the labor-management committee appointed to complete the code by resolving the sleeper-berth dispute never came to an agreement. The union side saw insistence on compensation while resting en route as an effective gambit to reach its real objective of the elimination of all onboard beds. Reports that more truck owners were wedging makeshift benches into their trucks stiffened the Teamsters' adamancy. In May 1935, the Supreme Court declared the National Industrial Recovery Act unconstitutional, pulling down the trucking code along with the entire rickety edifice surrounding it.[10]

Even while the NRA occupied center stage, plans were well underway to place the trucking of freight under the authority of the Interstate Commerce Commission (ICC), which had regulated rail shipping since the 1880s. In 1933, President Roosevelt appointed ICC fixture Joseph Eastman to the newly established position of federal coordinator of transportation. Eastman welcomed the presidential assignment to analyze the turbulent situation. With characteristic efficiency and thoroughness, Eastman examined the operating practices of this upstart rival to the railroads. His first report, issued in early 1934, painted an ugly picture of disorganization and cut-throat competition. As expected, his assessment of the melee concluded with a recommendation for federal regulation of interstate hauling. At this juncture, Eastman did not broach the specific topic of limiting driving hours. He did, however, indicate that various interest groups were supporting hours-of-service restrictions and that intervention by Washington might be "necessary for the protection of the public safety and of labor."[11]

Legislative action followed quickly. Congressional deliberations extended to regulation of working time and its implications for rest. In February 1935, Eastman informed a Senate committee that indebtedness commonly reduced owner-operators to sleeping in their vehicles. Another witness before this panel knew of whole families trying to live in trucks. In endorsing federal intervention, the IBT contended that state laws to curb hours on the road had failed dismally. The union's ideas for reform held obvious value with respect to meeting haulers' needs for sleep. It favored limiting daily hours to ten, with time-and-a-half pay after eight hours. It also wanted a minimum requirement of two days off per week. No other interested party came forward to support the Teamsters' plan to cap weekly hours at fifty in this manner. Eastman quietly opposed any legislated eight-hour standard. The ATA objected to federal intervention into any of their affairs. In passing the Motor Carrier Act in August 1935, Congress acted primarily to address the oversupply of small operations by giving the ICC the power to impede entry into the hauling market and to set interstate freight rates. Rather than place any limits on working time, the lawmakers incorporated Eastman's proposal to authorize the Interstate Commerce Commission to explore this issue further and make rules it deemed necessary.[12]

As Joseph Eastman and his associates launched their investigation, they were undoubtedly aware of accumulating criticism of the dangers associated with overwork. For years, the Brotherhood of Teamsters had condemned accidents caused by truckers losing consciousness after too many hours on the road. The union's opposition to onboard sleeping arrangements was also a matter of public record. In 1935, the National Safety Council amplified on the growing crisis of highway safety. At its annual meeting in October, the council's James Baker deplored the growing rate of driver-asleep crashes. Baker's research showed that these accidents occurred far more commonly among operators of trucks than cars and that they most frequently happened between five and seven in the morning after a night or more on duty. His field work identified many futile methods of fighting off sleep, such as using an onion to moisten dry eyelids. Baker and his colleague Oscar Gunderson expanded on this analysis in *Too Long at the Wheel: A Study of Exhaustion and Drowsiness as They Affect Traffic Accidents*. Based on extensive fact finding across the country, Baker and Gunderson concluded that truckers commonly put in extremely long hours, a practice unimpeded by state regulations. In their assessment, "in many states there is no attempt whatever at enforcement" of hours rules. They determined that for-hire driving by owner-operators led to the most flagrant violations. Overextended owner-operators regularly drove up to eighteen hours a day and often were "not out of their clothes for a week at a time." The Safety Council elaborated on the variety of methods truckers used to stay alert. Beyond the conventional reliance on caffeine in all its forms, commercial haulers turned to seemingly anything smelling or tasting foul enough to jar their exhausted senses: "Ammonia as an inhalant is useful, but its effect is not lasting. Some drivers are even reported to resort to sipping urine in emergencies." This investigation also catalogued a range of dubious sleeping places. "If the truck is full," Baker and Gunderson noted, "they must sleep sitting up in the cab; if partly empty, they make a bed on the load in the truck." The study documented frequent accidents involving unconscious truckers. The safety officials portrayed an altogether degraded situation.[13]

Joseph Eastman and his bureaucratic operatives added further evidence of wholesale disarray. In late 1936, he and his colleagues published their distillation of the data collected by the transportation coordinator's office over the past three years. In 1933, about a third of highway truckers were at work more than sixty hours a week. Fewer than one in four trucking firms set any limit on their employees' daily hours. Among those that did so, about a quarter let men work from sixteen to twenty hours a day. Indeed, a five-state field survey in the winter of 1933–34 discovered that a quarter of stints behind the wheel lasted at least sixteen hours. One independent hauler made regular sixty-hour nonstop runs delivering tires from Akron, Ohio, to Sioux City, Iowa.[14]

This report confirmed that sleep deprivation was rampant among over-the-road haulers, particularly among owner-operators. One Michigan-based solo operator, fearing repossession of his truck, got fourteen hours sleep in five days while bouncing around the Midwest. Another midwesterner received only twenty-two hours' sleep one week, while completing seven round-trip routes that consumed 137 hours on duty—driving, loading, or unloading his vehicle. An employee of a small upstate New York company endured a three-week stretch that averaged over ninety hours a week. During that time, this driver had one sixty-two-hour sleepless stretch of continuous driving and another fifty-hour turn. Contributing to difficulties getting real rest were rude facilities, such as bunks or bare concrete floors in noisy warehouses and, of course, the front seat of the truck.[15]

The consequences of this behavior were always bad. After several days of short sleep, drivers experienced hallucinations. They manifested plain evidence of shift work sleep disorder, nodding off during conversations or while carrying out routine tasks in terminals. One wasted man had the good fortune to have a helper accompanying him to advise him when he tried to park his rig in the middle of the road. Others had worse luck. Numerous collisions involving sleepy haulers came to light. In one case, the operator ignored a crossing signal and drove into the side of a moving train. Making the obvious links, the federal investigators maintained that "long hours of continuous road service are a factor in producing drivers' fatigue and [are] a cause of truck accidents." However, Eastman hastened to warn that if the rationale for intervention was transparent, the severity of proper restrictions was not. His agency's review of existing public and private rules had discerned no consensus on safe limits on working time. "Interfering with closer agreement," Eastman explained, "is a lack of knowledge of the governing facts, principal

among which is the number of hours which drivers can work without becoming over-fatigued." The slippery nature of fatigue and an unwillingness
to validate subjective self-reports of feelings of tiredness and drowsiness already had the regulators in a quandary. For an unreconstructed Progressive
bureaucrat like Joseph Eastman, a stalwart member of the commission since
1919, the absence of authoritative empirical guidance presented a steep obstacle to state action.[16]

To elicit further information, the ICC's skeletal motor-carrier staff managed to hold a series of hearings in eight cities around the country in late 1936
and early 1937. The core question of daily working time remained a bone of
contention throughout the sessions. Most business owners pressed for the
same sixteen-hour day granted to the railroads. A witness from the Wisconsin Public Service Commission, which regulated truckers' hours, delivered
quantitative evidence that accident rates went up for drivers who had spent
more than eight hours behind the wheel. However, this witness also testified
that his state allowed commercial operators to drive up to twelve hours a day.
Teamsters' top leadership advocated the eight-hour day as an absolute limit,
not as a threshold for imposition of premium pay. Daniel Tobin contended
that long-hauling overtime "destroys body and soul." Offering a glimpse of
the ramifications of overwork, one Chicago IBT leader told the ICC that
members who drove excessive hours drew disproportionate amounts of
union sick benefits. The union position on daily restrictions translated into
support for a forty-eight-hour weekly limit. William Green, president of the
American Federation of Labor, of which the IBT was an affiliate, went much
further. Green weighed in with a recommendation that the ICC impose the
thirty-hour week, both to share the available work and to minimize its safety
hazards. This radical proposal from a top labor leader elicited a perfunctory,
noncommittal reply from Commissioner Eastman. The management side
united behind the sixty-hour ceiling, though owners of refrigerated equipment pleaded that they could not turn a profit unless their men drove at least
seventy-two hours.[17]

The sleeper cab remained controversial. Technology was advancing rapidly, and cabs with integrated soft beds and some protection from noise and
light were becoming more widely available. In general, employers and the
self-employed who testified in the ICC hearings praised the devices as an
upgrade from crude makeshifts consisting of little more than a couple planks
and a blanket. However, a manager at Keeshin Motor Express Company, a
prominent Chicago firm, testified that his company refused to use sleeper

units, based not only on interviews with employees but also on the haggard appearance of men who had spent time in them. The very recent emergence and ongoing evolution of these onboard facilities precluded the accumulation of relevant statistical data on their performance with regard to accident rates. Not surprisingly, the cacophonous exchange of anecdotal claims and counterclaims fell far short of producing the enlightenment sought by a studious, cautious administrator like Eastman.[18]

In July 1937, R. W. Snow, who had overseen the hearings, submitted his findings to his superiors at the commission. Snow had learned that it was not unusual for drivers to work up to sixteen hours every day, regularly putting in over one hundred hours per week on the road. Some truckers drove eighteen to twenty hours a day for extended periods of time. The examiner recommended curtailing freight haulers' hours to twelve hours a day driving and fifteen hours of total service. He proposed that on-duty hours be limited to sixty per week and seventy per eight-day period. Recognizing that the numbing rhythms of highway driving induced drowsiness and inattentiveness and, in turn, that this condition could be alleviated by periodic breaks that might allow brief naps, he suggested giving drivers a right to make an unlimited number of stops for short rests. Snow refused to ban the sleeper cab, instead recommending that the ICC set minimum standards of comfort such as requiring installation of mattresses, bedding, and adequate ventilation.[19]

Snow offered his proposal on hours as a tentative solution only. He urged a definitive federal study of the critical nexus between operator fatigue and highway accidents, which might well lead to revised regulations. In addition, he expressed the ambitious hope that such an investigation might "produce useful data on the general subject of the physical and mental well-being of drivers." The reception of Snow's report was predictably mixed. The Teamsters judged the weekly and eight-day hours limits to be far too lax. Their written objections argued that an employer could have a man drive seventy hours in five consecutive days, a patently unsafe demand. In testimony during further hearings in October 1937, the union continued to press for the eight-hour day. The ATA, on the other hand, applauded Snow's plan and took a wait-and-see attitude regarding any possible shortcomings.[20]

On December 29, 1937, the ICC finally came out with its Hours of Service Regulations, covering for-hire motor carriers, to take effect on July 1, 1938. In its introductory comments, the commission posed the problem as one of "excessive fatigue." In doing so, it trivialized lesser conditions and signaled an acceptance of impaired drivers. The regulators explicitly endorsed

keeping drowsy truck drivers on the public roadways: "For the present purpose it suffices to distinguish between mere drowsiness and fatigue of a type
which requires considerable periods of rest for full recovery and which, if
carried too far, results in exhaustion." From this dismissive perspective,
drowsiness resulted mainly from the monotony of driving and was easily re-
versible by short rest breaks. The ICC agreed with its hearings officer that
there was "little definite evidence in existence showing the effect of fatigue
on accidents." Moreover, in the commission's assessment, "The data which
are available do not show definitely that the average qualified driver becomes an unsafe driver at the end of any specific period within the limits
recommended by the proposed regulations." The old Progressive approach
to reform was that policy had to rest on a sound factual basis: experts found
facts, spoke truth to power, and power listened. Standing Progressivism on
its head, the regulators in this instance manufactured ignorance by failing to
heed the Wisconsin revelations that accident frequency rose after eight hours
driving and then let supposed ignorance be their guide. Having thus cleared
the way for minimal protection, the commission promulgated rules embody-
ing R. W. Snow's recommendations. That is to say, it approved the fifteen-
hour day (with the limitation that the fifteen hours on duty could involve
only twelve hours of driving, loading, or other activity), the sixty-hour week,
and the use of sleeper cabs with amenities. Drivers were required to fill out a
log accounting for their time; their employers were obliged to send these to
the ICC's Bureau of Motor Carriers. That bureau could fine violators willing
to self-report infractions.[21]

The December 1937 announcement promised that "these preliminary
regulations will be revised if and when information is obtained which shows
need therefor." On January 7, 1938, Eastman replied to William Green's de-
nunciation of the "patent unreasonableness of a fifteen-hour day" with the
conciliatory characterization of this measure as "a first step." Further evidence that the commission viewed the hours determination as tentative came
when the regulators immediately began tinkering with their provisions. In
July 1938, the ICC limited consecutive hours of driving to ten and mandated
an uninterrupted eight-hour rest period before resumption of driving, with
the exception that in sleeper cabs the eight hours off could be broken into two
segments. The ten-on-eight-off stipulation opened the possibility of spending
sixteen hours behind the wheel within a twenty-four-hour span. It also con-
tradicted the commissioners' earlier position, declared in the introduction to
its original regulations, that approximately eight hours sleep was necessary

and that "allowance must be made for eating, dressing, getting to and from work, and the enjoyment of the ordinary recreations." Seven months later, the agency further relaxed its strictures by granting the right to drive for twelve straight hours if extreme weather or other emergency conditions detained a driver. Both revisions underscored the commission's devotion to promoting flexibility to accommodate shippers and the carriers who served them. When the second revision went into effect in March 1939 and was extended the following year by identical rules governing private carriers (i.e., companies that operated trucks solely to move their own products or supplies), few observers of this industry would have predicted this set of standards would remain in place, essentially unchanged, for more than six decades.[22]

Potentially the best opportunity to repair this set of weak regulations arrived with the renewed search for relevant information on long-haul hazards. In promulgating its original decision on hours in December 1937, the ICC announced its intention to have "a comprehensive, scientific study made of the causes and effects of driver fatigue." The commission tantalizingly suggested that "this study may well be broadened to include the possible long-run effect of driving on the health of the driver." Teamsters leaders, not government technocrats, were the primary advocates of deeper investigation of these questions. The union resented Snow's refusal to consider expert testimony on the strain of driving. It had demanded that the ICC postpone any hours regulations until after a comprehensive scientific inquiry produced additional knowledge on the meaning of overwork. By appearing to accede, albeit belatedly, to the union demand, the regulators were bringing biomedical authority to bear on unresolved questions at a formative stage of policy development, before inertia set in and too many parties became inured to the primitive system. By June 1938, Eastman had arranged for the U.S. Public Health Service (PHS) to investigate immediately. Early in the planning process, Surgeon General Thomas Parran cautioned that "no assurance can be given at this time that such a study will yield data sufficiently definite to support the Interstate Commerce Commission in establishing [limits on] hours of work." Bureaucratic hedging also found its way into the formal interagency agreement, which acknowledged that the subject of fatigue was "a difficult one" for which research methods were "not well standardized." On the still-more-nebulous subject of the general health effects of trucking, the PHS promised only to make such observations "as time and funds may allow." These preemptive exonerative moves provided fair warning as to the limits of scientific authority for shaping policy.[23]

The Public Health Service researchers, led by veteran industrial physician R. R. Sayers, failed to focus on the critical issue of the relationship of working time to road accidents and other ill effects of long-haul labor. Rather than adopt an approach that sought to correlate accidents or other errors in performance with time on duty, the PHS drifted off into exploration of fatigue. Fatigue was a notoriously intractable entity in any circumstance, and certainly not one amenable to elucidation in as limited a project as this. Nonetheless, the investigators set out on a chimerical quest to find practical, objective methods of measuring fatigue in drivers. However worthy this effort may have been for elucidating the miserable condition of overworked truckers, it did not help solve the immediate problem of setting a safe limit on driving time.[24]

Beginning in the summer of 1938, the public health staff conducted preliminary assessments on U.S. Marine truck and tank drivers at a newly constructed laboratory in Quantico, Virginia. Here began the attempts to find the "ideal test to reveal the fitness of the driver for the responsibility of his task." Trials using electroencephalography and blood tests of lactic acid levels proved unhelpful to that end. The main study, conducted in late 1938 and early 1939, put almost nine hundred commercial drivers in Nashville, Chicago, and Baltimore through a battery of tests of reaction time, steadiness, and other psychomotor indicators of fatigue immediately after they had completed drives of varying durations. With the variables under consideration shifting away from physiology and toward psychology, the medically oriented PHS brought in leading academic psychologists as consultants to assist in interpreting its findings. R. R. Sayers considered the results of this investigation "encouraging as to the possibility of developing satisfactory fatigue tests to meet the specific needs of the motor transport and other industries." The thrust of the inquiry swerved away from protection of workers and the traveling public and toward aiding employers in identifying fatigue-resistant job applicants.[25]

In 1941, the Public Health Service published *Fatigue and Hours of Service of Interstate Truck Drivers*. The researchers unsurprisingly found that those who had driven longer displayed slower reactions, less steadiness, and additional signs of fatigue. Other tests also confirmed the expected relationships without shedding much light on practical implications. For example, men who finished their driving and then were allowed to sleep for varying lengths of time (usually six hours or more) before taking psychomotor tests performed better than their unrested counterparts. But because the PHS did not correlate length of sleep with performance, it could give no guidelines for roadworthiness, conceding that its data were "not sufficient to answer the question of how many hours of sleep are required for complete recovery." In a brush with a more fruitful approach, the PHS's review of the literature took note of driver-asleep accident data gathered by other sources. It took cognizance of the National Safety Council's compilation of state data, which showed that eight in ten truck drivers had failed to obtain "normal sleep" (which the council defined as seven to eight hours) during the twenty-four hours prior to their accident. From ICC statistics based on truckers' self-reports, the authors had learned that a disproportionate share of events involved men on duty more than ten hours. But the public health team did not pursue this line of inquiry by mining or expanding upon this body of material. Such an exercise might well have yielded estimates as to what combinations of working time and sleeping time tended to be more associated with accidents. Even though epidemiology has always been the fundamental science of public health, the PHS did not take that route.[26]

The Public Health Service document attempted to profile driving fatigue as a discrete disease entity. To that end, it reiterated its findings regarding the several etiological factors involved and the performance symptoms of this syndrome. However, on the bottom-line question of regulatory standards, the PHS was perfectly vague: "While many factors in the daily lives and backgrounds of the drivers may operate to reduce efficiency and, therefore, the safety of driving, long hours of driving have been shown to be important in this respect. Furthermore, hours of driving are controllable while many of the other factors are not readily controlled except by the drivers themselves. It would therefore appear that a reasonable limitation of the hours of service would, at the very least, reduce the number of drivers on the road with very low functional efficiency." Nowhere did the federal health authority give its operational definition of "reasonable limitation" in terms of daily or weekly hours. In his foreword to the report, Joseph Eastman politely commended the PHS for its work. He had valid reasons to appreciate the solid substantiating evidence that driving performance declined after long hours at that task. Moreover, this exercise in political science gave the ICC the protective cover of having diligently sponsored a study by reputable investigators. However, its irresolute outcome left the commission about where it had started in terms of improving regulations promulgated as a provisional first step.[27]

For the International Brotherhood of Teamsters, the frustrations of dealing with the ICC were counterbalanced by breakthroughs in recruiting long-haul workers and representing their sleep-related interests in direct relations with employers. In the 1930s, the union greatly extended its reach beyond its traditional bastion in local delivery work in urban areas. Conventional union priorities of improving wages, hours, and working conditions spoke compellingly to highway drivers. In making its appeal to the unorganized, the IBT began with its bedrock objective of the eight-hour day, a standard for which it and its predecessors had fought since the turn of the century. Milk-wagon drivers and other delivery workers had suffered through sixteen-hour days, seven days a week before the union transformed their terms of employment. By the 1930s, the avowed policy of the organization called for the five-day week wherever possible. One recurrent theme in the rationale for reduced hours was the health benefit of recuperative time off. Although the union used the two-edged instrument of premium pay to discourage long hours, it also sought to apply this penalty to hours worked under nonstandard schedules, attacking night and Sunday work. In a 1936 review of its leading accomplishments, President Tobin proudly listed the virtual elimination of Sunday labor, with a compensatory weekly day off for the few still required to drive that day. By the time it seriously entered the long-haul field, the brotherhood could boast of many agreements limiting its members working time to between forty and forty-eight hours. Teamsters recruiters also consistently raised the issue of the poor quality of accommodations and arrangements for men trying to rest away from home. Organizers never passed up a chance to blast non-union employers who forced men to sleep in their vehicles.[28]

Initially, the main organizing frontiers for long-haul drivers were the upper Midwest and the Pacific Coast. Recruitment drives radiating from Minneapolis, Seattle, San Francisco, and other metropolitan sites rapidly brought masses of overworked truckers into the IBT fold. When it expanded its campaign among over-the-road employees in 1937, the North Central District Drivers Council distributed a questionnaire to gauge interest in various issues. One battery of questions inquired as to how long one could safely drive, how much rest was necessary between runs, and whether it was possible to rest properly in a sleeper cab. The survey determined that many non-union drivers put in seventy to ninety hours a week. Young James Hoffa began signing up car haulers out of Detroit in 1936. His nighttime roadside recruitment methods required lucky timing: "Some of those fellows would light a cigarette and sleep until it burned down and awakened them by scorching their fingers. They had to rest, but they couldn't rest long. We would catch them

in the short interval." Because many of these candidates for union membership slept with tire irons in their hands, Hoffa learned to explain himself
very quickly when awakening a dozing driver. Amid a contagious upsurge
in working-class collectivism that saw American union membership triple
between 1933 and 1941, rank-and-file drivers sometimes did not wait for IBT
staff to approach them. In 1939, one group of Kansas long-haulers who were
regularly on duty sixteen hours a day every day of the week went looking
for representation. At the same time, a disgruntled trucker in New England,
weary of working as much as thirty hours at a stretch and sleeping on the
side of the road, contacted union officials in search of assistance. Despite stiff
resistance from employers, the Teamsters quickly made deep inroads into the
long-haul workforce.[29]

Union leaders wasted no time winning collective bargaining agreements,
often with the aid of work stoppages. As expected, the main thrust in its on-
slaught on overwork was the limitation of hours by the standard device of
punitive premium pay. A 1935 California contract imposed an overtime differential, but only after sixty hours. Two years laters, the California Highway
Drivers Council reduced the overtime threshold by five hours. Numerous
IBT affiliates won deals with better terms than those. Led by Trotskyist radi-
cals, highway drivers operating out of St. Paul, Minnesota, won the forty-
eight-hour week in 1935, with overtime compensated at time and a third.
Over-the-road bargaining units in Spokane, Peoria, Oklahoma City, Philadelphia, and elsewhere gained the forty-eight-hour week around the same
time. New overtime penalties raised a hurdle to using workers on Sundays.
The standard contract in the upper Midwest called for double time on Sunday and required that anyone forced to report that day receive some other
day off. This agreement also introduced a requirement that anyone who had
to lay over away from home more than forty hours be paid for their time.
This move enabled employees to do more sleeping in their own beds by giving their employers a plain incentive to schedule carefully enough to avoid
unduly stranding them at a distant terminal. One Boston contract promised
nine hours off to rest between stints. Particularly where long-haul groups
were being folded into existing locals dominated by short-haul employees,
the Teamsters simply extended their regular terms for working time across
their expanding jurisdiction.[30]

The earliest long-haul agreements addressed grievances over sleeping
conditions. The main object of contention remained the sleeper cab. The 1935
agreement covering Local 120 in St. Paul required two drivers on all trips over

350 miles and mandated that both receive wages for all time spent in the truck, forcing companies to pay men while they endured low-quality sleep jostling about in an onboard compartment. This provision aimed primarily to deter, not compensate, sleeping in the vehicle. In the contract renewal completed in 1936, Local 120 confirmed that management was responsible for overnight lodging of employees running rigs without sleeper cabs. The following year this branch and a neighboring one in Minneapolis went as far as to place any use of sleeper cabs at the driver's option. In its most daring advance, union councils in some places on the West Coast and in the northern Midwest prevailed on management to reorganize fundamentally its operations to eradicate the sleepers and to curtail all forms of layover. The IBT insisted on the creation of a relay system in which drivers ventured only a half day or day's journey to a transfer point, at which their load passed to another trucker. The first driver then either returned home that day or spent one night in a company bunk before heading back. By August 1937, Daniel Tobin was already boasting of progress in the battle against onboard slumber: "The slogan 'sleep in a bed in a room and not in the cab of a truck' is having a good effect as many of the new agreements sent here for approval have among the many articles one providing that drivers shall not be required to sleep in the cabs of their trucks." Not all advances could be as sweeping, however. The freight haulers in Toledo achieved mixed results when Local 20 managed to get employers to guarantee acceptable lodging but allowed time spent resting in a sleeper to be treated as time off duty. By 1939, the union had centralized midwestern negotiations to such an extent that the same terms covered over three hundred thousand drivers in a dozen states. This contract pledged signatories to furnish "comfortable, sanitary lodging" to employees on the road. Within the span of a few years, the Teamsters thus eradicated the practices of slumping in the driver's seat or reclining in the trailer atop a pile of freight.[31]

Many of these gains did not last long. The Second World War prompted either the temporary suspension or permanent reversal of basic terms and conditions of trucking employment related to sleep. In the intense mobilization after Pearl Harbor, patriotic fervor swept away safeguards against overwork. "Labor must work faster, harder and longer," declared the *International Teamster* in September 1942. In its next issue, the Teamsters' newspaper denounced slackers and reminded readers that the nation's armed forces, which included fifty thousand IBT members, were "not worrying about their hours." The paper claimed that the American soldier "sleeps only when there is nothing else to do." In mid-1943, its article by General Raphael Chavin, in charge of supply operations in Tunisia, described military truckers working themselves into exhaustion delivering ammunition under heavy enemy fire. Along the same lines, employers and government officials pushed drivers as hard as possible. Federal labor-relations administrators took a dim view of overtime premium rates that might act to curb long hours. Whereas some American workers gained higher wages for taking late shifts during the war, the U.S. Trucking Commission denied that type of wage differential for truckers with the argument that motor-freight workers' stints came up so erratically that no regular shifts existed. The result of this confluence of forces was a reversion to onerous versions of nonstandard scheduling and nonscheduling, with many drivers on duty at all times of day and night up to ninety hours a week without overtime compensation. By late 1943, however, the IBT was beginning to think about its counterattack, as it contemplated both bargaining for reduced working time after the war and wiping out the chiseling independent operators who so often drove the longest hours.[32]

The drivers' union accepted longer hours and other regressive changes in support of the war effort but rejected one progressive change that would have served the patriotic cause. Loads went undelivered in Detroit while Local 299 fought to keep African Americans out of long-haul jobs. From late 1942 to the end of the war, this large IBT branch blocked a series of attempts by experienced black truckers to break into highway driving. In stark contrast to its lack of creativity in devising ways to bring down the color bar, Jimmy Hoffa and other union leaders came up with an endless stream of pretexts for avoiding integration of this relatively well-paid work. Throughout the course of its maneuverings, the lynchpin in the racist defense remained the contention that overnight runs necessitated sharing of sleeping quarters, either in trucking terminal bunkhouses or, most intimately, in the vehicle itself in two-man operations. Local and national Teamsters' officials fended off the demands of the federal Committee on Fair Employment Practices with vague promises, pleas for patience, veiled threats that integration would breed rank-and-file violence, and other evasive tactics. At one fruitless meeting with representatives of the antidiscrimination committee in August 1944, President Tobin blamed the problem on civil-rights agitators, opportunistic employers, and his own backward rank and file, before he "let slip that personally he would not want to sleep with a Negro." The federal investigation produced not only ample evidence of racial exclusion by the Detroit local but also signs of a tacit understanding that African American men could not receive assignments to long-haul jobs anywhere in the upper Midwest, even where they were IBT members in good standing. The white-controlled brotherhood deemed only lower-paid and more arduous work on loading docks, in warehouses, and in some local hauling appropriate for black men. Segregation of that sort did not venture into the dangerous realm of "social equality," as Hoffa put it. The ineffectual fair-employment agents accomplished nothing in Detroit.[33]

As organizing drives, bargaining sessions, work stoppages, and other employee-employer clashes sharpened class divisions in the 1930s and 1940s, the intermediate and often contradictory location of owner-operators became more contested. The Teamsters' ambivalent stance went back to its founding days. Many of its original bases of support in short-distance work—among men handling milk delivery, laundry routes, and so on— involved driver-salesmen or others who owned a single vehicle or a few pieces of equipment and did not simply toil for a wage but often worked on commission. The indeterminate status of these individuals continually discomforted IBT leaders, who appreciated that these small operators had often come out of the wage-earning ranks, that they might soon return to straightforward employee status, and that they did not control anything like a fleet of trucks. Yet the organization barred truck owners from voting on contracts and strikes involving journeymen and generally viewed owners with distrust. The notorious untamed individualism of this fraction of the driving force, particularly that of farmers and others from rural areas (a group well explained in Shane Hamilton's work), always posed an obstacle to collectivism. Amid the late 1930s organizing surge, union leaders fielded numerous complaints about uncontrollable owner-operators who ran endlessly, undercutting union standards. At the same time, Teamsters negotiators fought to win shorter hours, overtime pay, and decent sleeping places for owner-drivers who did choose to join the organization. Behind the scenes, General Counsel Joseph Padway in 1941 damned employers who sponsored "the so-called independent contractor or business man" in order to have their cargo delivered without having to make contributions for Social Security, workers' compensation, or other mandatory assessments under employment laws. Padway advised IBT leaders that they had no choice other than to continue to try to regulate the hours and conditions of owner-operators by organizing them. In his view, the dire alternative was a system of individual cut-rate deal making that would "emasculate, and even render useless, the benefits of collective bargaining." During the especially hectic conditions of the war, the union ripped one-man outfits that occasionally hired a union member to drive and then kept him on the road for excessive hours. Under any circumstances, the relationship between the Teamsters and these micro-capitalists was destined to be tense and fraught with boundary skirmishes.[34]

In the postwar years, relations between the independents and organized labor deteriorated further. Benefits under the GI Bill financed driver training and offered loans for the purchase of equipment on a large scale, flooding the motor-freight market with neophyte owner-operators. The military added fuel to the fire by selling off surplus vehicles at low prices. In 1950, about 130,000 self-employed truckers roamed the highways, including a large fraction who had borrowed heavily to start their businesses. The threat to union standards became more critical, and the IBT's ambivalence turned to unalloyed opposition. Nobody hated the undisciplined individualists more than Jimmy Hoffa. Hoffa's apprenticeship with Farrell Dobbs in Minnesota had not made him a Trotskyist but had confirmed a hard-line, class-against-class worldview. In a 1945 meeting of the union's largest long-haul representative, the Central States Drivers Council, Hoffa, as chairman of the committee on owner-operators, declared that "we are all of the same opinion, and that is to get rid of them." Particularly galling to the IBT was the spread of trip leasing, a stratagem largely motivated by fleet owners' desire to circumvent union rules. Under this system, the owner-operator leased his equipment to a company for a short term, often only one trip, and then drove the trip himself, usually on a cut-rate contingent form of compensation that made it necessary to dispense with sleep and ignore the ICC hours limits. Throughout the decade following the war, the Teamsters wrestled with this growing threat to its members' livelihoods. The union secured restrictive clauses in long-haul contracts but then had the ongoing test of trying to enforce them. The brotherhood pressed the ICC to close the loophole that authorized loose leasing schemes. A marathon series of reform petitions, hearings, administrative decisions, and court challenges involving the commission ensued, along with legislative reform proposals, and resulting congressional deliberations. At one point deep in these proceedings, IBT attorney Edward Wheeler, perhaps only slightly hyperbolically, told a Senate committee that "the conditions which currently prevail in the trucking industry are virtually identical with the conditions which prevailed prior to 1935." When this process concluded in the late 1950s, gaping regulatory loopholes remained, especially for those drivers carrying agricultural commodities exempt from federal control. The Transportation Association of America in 1963 estimated that two-thirds of trucked freight moved outside ICC jurisdiction. When owner-operators could not escape regulations through a loophole, many simply took their chances and defied the rules.[35]

The overwork and lost-sleep ramifications of this situation were profound. Of course, the primary victims were the owner-drivers themselves, taking too many trips in order to keep up the payments on their equipment. In the late 1940s, Ralph Nordan, an owner-operator based in Baltimore, often drove without a rest break for twenty-four hours and not infrequently fitted in only two or three hours' sleep between hauls. Several weeks of that routine would leave Nordan "dead tired and fighting to keep awake while driving." In his estimation, the outlaw fraction of the trucking fraternity constituted 90 percent of the traffic through Baltimore, and southern routes were filled with wildcatters violating federal regulations. Joseph Ricci operated out of Providence after completing military service in 1945. Foundering in his attempts to pay for his rig, Ricci once made a restless thirty-six-hour run from Nashville to New York City. "If I was to get twenty hours of sleep per week," he recalled, "I would be lucky." Like Nordan's solo enterprise, Ricci's business went under after a few years. Indebted owner-operators often gained little from IBT protection. One independent who was supposedly bound by union-negotiated rules told the ICC in 1949 that he constantly violated the hours-of-service code, kept fake logs to conceal this behavior, and once drove for twenty-nine hours. Another admitted that he had performed for thirty-six hours straight and often slept only two or three hours a day. Journalist Harry Henderson rode with "the strangest, most nomadic and independent workers America has" in 1951. His account, titled "Hell on Wheels," described an owner-operator who drove twenty-three hours, napped for one hour, and then resumed hauling. Henderson observed his subject nodding out at the wheel, his vehicle weaving around the road. The forty-one-hour round-trip between New York and Florida was interrupted by only two hours of slumber. Richard Vickery relied on No-Doz to persevere at his one-man business sixteen to eighteen hours a day, seven days a week. Vickery saw a direct link between financial worries and sleep deprivation: "I never took more than a few hours' rest before I was afraid of being stranded without anything to live on or money to meet my equipment payments." His colleague Clarence Voss endured the same long days and nights to quell similar fears. His roadside naps sometimes did not suffice: "To meet my payments, I drove until I was so exhausted that I fell asleep at the wheel." With assignments of widely varied and unpredictable duration, the irregularity of working time exacerbated the sheer number of hours on duty.[36]

The presence of tens of thousands of essentially uncontrolled operators contributed to the insidious undermining of union terms and conditions. This was the period when IBT leaders had seemingly triumphed in the long struggle to standardize the treatment of long-haul workers, capped by the signing of the first National Master Freight Agreement (NMFA) in 1964. Yet national standards did not apply to hours. Neither the original master agreement nor its periodic renewals contained a clause on working time, a thunderous silence. Supplemental agreements at subnational levels do not appear to have set any limits. The union thus abandoned its traditional role as advocate for and guarantor of the eight-hour day. To be sure, long-haul contracts did set mandatory off-duty periods of at least ten hours between work stints, a marked improvement over the ICC requirement of eight hours respite. The 1961 deal covering highway drivers in eleven western states called for double pay on the seventh day in a row worked. But for the most part, the IBT leadership slid into a tacit policy of accommodating both signatory employers beset by non-union rivals and that share of union members willing to subject themselves to long hours for the high wages that constituted the union's primary accomplishment. Concessions were deemed preferable to losing the loads, and the union jobs they made possible, to the outlaw elements. By the 1960s, Teamsters' executives directly took up the question of overwork only when excoriating load-stealing "gypsies." After a truck driver killed T. Ashton Thompson, a member of the House of Representatives from Louisiana, in 1965, President Hoffa condemned the "gypsy operator who had been on the highway twenty-one consecutive hours." He also used that occasion to remind Congress of an accident in which "a gypsy driver . . . sound asleep at the wheel" killed a family of five. However, too many politically powerful shippers valued the flexibility and savings made possible by a shady minority of owner-operators for Congress to take remedial action.[37]

Union negotiators performed better in guaranteeing decent accommodations on the road. Consistent with the larger goal of bringing truckers a middle-class standard of living, long-haul agreements pressed for the amenities that were becoming commonplace in affluent postwar America. Some non-union drivers had to share a hotel bed or sleep on their truck seats. Others stayed in rude dormitories attached to truck stops. Truckers damned the discommodations at Tooley's Truck Stop in Jersey City in 1954: "The atmosphere around this bunkhouse was not very conducive to rest. In fact, the bunkhouse represents just a large flophouse and the facilities are very primitive." In contrast, Teamsters' collective agreements specified that drivers never share a bed and were to have no more than one roommate. Contracts called for clean linens, hot water, good ventilation, and ready access to restrooms. By 1964, IBT freight haulers in New York enjoyed a right to air-conditioned rooms. On the other hand, consistent with the general stance of American unions throughout the nation's history, opposition to technological innovation faded away as more comfortable sleeper cabs became available. In fact, by the early 1960s the union praised sleepers as marvels of modern efficiency. Here again, owner-operators had functioned as an entering wedge. Too many independents essentially lived in their sleeper-equipped vehicles and thereby provided superior flexibility. In this bind, the union understandably shifted its efforts to upgrading the sleeper cabs. The 1967 NMFA forced employers to have air conditioners in all new sleeper units. At the same time, unionists sought other changes in trucking equipment that would prevent unwanted outcomes of sleepiness. After failing the previous year to obtain federal legislation mandating installation of anti-drowsy-driving technology in all new American trucks, the union pursued this objective in the 1967 round of bargaining. However, management rejected demands for installation of the "Drive-Alert" device, which would automatically stop a vehicle whenever both the driver's foot left the accelerator and his hands left the steering wheel. Overall, after 1960 the IBT fell back to a defensive stance but still delivered a higher probability of reasonable sleep for its constituents.[38]

Widespread use of amphetamines added a potent ingredient to the recipe for sleep deprivation by mid-century. Many truckers had wartime exposure to these stimulants both through military service and on the home front. Trucking safety expert O. D. Shipley, in a 1955 article in *Drivers' Digest*, traced the current problem to issuance of amphetamines to troops serving in the Second World War and the Korean War. Shipley criticized the armed services for failing to advise drug recipients of their health hazards. Throughout the postwar era, ample supplies of Benzedrine, Dexedrine, and Methedrine flowed to trucking employees and the self-employed. Drivers received drugs that had been diverted from legitimate pharmaceutical distribution channels. Legal output in 1958 stood at around 3.5 billion tablets and almost tripled from that level by the end of the 1960s. Smugglers brought in loads of stimulants from Mexico. Underground manufacturers churned out large quantities, often counterfeit versions of brand-name products. Truckers effortlessly obtained bennies and the other wakefulness aids at truck stops, gas stations, brothels, and other roadside establishments. A 1959 journalistic assessment of the situation characterized amphetamine bootlegging as "an established, profitable, nationwide business" with long-haulers as important customers. Drivers also acquired prescriptions from medical practitioners for treatment of real or feigned depression or weight problems. Some employees received pills or capsules directly from their employers. For the majority of over-the-road truckers who had to function alone, Benzedrine and the other amphetamines became a fictive partner. Exhausted truckers commonly joked that "Bennie" would be taking over for the driving. By the time furniture movers Earl Green and Carl Montgomery wrote the popular country song "Six Days on the Road" in 1963, truckers (and many others) had no trouble interpreting these lyrics: "I'm taking little white pills/And my eyes are open wide."[39]

Competitive pressures made owner-drivers most likely to abuse amphetamine. Harry Henderson's 1951 article explained that owner-operators' thirty-six-hour turns at the wheel were "only accomplished with the help of Benzedrine, which nearly all drivers carry." Struggling independent Thomas Kirby admitted to relying on bootleg stimulants for sleepless coast-to-coast jaunts in the early 1950s. At the same time, fellow owner-operator Ovila LeClair bought black-market drugs to sustain a routine of twenty-hour days. Owner-operators soon realized that no one retaining them bothered to inquire about how much sleep they had gotten prior to being entrusted with their cargo. A 1964 exposé by the trade journal *Fleet Owner* contended that amphetamine consumption was concentrated among solo operators, with the heaviest use on the fresh-produce runs between Florida and New York. The owner-drivers' greater probability of getting unrefreshing sleep in inhospitable places also led them to fight drowsiness with stimulants. Moreover, the independents were more likely to turn to barbiturates to combat the effects of amphetamine, setting in motion a vicious cycle of grogginess and extended wakefulness. All these factors created a downward spiral of drug dependence and sleep loss. In 1971, veteran independent steel hauler James Leavitt illuminated for Senate investigators a "brutalizing lifestyle" of forty-to-fifty-hour sleepless stints, irregular schedules, and brief attempts to recover in "flea-bag hotels and filthy, oppressive terminals." Leavitt maintained that stimulant use was rampant and accepted as a necessary fact of life in these trying circumstances.[40]

After 1950, mass consumption of illicit stimulants by operators of heavy trucks alarmed some public officials. In response, the U.S. Food and Drug Administration (FDA) mounted the first undercover investigation in its history. The FDA conducted large-scale inquiries in 1954 and 1959, using agents posing as truckers, with significant investigatory work done in the interim as well. These field studies disclosed the scope, structures, and practices of a thriving drug culture, one by no means limited to wildcatting small businessmen along a few routes. The 1959 phase of the project located over two hundred truck stops selling "road aspirin," one of many common terms in the drivers' parlance for these ubiquitous substances. One inspector, posing as a trainee, rode along with a driver on a forty-four-hundred-mile round-trip between the Southwest and Maine. The veteran trucker-instructor did all but four hundred miles of the driving, propped up by Benzedrine and coffee. He slept a total of about six hours over the course of more than five days on the road. When the driver turned around the following day to start another cross-country run, the frightened FDA agent refused to accompany him. Discussions with a driver who had made numerous wildcat trips between Texas and California brought to light his habit of procuring stimulants in Arizona and Mexico, so that he could complete frenetic journeys during which he drove at speeds up to ninety miles an hour despite occasional hallucinations. The experience of undercover agent Robert Palmer, who shared a house with several other drivers in Charlotte, North Carolina, afforded insights into the sleepless realm. In Palmer's assessment, some of his housemates were "burning the candle at both ends. They got back from their trips and they didn't sleep. They went out for a good time, and they were living on bennies." Even the drug-free Palmer considered it "more than unusual to get a full night's sleep," because of the extreme irregularity of long-haul working time. FDA inspectors lacked the power to arrest those observed engaging in illegal actions. Instead, they could only relay their discoveries to law enforcement authorities. The Food and Drug agents provided further compelling evidence of wholesale circumvention of the federal hours-of-service regulations. Yet the well-publicized results of this exercise appear to have made no impression on the regulators at the ICC. Here again, the federal government remained primarily a spectator.[41]

The most disturbing revelations from the federal investigations demonstrated the intertwined roles of drugs, overwork, and sleep deprivation in the causation of truck accidents. In some instances an inexplicable accident served to trigger the FDA's fact-finding work. Drivers told undercover agents numerous stories of wrecks attributable at least in part to chemical stimulants. Inspector John Van Allen, posted in Philadelphia in 1958, delved into a local fatal crash in which a truck driver at three A.M. plowed into a string of parked, easily avoidable railroad cars. Van Allen learned that police had recovered a bottle of methamphetamine pills from the cab of the truck and that the coroner's office had determined that the operator had taken a heavy dose of at least fifty milligrams of the potent drug prior to his death. The mass media grabbed the most lurid aspects of the FDA findings. In early 1956, the *Saturday Evening Post* carried a lengthy account of the federal probe that featured the case of a drug-addled driver whose rig crashed after he decided to crawl into the sleeper berth of his moving vehicle, on the deluded belief that he could "let Benny drive" for him. Publicity on such bizarre episodes lent further corroboration to a pattern recognized by other observers of highway safety. In 1957, *Alabama Trucker* warned its readers that amphetamines were "playing a major part in the overall truck accident picture." The magazine argued that the drugs fostered an overconfidence that encouraged risk taking. It also noted that some mishaps resulted from visual hallucinations, which made truckers swerve to avoid nonexistent objects. The immediate outcomes of all the lurid findings of the FDA inspectors were meager. The trucking industry undertook an educational campaign. To that end, a trade journal advised that the exhausted trucker on amphetamines "risks sleeping with his eyes open—like a zombie." In addition, prosecutions in some jurisdictions yielded a few convictions for drug trafficking, none of which resulted in imprisonment.[42]

Unfortunately, the ICC was not disposed to capitalize on the sorry state of affairs exposed by their colleagues at the FDA and amplified further by the media. The commission sat on a wealth of its own evidence of hours-of-service violations and vehicle crashes but apparently chose not to mine or supplement this data to search further for links to sleeplessness, whether induced by drugs or other factors. Most remarkably, just prior to the FDA's revelations, the ICC had chosen to discontinue its series of annual reports of driver-asleep accidents. Even though these reports were based on self-disclosure and, accordingly, represented in all probability only a small fraction of the actual occurrences, they had totaled over two hundred accidents in each of the previous two years in which such information was available. For purposes of amending public policy, the FDA's body of information connecting sleeplessness, hours violations, and accidents had no practical effect on the ICC.[43]

Instead of seizing an opportunity to tighten its hours-of-service standards, the ICC moved in the opposite direction. Its timing stood out as all the more remarkably disturbing because of recent scientific advances in grasping the importance of circadian rhythms. Experiments by Franz Halberg, a physiologist at the University of Minnesota, and others in the emerging field of chronobiology established the profound influence of these rhythms on the functioning of the human organism. But cutting-edge work of this sort had no leavening influence on regulatory action. To add another element of perversity to the sanctioning of bad sleep, the Teamsters openly opposed stronger hours rules, in the interest of promoting flexibility. Plainly, the unionists' understanding of the postwar accord with employers was that concessions on working time constituted part of the price of their members' middle-class standard of living. Unhindered by their traditional adversary, the industry won a significant relaxation in the hours-of-service regulations in 1962. The ICC allowed the work-rest cycle to be calculated on an eighteen-hour, not twenty-four-hour, basis. A trucker could be placed on a schedule of repeated sequences of driving ten hours and taking eight hours off duty. This derangement plainly ran counter to fundamental physiological rhythms attuned to a diurnal period. On the other hand, in an attempt to curtail driving by those held on duty (but engaged in nondriving tasks) for long hours, the revised rule barred drivers who had been on the job for thirteen hours from operating a truck for more than two hours. However, the disruptive abandonment of the twenty-four-hour cycle more than offset this small gain.[44]

By the 1970s, the old safeguards of the New Deal system in long-haul were already badly eroded and eroding further. The federal bureaucracy and organized labor did less and less to sustain even minimal restrictions on working time. Transfer of regulatory authority from the ICC to the newly created Department of Transportation (DOT) in 1967 left untouched the established policy of passivity. The Teamsters lacked any semblance of real leadership, with organized crime influence becoming much stronger after Jimmy Hoffa went to prison in 1967. A highly determined, ideologically informed, and virtually unimpeded drive for formal deregulation intensified. This movement accelerated destabilization even before its official triumph at the end of the decade. With lower barriers facing those interested in trying long-distance hauling, a steady supply of fresh owner-operators, including another sizable cohort of "country boys," took advantage of this fluid situation to try their luck as independent businessmen. By the mid-1970s, owner-drivers handled up to 40 percent of the nation's intercity cargo. Their efforts to avert bankruptcy were complicated not just by the usual host of competitors but also by soaring fuel prices brought on by the aggressive policies of the powerful Organization of Petroleum Exporting Countries cartel.[45]

The pursuit of independence continued to lure men into the overwork necessitated by severe competition. Disregard for federal hours-of-service limits became even more of an open secret. A 1972 survey of owner-operators found that one in fifty worked a forty-hour week. The surveyors did not inquire as to how many violated the seven- and eight-day limits, but over 80 percent of respondents claimed to be putting in the maximum allowable working time over those intervals. In a study that dared to explore illegal behavior, the extent of illicit activity was striking, as was the abiding value of IBT representation. Only 5 percent of unionized employees admitted regularly entering false data in their logbooks, compared with 38 percent of non-union owner-operators. Three percent of unionized employee drivers regularly drove more than ten hours a day; 32 percent of independents did so. Owner-drivers more frequently voiced their resentment of regulations and joined the chorus calling for greater laxity, operationally defined as the right to drive more than sixty hours a week. Unsurprisingly, sleep deprivation tormented many in the long-haul game in the 1970s. Independent operator James Johnston portrayed his quandary as one in which he had no choice but to violate the hours-of-service rules: "If I get to a warehouse at five o'clock in the morning after driving ten hours, there is no way I can lay down and go to bed. If I lay down and go to bed, there are going to be ten trucks in there ahead of me and I may not get unloaded that day." Some drivers who obeyed the federally mandated highway speed limit of fifty-five miles per hour slept only three to four hours per night because delivery schedules were not always adjusted to allow slower rates of travel. Not surprisingly, Harvard Business School professor D. Daryl Wyckoff's 1979 study of driving behavior reconfirmed that dozing on the job was widespread, with one-third of haulers of hazardous materials admitting to falling asleep on the road either occasionally or regularly.[46]

Enactment of the Motor Carrier Act of 1980 culminated the formal process of deregulating freight hauling. Anarchy ensued. The flow of newcomers into the ranks of the owner-operators became a flood. In the early 1980s, dozens of large unionized companies collapsed while others survived only with massive layoffs. The IBT's bargaining leverage declined further as it came to represent a much smaller share of over-the-road workers. With the proliferation of just-in-time inventory plans and other tighter demands for supply-chain efficiency, the irregularity and unpredictability of long-haul work worsened. The tyranny of one-sided flexibility left a growing share of both self-employed and employed truckers expected to display superhuman capabilities in making fast deliveries. By the late 1990s, relatively few drivers enjoyed a standard daylight schedule. An ATA survey disclosed that almost half of the nation's truckers essentially had no schedule and drove "whenever the work requires." The title of Michael Belzer's *Sweatshops on Wheels* incisively conveyed the dismal plight of a growing proportion of truckers. While acknowledging that he "had not dwelt on safety and working conditions," Belzer called attention to the fact that "rest areas and truck stops fill to overflowing every night with truckers who live in their trucks." His account, like those of other close observers, left no doubt that intense competition could only be exacerbating the chronic challenges of overwork and sleep deprivation among the truck residents and others forced to match their exertions.[47]

By the late twentieth century, neither the many causes nor the most dramatic effects of inadequate sleep among long-haul truckers remained mysterious. Yet well-known problems persisted. Bad roads, for example, had long discommodated any member of a two-man crew trying to rest in a sleeper cab while the vehicle was rolling. In 1985, Otto Riemer provided this reminder that the many amenities of modern equipment had not overcome this elemental obstacle: "Hoping for some rest, you find yourself tossed around like a cork on a stormy sea instead. (Individuals wearing dentures would be advised to keep their mouths closed lest the jarring shake them loose.)" For those trying to snooze in stationary sleepers in truck-stop parking lots, the perennial nuisance of sex workers' insistent solicitations continued unabated. "I've had them knock on my door every twenty minutes when I'm trying to sleep," reported trucker Steven Maldonado in 2006. A study of fatal accidents involving heavy trucks, published by the National Transportation Safety Board itself in 1990, merely reconfirmed the unhealthful pattern—long hours on duty, little or no sleep immediately prior to the fatal event, dependence on stimulants, disregard for hours regulations. One driver who died in a 1988 crash was reportedly working about 125 hours a week, sleeping four or five hours a day, and using methamphetamine and cocaine. The board's analysis of a large number of cases did not attempt to address its own question of national prevalence. In the early 1990s, about one in five long-haul drivers admitted falling asleep at the wheel during the past month. By the late 1990s, that rate had almost doubled, and almost a quarter of drivers slept five hours or less a day. In the absence of more than impressionistic evidence of trends in truckers' sleeplessness, it is impossible to say with any certainty whether deregulation exacerbated the existing difficulties. However, there are certainly some indications that it did so.[48]

The more subtle consequences of insufficient and unrefreshing sleep came more clearly into view in the last two decades of the twentieth century and the first decade of the twenty-first. Investigators drawn from several scientific disciplines and practitioners in sleep medicine and other medical specialties transformed the depth and breadth of understanding of the insidious costs of overwork in many occupations, including truck-driving. In one sophisticated field project reported in the *New England Journal of Medicine* in 1997, Merrill Mitler and his coworkers gathered polysomnographic data showing that truckers resting in rooms on the road obtained less than five hours sleep a day. Monitoring of driving behavior demonstrated that most men went through periods of drowsiness. Perhaps most disturbingly, during this brief five-day study, Mitler's team identified by means of electroencephalography a number of episodes in which drivers entered into stage one sleep while piloting heavy trucks at highway speeds. This investigation also detected two previously undiagnosed cases of sleep apnea. Expert research of this nature was all the more crucial because truckers themselves and their union leaders appear to have recognized and articulated their problems to a lesser extent than their counterparts in some other sleep-compromised jobs. Drivers relatively infrequently sought health care, limiting both their own awareness of conditions and that of providers of clinical services. When in 1980 Teamster dissident David Gaibis observed that "many drivers suffer from hypertension and debilitating fatigue because they cannot get enough rest" owing to long hours, he delivered an exceptional insight. With few lay observations reaching wide public attention, academic authorities became indispensable for elucidation of shift work sleep disorder and other sleep-related disorders that were complex and overshadowed by traumatic injuries incurred in collisions. Rigorous research also added further proof that somnolent truck operators lost alertness and otherwise suffered from diminished performance on the road.[49]

The flood of insights regarding adverse outcomes of extended driving time made the federal hours rules even more untenable. In 1989 the NTSB helped instigate a reconsideration of the antiquated hours-of-service rules, giving federal regulators their opening to make use of the latest science. The 1962 provision for an eighteen-hour restart of the work-rest cycle came under particularly sharp attack. An expert panel in 1998 told DOT to discard that enervating rhythm, which, it contended, "violates everything that is known about circadian cycles," and to return to a twenty-four-hour cycle. This advisory body criticized any form of onboard sleeping and recommended additional off-duty recovery time. Unfortunately, these advisors used a sophisticated grasp of the science of sleep and wakefulness to analyze only risks of traumatic injury, not the quieter forms of damage to mind and body inflicted through years of poor sleep. In 1999, the transportation agency produced a review of the rapidly growing body of literature that did call attention to the more insidious consequences of prolonged sleep deprivation. But observations of that sort fell on deaf ears. DOT leaders stayed focused on accident prevention, with its obvious second-party risk to the motoring public and others endangered by out-of-control trucks, and did not factor into their decisions either the scientific literature on shift work sleep disorder (an officially recognized disease entity in America since 1980) or the literature on the association between bad sleep and psychiatric, gastrointestinal, and cardiovascular conditions. Moreover, regulators did not grapple with the fact that a sizable share of long-distance drivers ran not as much on a nonstandard schedule of shifts as on a chaotic unscheduled basis. In 1997, a DOT-commissioned study found that over 80 percent of over-the-road truckers worked irregular hours and followed irregular routes on trips that lasted an average of thirteen days.[50]

The revised regulations set forth in 2003 did acknowledge some of the verified risks of overwork. DOT's Federal Motor Carrier Safety Administration (FMCSA) discarded anti-circadian eighteen-hour cycling and put the duty periodization back on a twenty-four-hour basis. The FMCSA chose to retain the limits of sixty hours for seven days and seventy hours for eight. Although it let operators drive for eleven hours a day, that is, one hour longer than previously, that stint had to be preceded by at least ten hours off duty, a period deemed sufficiently long to permit eight hours' sleep. The updated rules failed to require installation of onboard fatigue-monitoring technology despite abundant evidence of its efficacy and feasibility. In justifying their regulatory approach, federal officials made clear that they had drawn on biomedical knowledge only with respect to assessing risks of vehicular accidents. Whether drivers risked cardiovascular disease and ulcers or lived in a stuporous fog of drowsiness lay beyond their interest.[51]

The agency held to this narrow perspective in the face of a series of challenges led by the progressive advocacy group Public Citizen. In 1999, Public Citizen president Joan Claybrook had condemned "the sorry record" of federal regulators and noted that the weak hours regulations "exist only because of a statutory exemption granted in 1937 to the Fair Labor Standards Act which has sustained a pre-Depression approach to the use of labor." In 2000, Michael Belzer had advised that "new hours-of-service rules should . . . structure work schedules to enhance the long-term health of employees, as irregularity must have a deleterious effect on drivers' long-term health." Public Citizen and its partners greeted the 2003 regulations with dismay and immediately took DOT to court. A federally sponsored conference held shortly after the issuance of the revised rules added further evidence of ill health. At this event, the Owner-Operator Independent Drivers Association announced that the average life expectancy of its members was just under fifty-six years. A federal court in mid-2004 found merit in the objections. Judge David Sentelle observed that "the FMCSA points to nothing in the agency's extensive deliberations establishing that it considered the statutorily mandated factor of drivers' health in the slightest."[52]

The George W. Bush administration's motor-carrier regulators responded grudgingly to their judicial rebuke. The FMCSA went through the motions of assessing health aspects of overwork. The safety administration then reissued essentially the same rules in 2005. After acknowledging that shift work contributed to gastrointestinal, cardiovascular, and reproductive disorders, the regulators begged the question of ameliorative action by perversely using the deficiencies of previous regulations to justify continued obliviousness to the outcomes of nonstandard schedules, erratically changing schedules, and fragmented sleep: "The rule is 'shift-neutral' with regard to driving during the daytime or nighttime. Therefore, in the Agency's best judgment, the final rule should pose no greater risk to driver health than the pre-2003 and 2003 rules with respect to shift work." The only health-promoting concession required that rest taken in a sleeper berth occur in one unbroken interval, not two phases, as it had previously allowed. The agency seized on one study that had found drivers managing to sleep slightly more than six hours a night under the 2003 regulations and proclaimed that amount sufficient for maintaining "a healthy lifestyle" (though any study based on those following the legal limits ignored the problem of widespread evasion of those limits). The study found "only a weak association" between a career in trucking and heart disease and dismissed any notion that long hours in and of themselves represented a threat to well-being. Predictably, this dismissive stance led to another legal challenge by Public Citizen and other parties. In July 2007, the U.S. Circuit Court of Appeals threw out the rules, for their inadequate treatment of the safety issue, without reaching the question of health effects. During the lame-duck phase of the Bush presidency, DOT administrators defiantly reinstated the discredited rule. Opponents immediately petitioned their successors to set aside these regulations and write new ones. In its letter to Transportation Secretary Ray LaHood on March 9, 2009, reformers maintained that the preceding administration "threw up its hands and refused to factor in the health consequences of its rule into its regulatory impact analysis *at all.*" Neither side was giving any ground.[53]

Somewhat more surprising than the Bush administration's intransigence was the modest nature of the revisions proposed by the Obama administration in 2010. Rather than recast the issue to confront the overwork ingrained in this industry's work practices, the FMCSA stuck with the sixty-hour week and the seventy-hour maximum for eight days. The agency declared itself undecided on whether to reduce the daily ceiling to ten hours. It did, however, propose that the thirty-four-hour off-duty period, which functioned as a sort of weekend for purposes of restarting weekly duty restrictions, had to encompass two periods between midnight and six A.M., in recognition of the value of nighttime sleep. In estimating the regulatory benefits entailed by improving drivers' sleep, the FMCSA ventured across the frontier by including benefits that would be realized from decreases in obesity, hypertension, diabetes, cardiovascular disorders, and other ailments. This departure at least pointed in the direction of a fuller acknowledgment of the wide-ranging damage inflicted on drivers beyond traumatic injuries. The proposal also recommended that FMCSA "review studies that were not considered under previous rulemakings (e.g., shift work studies and epidemiological research findings that are related to driver health and HOS)." In early 2011, the Obama administration sought to require electronic onboard monitoring technology, replacing the widely falsified logbooks for enforcement of hours rules. If the preceding phases of this bureaucratized, legalistic battle have any predictive value, the latest proposals will be embroiled in controversy for many years to come.[54]

The inconclusiveness of this protracted adversarial proceeding is emblematic of the official disregard of the truck drivers' need for a reasonable amount of sleep. For several decades, those in a position to set limits that would make adequate allowance for critical human needs have been unwilling to do so. Underlying this refusal to act has been a market shaped by a sizable contingent of self-employed men who believe that they either have to work excessive, irregular hours or go bankrupt. Indeed, owner-operators have been much more likely to plead for relaxed regulations than for relief from sleep-depriving overwork. The resulting predicament, so often glossed over in romantic sketches of manly entrepreneurial freedom, has taken a toll on drivers' well-being that remains hard to estimate. In 2007, the National Institute for Occupational Safety and Health made a provocative call for a more expansive research program. Among its many ideas for broadening understanding of truckers' health, NIOSH proposed combining epidemiological and economic analysis, undertaking studies of the deleterious effects of long or irregular hours, and determining "the relationship between sleep debt and both obesity and metabolic function in transportation workers." In pursuit of these concerns, the institute launched an investigation of truckers with research questions that extended to the prevalence of "health conditions and sleep disorders" and any association between working conditions and overall health status.[55]

Of course, broadly conceived and meticulously executed science can carry the reform process only so far. Steelworkers struck in 1919 to dramatize their opposition to overwork; sleeping-car porters made sleep a prominent organizing and bargaining issue. Organized truckers have done fairly little in the past half century to create the pressure necessary to make either employers or the state address questions of overwork and sleep loss. The International Brotherhood of Teamsters has had a less-than-stellar record on this score because of a shortage of internal health expertise and, most important, a swarm of other priorities related to the crisis of deregulated hypercompetition. Constantly adding fuel to the competitive fires and thus hindering collective action at every turn—and a factor absent from employment relations in steel manufacturing and passenger rail service—has been the menace posed by individualistic owner-operators. Dreams of individual freedom for some drivers have thus meant a nightmare of sleeplessness for others, and for many of the dreamers themselves as well.

Conclusion:
The Employers' Dreams

Corporations cherish flexibility, leanness and just-in-time management.
"Creative destruction" is the rule. Men—and, this time around, women—
of ambition seek their fortunes not in bureaucratic conformity but in
adaptability.

             —Virginia Postrel, 1999

It is in the name of this model [of globalization] that flexible working,
another magic word of neo-liberalism, is imposed, meaning night work,
weekend work, irregular working hours, things which have always been
part of the employers' dreams. In a general way, neo-liberalism is a very
smart and very modern repackaging of the oldest ideas of the oldest
capitalists.

             —Pierre Bourdieu, 1998

Flexibility has become a catchword of the current age. Just as efficiency served
as the shibboleth at the turn of the twentieth century, a cult of adaptability
has arisen at the turn of the twenty-first. From the popularity of yoga through
the vogue of the lean and virtual organization, American culture celebrates
individuals and organizations with the capacity to initiate endless changes,
engage in nimble multitasking, and adjust smoothly to unexpectedly changing conditions. Especially within the business community, with its cultural
power, flexibility has become a mantra. Wal-Mart Stores transformed corporate thinking on fluid methods of moving merchandise. Best sellers like *Who
Moved My Cheese?* derided rigid characters unable to reinvent and rebrand
themselves continually. Sleep deprivation now resides within a repertoire of
practices deemed essential to survival in a globally competitive world—along
with attributes such as constant availability, ability to function competently
after crossing several time zones, close coordination within thrown-together

teams, and other routine feats of adaptation. More so than in the time of Thomas Edison, depriving oneself of necessary rest or denying it to those under one's control is considered necessary to success in a 24/7/365 society. Americans have a stronger ideological rationale than ever to distrust any sort of dormancy.[1]

The proliferation of nonstandard work schedules and the outright abandonment of schedules reflect the mounting demands for flexibility. In manipulating employee insecurity to tolerate unreasonable commitments to time at work, globalization has served as an ever-looming threat, even in circumstances where no real possibility for job exporting exists. Taken together, night, weekend, rotational, and other forms of biologically confusing plans now challenge about 20 percent of the U.S. workforce. For the most part, in recent years American workers have held little control over the specific terms of temporal arrangements that tend to compromise sleep time. Flextime has generally operated within narrow bounds, with options as to starting and ending times for shifts often available only in exchange for putting in excessive hours. Other accommodations for juggling work and family obligations are usually quite limited. For the most part, flexibility lies under the control of managers, not rank-and-file employees, especially in the predominant non-union setting. By one recent estimate, only about a quarter of the workforce exercises significant control over its scheduling.[2]

The drive to configure working time in physiologically unnatural ways threatens to derange the sleep of a growing share of American workers. The sleep deficits associated with extreme and demanding jobs point to a deep disparity, a sort of sleep divide, in American society, that separates a perpetually drowsy segment of the workforce from the well-rested majority. The inordinate attention paid to elite short sleepers conceals the fact that a large share of those on the disadvantaged side of the sleep divide appear to be low-wage employees—cashiers, waitresses, domestic servants, janitors, and other service-sector workers. A recent epidemiological study concluded that "the opportunity for sleep of adequate duration may be hindered in low income and education groups, and among those of African-American and Hispanic descent." Besides living in a dysfunctional somnolent state, sleep-deprived workers are known or suspected to be at greater risk of several diseases. The full range of adverse effects of insufficient sleep is surely not understood, particularly as trends like the spread of on-call work and the growing phenomenon of individuals holding multiple jobs exacerbate the fragmentation of rest time. The full prevalence of ill effects is also a mystery. Christopher

Drake and his associates have put the prevalence of shift work sleep disorder among employees on night and rotating shifts at about 10 percent. Future epidemiological research illuminating the elevated frequency of other conditions—such as ulcers, workplace and commuting injuries, hypertension, and psychiatric disorders—would contribute to estimating the full human cost of flexible business systems.[3]

Yet nonstandard schedules need not be so deleterious. Naps can prevent and repair some damage. Considerable research and real-world experimentation have laid the groundwork for acceptance of napping on the job. For at least a quarter century, the American military has invented and administered sleep management plans that incorporate short rest periods. Scientists at the National Aeronautics and Space Administration have become proponents of polyphasic sleep regimens that incorporated short naps. David Dinges of the University of the Pennsylvania School of Medicine and a number of other biomedical investigators have demonstrated the value of this form of rest.[4]

Based on these insights and accumulating experience, managerial acceptance of workplace napping has grown in recent years. Enlightened employers began to introduce brief, nonsleeping respites from work activity a century ago, convinced that these breaks would raise productivity and enhance performance quality. Today, a growing number of companies permit napping on their premises. In 2011, *Huffington Post* publisher Arianna Huffington reacted strongly to Secretary of Transportation Ray LaHood's refusal to let air traffic controllers sleep for short periods during their shifts, despite a series of reports of controllers dozing on duty: "We have a pair of napping rooms—christened Napquest I and Napquest II—where sleepy editors and reporters can refresh and recharge. Shouldn't those making sure planes take off and land safely be given the same option? As someone who flies a lot, I much prefer the idea of paid naps than of bleary-eyed, sleep-deprived air traffic controllers." Though no panacea, naps can offer a measure of relief from the loss of sleep imposed by overwork, irregular work hours, or unavoidable nonwork commitments. If employees can receive paid time off to consume coffee or tobacco, then it is no great leap to grant this modest benefit.[5]

In unionized sites, workers' representatives may have openings to negotiate for rest breaks and other ameliorative steps. The American labor movement's well-known priorities of wages and hours have relevance to matters of overwork and sleep denial. In recent years, unions have made significant advances in limiting or eliminating mandatory overtime. Of course, they also have a long record of discouraging nonstandard schedules by winning premium pay for evening and overnight work. They have raised similar financial disincentives for unscheduled or loosely scheduled operations by imposing punitive pay rates of double time or more for weekend work and call-in assignments. Some unions have won reduced hours for those stuck working nights or weekends. Moreover, as work-related sleep difficulties gain greater recognition as legitimate health concerns, the unions' traditional role as advocates for workers' physical well-being may aid in recruiting new members, particularly employees on unconventional schedules. Indeed, workplace health and safety currently ranks as the most important consideration in American workers' decisions to support union representation. In 2005, the AFL-CIO launched an initiative to assist its affiliated unions in using health grievances in organizing campaigns.[6]

Beyond the horizon of realistic immediate possibilities, public policy innovations could do much to alleviate shift work sleep disorder and other maladies following from chronic shortfalls of unconscious rest. American political leaders might reconsider the nation's disregard of Article 24 of the Universal Declaration of Human Rights: "Everyone has the right to rest and leisure, including reasonable limitation of working hours and periodic holidays with pay." If the United States were to join the more than ninety other nations that require by law that workers receive at least one day off a week, that departure would offer a substantial number of men, women, and children a chance to catch up on lost sleep. In the same vein, benefits would follow a decision to join the more than eighty nations in which protective legislation sets a maximum length of the work week that covers more than merely the few employees whose sleepiness endangers large numbers of other people. Increasingly, foreign legislation acknowledges the need for some flexible assignments but places this concession within limits and grants employees a voice, individually or collectively, in determining schedules. American policy makers at the local, state, or national level might, for example, curtail the graveyard shift by closing some nonessential commercial establishments now permitted to operate twenty-four hours a day. Sociologists Rick Fantasia and Kim Voss have noted that the elevation of consumer rights has hidden costs: "On the other side of the smiling face of endless consumer 'convenience' is · the stern regime of coerced labor 'flexibility.'" In balancing workers' rights to sleep against consumers' rights to shop at any time, lawmakers might take into account widespread public support for limitations on working hours. Among Juliet Schor's many imaginative proposals for amending the Fair Labor Standards Act to give employees greater flexibility in putting in their working time is her recommendation to ban discrimination against workers who refuse night or weekend work.[7]

In the regulatory realm, it is conceivable that under progressive leadership the Occupational Safety and Health Administration would construe sleep-denying arrangements of working time as legitimate workplace hazards and, therefore, set standards to control them. The labor agency could consider either the disabled state of victims of shift work sleep disorder in its own right or the elevated risk of occupational injuries faced by somnolent workers. In proceeding along the path toward hazard prevention, OSHA could draw on the expertise of their colleagues at the National Institute for Occupational Safety and Health, who have been examining the damage wrought by overwork and sleep disruption since the 1970s. Combined with private measures, imaginative public intervention could do much to usher in a new era in which America comes to define dangerous sleepiness more broadly.[8]

Historians can play a significant part in the ongoing process of recognizing the human cost of lost sleep. The traditions of sleep deprivation in female-dominated occupations, like nursing and domestic service, remain virtually unmapped. Certainly, future research may help us to understand both the general ramifications for sleep and sleeplessness of the evolution of the division of labor within households and the particular burdens loaded on employed mothers. This book suggests that inappropriate standards of overwork have arisen based partly on men's workplace performance, involving patterns of time allocation that generally have not been constrained by time-consuming domestic tasks. Future work may well examine the changing standards set for women workers and the notions of strength and stamina on which they rested, as well as investigating sleep negotiations within domestic partnerships.[9]

This small exploratory study has suggested that America has a long history of experimenting with male workers to see how much flexibility it can attain at the expense of sleep. The experiences of the steelworkers, Pullman porters, and long-haul truckers all reveal moments of strong, and sometimes effective, resistance to flexploitation. Perhaps those seeking to improve the plight of all those who are dangerously sleepy in today's workforce can take encouragement from an awareness of earlier struggles both to bring to light this hidden injury of working life and to curtail it. Efforts to forge a right to sleep will almost certainly confront stiff opposition. After all, American employers tend to treat their employees' sleep problems as disciplinary, not medical, matters. Accordingly, knowledge of past encounters on this terrain may be useful to those contending for progress toward a decent quality of life.[10]

Notes

Preface

Note to epigraph: U.S. National Commission on Sleep Disorders Research, *Wake Up America: A National Sleep Alert: Report of the National Commission on Sleep Disorders*, by William Dement et al., 2 vols. (Washington, D.C.: Government Printing Office, 1993), 1:22 (quotation), 47–48.

1. Juliet B. Schor, *The Overworked American: The Unexpected Decline of Leisure* (New York: Basic Books, 1993), 29; Lonnie Golden and Deborah M. Figart, eds., *Working Time: International Trends, Theory and Policy Perspectives* (New York: Routledge, 2000); Sangheon Lee, Deidre McCann, and Jon Messenger, *Working Time Around the World: Trends in Working Hours, Laws and Policies in a Global Comparative Perspective* (Geneva: International Labor Office, 2007); Sara E. Luckhaupt, Sangwoo Tak, and Geoffrey M. Calvert, "The Prevalence of Short Sleep Duration by Industry and Occupation in the National Health Interview Survey," *Sleep* 33 (2010): 149–59; Bruce Rolfsen, "Employers Urged to Deal with Increase in Workers Not Getting Adequate Sleep," *Bureau of National Affairs Daily Labor Report*, Nov. 6, 2012, A-6.

2. Harriet B. Presser, *Working in a 24/7 Economy: Challenges for American Families* (New York: Russell Sage Foundation, 2003); Richard M. Coleman, *The 24-Hour Business: Maximizing Productivity Through Round-the-Clock Operations* (New York: AMACOM, 1995); U.S. Congress, Office of Technology Assessment, *Biological Rhythms: Implications for the Worker* (Washington, D.C.: Government Printing Office, 1991), 69–84, esp. 71–72; Thomas Beers, "Flexible Schedules and Shift Work: Replacing the '9-to-5' Workday?" *Monthly Labor Review*, June 2000, 33–40; Nancy Gordon et al., "The Prevalence and Health Impact of Shift Work," *American Journal of Public Health* 76 (1986): 1225–28; Eva E. Jacobs and Mary Meghan Ryan, eds., *Handbook of U.S. Labor Statistics: Employment, Earnings, Prices, Productivity, and Other Labor Data*, 9th ed. (Lanham, Md.: Bernan Press, 2006), 79–81; Kathleen Barker and Kathleen Christensen, eds., *Contingent Work: American Employment Relations in Transition* (Ithaca, N.Y.: ILR Press of Cornell University Press, 1998); Francoise Carre et al., eds., *Nonstandard Work: The Nature and Challenges of Changing Employment Arrangements* (Champaign, Ill.: Industrial Relations Research Association, 2000); Erin E. Hatton, *The Temp Economy: From Kelly Girls to Permatemps in Postwar America* (Philadelphia: Temple University Press, 2010).

3. For emphasis on more sensational parameters, see, among others, Michael S.

Kimmel, *Manhood in America: A Cultural History*, 2nd ed. (New York: Oxford University Press, 2006); Clifford Putney, *Muscular Christianity: Manhood and Sports in Protestant America, 1880–1920* (Cambridge, Mass.: Harvard University Press, 2001); John Pettegrew, *Brutes in Suits: Male Sensibility in America, 1890–1920* (Baltimore: Johns Hopkins University Press, 2007); Gail Bederman, *Manliness and Civilization: A Cultural History of Gender and Race in the United States, 1880–1917* (Chicago: University of Chicago Press, 1995); John Hoberman, *Testosterone Dreams: Rejuvenation, Aphrodisia, Doping* (Berkeley: University of California Press, 2005); Stephen H. Norwood, *Strikebreaking and Intimidation: Mercenaries and Masculinity in Twentieth-Century America* (Chapel Hill: University of North Carolina Press, 2002); Harrison G. Pope Jr., Katharine A. Phillips, and Roberto Olivardia, *The Adonis Complex: The Secret Crisis of Male Body Obsession* (New York: Free Press, 2000); Lynne Luciano, *Looking Good: Male Body Image in Modern America* (New York: Hill and Wang, 2001); Pierre Bourdieu, *Masculine Domination*, trans. Richard Nice (Stanford, Calif.: Stanford University Press, 2001). Among the projects that do take up male workers' stamina and perseverance are Melissa Dabakis, *Visualizing Labor in American Sculpture: Monuments, Manliness, and the Work Ethic* (New York: Cambridge University Press, 1999), 27–28, 96, 99, 124, 247n6; Daniel E. Bender, *Sweated Work, Weak Bodies: Anti-Sweatshop Campaigns and Languages of Labor* (New Brunswick, N.J.: Rutgers University Press, 2004); Edward S. Slavishak, *Bodies of Work: Civic Display and Labor in Industrial Pittsburgh* (Durham, N.C.: Duke University Press, 2008). For works exploring the relationship between aggressiveness and stamina, see Rupert Wilkinson, *American Tough: The Tough-Guy Tradition and American Character* (Westport, Conn.: Greenwood Press, 1984), 18–20; R. W. Connell, "An Iron Man: The Body and Some Contradictions of Hegemonic Masculinity," in *Sport, Men, and the Gender Order: Critical Feminist Perspectives*, ed. Michael A. Messner and Donald F. Sabo (Champaign, Ill.: Human Kinetics Books, 1990), 83–95.

4. Sylvia Ann Hewlett, *Off-Ramps and On-Ramps: Keeping Talented Women on the Road to Success* (Boston: Harvard Business School Press, 2007), 60 (quotation), 57–88; Joan C. Williams, *Reshaping the Work-Family Debate: Men and Class Matter* (Cambridge, Mass.: Harvard University Press, 2010), 5 (quotation), 88 (quotation), 79–80, 86–88; Arlie Russell Hochschild with Anne Machung, *The Second Shift*, rev. ed. (New York: Penguin Books, 2003), 10, 6. For one recent manifestation of professional women's striving to meet male standards of overwork, see *New York Times*, June 12, 2011, Week in Review, 9. For all its insights into working women's dilemmas, the American literature on work-family balance has shown little interest in sleep. For passing comments, see Schor, *Overworked American*, 5, 11, 13, 18; Marin Clarkberg and Stacey Merola, "Competing Clocks: Work and Leisure," in *It's about Time: Couples and Careers*, ed. Phyllis Moen (Ithaca, N.Y.: ILR Press of Cornell Press, 2003), 41; Ellen Galinsky, Stacy S. Kim, and James T. Bond, *Feeling Overworked: When Work Becomes Too Much* (New York: Work and Families Institute, 2001), 49, 52–53, 55, 56; Jerry A. Jacobs and Kathleen Gerson, *The Time Divide: Work, Family, and Gender Inequality* (Cambridge, Mass.: Harvard University Press, 2004), 148; Hewlett, *Off-Ramps*, 71, 73; Suzanne M. Bianchi, John

P. Robinson, and Melissa A. Milkie, *Changing Rhythms of American Family Life* (New York: Russell Sage Foundation, 2006), 89, 108, 218; Joan Williams, *Unbending Gender: Why Family and Work Conflict and What to Do about It* (New York: Oxford University Press, 2001), 125; Pamela Stone, *Opting Out? Why Women Really Quit Careers and Head Home* (Berkeley: University of California Press, 2007), 100, 102; *New York Times*, March 2, 2006, A1, C2. For exceptional attention to the issue, see David J. Maume, Rachel A. Sebastian, and Anthony R. Bardo, "Gender Differences in Sleep Disruption among Retail Food Workers," *American Sociological Review* 74 (2009): 989–1007; David J. Maume, Rachel A. Sebastian, and Anthony R. Bardo, "Gender, Work-Family Responsibilities, and Sleep," *Gender and Society* 24 (2010): 746–68. In Britain, Stella Chatzitheochari and Sara Arber pointed out that "sleep is absent from work-life balance debates" and proceeded to fill the void. See "Lack of Sleep, Work and the Long Hours Culture: Evidence from the UK Time Use Survey," *Work, Employment and Society* 23 (2009): 31 (quotation), 31–48.

5. Analyses of more nebulous conditions include Bender, *Sweated Work*; Tera W. Hunter, *To 'Joy My Freedom: Southern Black Women's Lives and Labors after the Civil War* (Cambridge, Mass.: Harvard University Press, 1997), 187–218; Alan Derickson, "Physiological Science and Scientific Management in the Progressive Era: Frederic S. Lee and the Committee on Industrial Fatigue," *Business History Review* 68 (1994): 483–514; Allison L. Hepler, *Women in Labor: Mothers, Medicine, and Occupational Health in the United States, 1890–1980* (Columbus: Ohio State University Press, 2000); Michelle Murphy, *Sick Building Syndrome and the Problem of Uncertainty: Environmental Politics, Techno-science, and Women Workers* (Durham, N.C.: Duke University Press, 2006).

6. Matthew J. Wolf-Meyer, *The Slumbering Masses: Sleep, Medicine, and Modern American Life* (Minneapolis: University of Minnesota Press, 2012), 27–78; Kenton Kroker, *The Sleep of Others and the Transformation of Sleep Research* (Toronto: University of Toronto Press, 2007) Although his study is global in scope, Kroker gives considerable attention to American scientific developments; Elizabeth Cromley, "Sleeping Around: A History of American Beds and Bedrooms," *Journal of Design History* 3 (1990): 1–17; John Shepard Jr. et al., "History of the Development of Sleep Medicine in the United States," *Journal of Clinical Sleep Medicine* 1 (2005): 61–82; William C. Dement, "History of Sleep Medicine," *Neurologic Clinics* 23 (2005): 945–65; Peter N. Stearns, Perrin Rowland, and Lori Giarnella, "Children's Sleep: Sketching Historical Change," *Journal of Social History* 30 (1996): 345–66; Alan Derickson, "'Asleep and Awake at the Same Time': Sleep Denial among Pullman Porters," *Labor: Studies in Working-Class History of the Americas* 5, no. 3 (2008): 13–44; Alan Derickson, "'No Such Thing as a Night's Sleep': The Embattled Sleep of American Fighting Men from World War II to the Present," *Journal of Social History* 47 (2013). For the provocation of early modern biphasic slumber, see A. Roger Ekirch, "Sleep We Have Lost: Pre-industrial Slumber in the British Isles," *American Historical Review* 106 (2001): 343–85.

7. David F. Dinges, "An Overview of Sleepiness and Accidents," *Journal of Sleep Research* 4: suppl. 2 (1995): 7 (quotation), 4–14; Committee on Sleep Medicine and

Research, Institute of Medicine of the National Academies, *Sleep Disorders and Sleep Deprivation: An Unmet Public Health Problem* (Washington, D.C.: National Academies Press, 2006), 149; Simon Folkard and Philip Tucker, "Shift Work, Safety and Productivity," *Occupational Medicine* 53 (2003): 95–101; Ronald Powell and Alex Copping, "Sleep Deprivation and Its Consequences in Construction Workers," *Journal of Construction Engineering and Management* 136 (2010): 1086–92; Merrill M. Mitler et al., "Catastrophes, Sleep, and Public Policy: Consensus Report," *Sleep* 11 (1988): 100–109; John K. Lauber and Phyllis J. Kayten, "Sleepiness, Circadian Dysrhythmia, and Fatigue in Transportation System Accidents," ibid., 503–12; Damien Leger, "The Cost of Sleep-Related Accidents: A Report for the National Commission on Sleep Disorders Research," ibid., 17 (1994): 84–93; National Commission, *Wake Up America*, 1:22–24, 36–37, 48–54, 56–57; Timothy H. Monk, "Shift Work: Basic Principles," in *Principles and Practice of Sleep Medicine*, 4th ed., ed. Meir H. Kryger, Thomas Roth, and William C. Dement (Philadelphia: Elsevier Saunders, 2005), 673–79; U.S. National Institute for Occupational Safety and Health, *Overtime and Extended Work Shifts: Recent Findings on Illnesses, Injuries, and Health Behaviors*, by Claire C. Caruso et al. (Cincinnati: National Institute for Occupational Safety and Health, 2004); Christopher P. Landrigan et al., "Effect of Reducing Interns' Work Hours on Serious Medical Errors in Intensive Care Units," *New England Journal of Medicine* 351 (2004): 1838–48.

8. Anders Knutsson, "Health Disorders of Shift Workers," *Occupational Medicine* 53 (2003): 103–8; X.-S. Wang et al., "Shift Work and Chronic Disease: The Epidemiological Evidence," ibid., 61 (2011): 78–89; Allene J. Scott and Joseph LaDou, "Shiftwork: Effects on Sleep and Health with Recommendations for Medical Surveillance and Screening," *Occupational Medicine: State of the Art Reviews* 5 (1990): 273–99; Gordon et al., "Prevalence and Health Impact," 1225–28; Anders Knutsson et al., "Increased Risk of Ischaemic Heart Disease in Shift Workers," *Lancet*, no. 8498 (1986): 89–92; James E. Gangwisch et al., "Short Sleep Duration as a Risk Factor for Hypertension: Analyses of the First National Health and Nutrition Examination Survey," *Hypertension* 47 (2006): 833–39; Sheldon Cohen et al., "Sleep Habits and Susceptibility to the Common Cold," *Archives of Internal Medicine* 169 (2009): 62–67; American Sleep Disorders Association, *The International Classification of Sleep Disorders: Diagnostic and Coding Manual* (Rochester, Minn.: American Sleep Disorders Association, 1990), 121–25; Christopher L. Drake et al., "Shift Work Sleep Disorder: Prevalence and Consequences beyond That of Symptomatic Day Workers," *Sleep* 27 (2004): 1453–62; Charles A. Czeisler et al., "Modafinil for Excessive Sleepiness Associated with Shift-Work Sleep Disorder," *New England Journal of Medicine* 353 (2005): 476–86; American Academy of Sleep Medicine, *The International Classification of Sleep Disorders: Diagnostic and Coding Manual*, 2nd ed. (Westchester, Ill.: American Academy of Sleep Medicine, 2005), 131–33; Torbjorn Akerstedt and Kenneth P. Wright, "Sleep Loss and Fatigue in Shift Work and Shift Work Disorder," *Sleep Medicine Clinics* 4 (2009): 257–71; Bonnie Dean et al., "Impaired Health Status, Daily Functioning, and Work Productivity in Adults with Excessive Sleepiness," *Journal of Occupational and Environmental Medicine* 52 (2010): 144–49.

9. Luckhaupt, Tak, and Calvert, "Prevalence of Short Sleep," 156. On flexploitation, see Pierre Bourdieu, *Acts of Resistance: Against the Tyranny of the Market*, trans. Richard Nice (New York: New Press, 1998), 34–35, 81–87.

Chapter 1. Sleep Is for Sissies

Note to epigraphs: "Edison's Prophecy: A Duplex, Sleepless, Dinnerless," *Literary Digest*, Nov. 14, 1914, 967 (Edison quotation); Ken Auletta, "The Dawn Patrol," *New Yorker*, Aug. 8, 2005, 75 (Ross quotation). In the same vein, see Walter Kirn, "Sleep Is for Sissies," *Time*, Dec. 20, 2004, 56, 59; and a Sleep Is for Sissies travel mug, available through cafepress.com in 2010. On the coining of the term "sissy" in the late nineteenth century, see Gail Bederman, *Manliness and Civilization: A Cultural History of Gender and Race in the United States, 1880–1917* (Chicago: University of Chicago Press, 1995), 17.

1. Matthew J. Wolf-Meyer, *Slumbering Masses: Sleep, Medicine, and Modern American Life* (Minneapolis: University of Minnesota Press, 2012), 51 (quotation), 51–55; Max Weber, "The Meaning of Discipline," in *From Max Weber: Essays in Sociology*, ed. and trans. H. H. Gerth and C. Wright Mills (New York: Oxford University Press, 1946), 253–64. On the dominant cultural authority of capitalists, see Alan Trachtenberg, *The Incorporation of America: Culture and Society in the Gilded Age*, 25th anniversary ed. (New York: Hill and Wang, 2007); Olivier Zunz, *Making America Corporate, 1870–1920* (Chicago: University of Chicago Press, 1990).

2. Daniel T. Rodgers, *The Work Ethic in Industrial America, 1850–1920* (Chicago: University of Chicago Press, 1978), 8–12; John Cawelti, *Apostles of the Self-Made Man* (Chicago: University of Chicago Press, 1965).

3. Benjamin Franklin, *Autobiography, Poor Richard, and Later Writings* (New York: Library of America, 1997), 458 (quotation), 483 (quotation), 464, 644–45, 649, 246–47; Edmund S. Morgan, *Benjamin Franklin* (New Haven, Conn.: Yale University Press, 2002), 22–25; Walter Isaacson, *Benjamin Franklin: An American Life* (New York: Simon and Schuster, 2003), 89–101; W. J. Rorabaugh, *The Craft Apprentice: From Franklin to the Machine Age in America* (New York: Oxford University Press, 1986), 11, 15. For Franklin's less disciplined style in his later years, see Isaacson, *Benjamin Franklin*, 352–53. On the Galenic framework within which Franklin valued moderation, see Stanley Finger, *Doctor Franklin's Medicine* (Philadelphia: University of Pennsylvania Press, 2006), 314–15, 325.

4. Franklin, *Autobiography, Poor Richard*, 480 (quotation), 490 (quotation), 556 (quotation), 513 (quotation, all italics in original), 547, 556–57.

5. John C. Gunn, *Gunn's Domestic Medicine, or Poor Man's Friend: A Facsimile of the First Edition* (1830; Knoxville: University of Tennessee Press, 1986), 103, 105; Michael O'Malley, *Keeping Watch: A History of American Time* (New York: Viking Press, 1990), 29–199, esp. 43–44, 196, 198.

6. Cynthia Shelton, "The Role of Labor in Early Industrialization: Philadelphia, 1787–1857," *Journal of the Early Republic* 4 (1984): 384 (quotation), 383–85; Robert F. Dalzell Jr., *Enterprising Elite: The Boston Associates and the World They Made* (New

York: W. W. Norton, 1993), 32–34; Herbert G. Gutman, *Work, Culture, and Society in In-dustrializing America: Essays in American Working-Class and Social History* (New York: Alfred A. Knopf, 1976), 3–77; David Brody, "Time and Work during Early American Industrialism," *Labor History* 30 (1989): 5–46, esp. 38; David R. Roediger and Philip S. Foner, *Our Own Time: A History of American Labor and the Working Day* (New York: Verso, 1989), 43–64, esp. 50; Rorabaugh, *Craft Apprentice*, 141; Bruce Laurie, "'Noth-ing on Compulsion': Life Styles of Philadelphia Artisans, 1820–1850," *Labor History* 15 (1974): 337–66; Mark M. Smith, *Mastered by the Clock: Time, Slavery, and Freedom in the American South* (Chapel Hill: University of North Carolina Press, 1997), 112–16; Clar-ence E. Glick, *Sojourners and Settlers: Chinese Migrants in Hawaii* (Honolulu: Univer-sity of Hawaii Press, 1980), 34. For the seminal studies, see Sidney Pollard, "Factory Discipline in the Industrial Revolution," *Economic History Review* 16 (1963): 254–71; E. P. Thompson, "Time, Work-Discipline, and Industrial Capitalism," *Past and Present* 50 (1971): 76–136.

7. David E. Nye, *Electrifying America: Social Meanings of a New Technology, 1880–1940* (Cambridge, Mass.: MIT Press, 1990), esp. 185–237; Betsy H. Bradley, *The Works: The Industrial Architecture of the United States* (New York: Oxford University Press, 1999), 106; Jane Brox, *Brilliant: The Evolution of Artificial Light* (Boston: Houghton Mif-flin Harcourt, 2010).

8. Andre Millard, *Edison and the Business of Invention* (Baltimore: Johns Hopkins University Press, 1990); Paul Israel, *Edison: A Life of Invention* (New York: John Wiley and Sons, 1998); Randall Stross, *The Wizard of Menlo Park: How Thomas Alva Edison Invented the Modern World* (New York: Crown, 2007); Brox, *Brilliant*, 110–24, 275. On Edison's dealings with the media, see Matthew Josephson, *Edison: A Biography* (New York: McGraw-Hill, 1959), 179, 268, 272; Israel, *Edison*, 146–47; Stross, *Wizard*, 62–64, 71–75, 98–104.

9. *Chicago Tribune*, Apr. 8, 1878, 3 (five quotations); "Science and Mechanics," *Pot-ter's American Monthly*, Nov. 1878, 397 (quotation); William H. Bishop, "A Night with Edison," *Scribner's Monthly*, Nov. 1878, 96 (quotation), 96–99; "Edison's Inventions, II: The Carbon Button and Its Offspring," ibid., July 1879, 450 (quotation); *New York Her-ald*, Dec. 2, 1874, 4, repr. in Thomas A. Edison, *The Papers of Thomas Alva Edison*, vol. 2, *From Workshop to Laboratory, June 1873–March 1876*, ed. Robert Rosenberg et al. (Balti-more: Johns Hopkins University Press, 1991), 668–69.

10. Sarah K. Bolton, *How Success Is Won* (Boston: Lothrop, Lee and Shepard, 1885), 192 (quotation), 191–92; "Edison's Home Life," *Scientific American*, July 27, 1889, 51 (quo-tation); untitled article, *Ladies' Home Journal*, Sept. 1889, 7; "Do You Share the Results?" *Godey's Lady's Book*, Aug. 1889, 174; Horace Townsend, "Edison: His Work and His Work-Shop," *Cosmopolitan*, Apr. 1889, 604. On the lighting work, see Robert Friedel, Paul Israel, and Bernard Finn, *Edison's Electric Light: Biography of an Invention* (New Brunswick, N.J.: Rutgers University Press, 1986); Israel, *Edison*, 16–229. On overwork and sleep loss outside the media spotlight during this period, see Thomas Edison to Edward Johnson, Oct. 16 and 27, 1879, in Thomas A. Edison, *The Papers of Thomas Alva*

Edison, vol. 5, *Research to Development at Menlo Park, January 1879–March 1881*, ed. Paul Israel et al. (Baltimore: Johns Hopkins University Press, 2004), 429, 459; Friedel, Israel, and Finn, *Edison's Electric Light*, 146–47.

11. "Killing Time," *Reformed Church Messenger*, Jan. 8, 1891, 7 (quotation); Franklin, *Autobiography*, 567; Horatio Alger Jr., *Ragged Dick, or, Street Life in New York with Boot-Blacks: An Authoritative Text, Contexts, Criticism*, ed. Hildegard Hoeller (1868; New York: W. W. Norton, 2008), 3, 9, 28–29, 50–54, 65, 69–70; H. A. Lewis, *Hidden Treasures, or, Why Some Succeed While Others Fail* (New York: A. W. Richardson, 1887), vi, 44, 64, 79, 498; James Platt, *Business* (New York: G. P. Putnam's Sons, 1889), vii, 22–25, 68, 70–106; Orison S. Marden, *Rising in the World, or, Architects of Fate* (New York: Success, 1897), 179; Judy Arlene Hilkey, *Character Is Capital: Success Manuals and Manhood in Gilded Age America* (Chapel Hill: University of North Carolina Press, 1997), 75; "Invention and Appetite," *Youth's Companion*, Apr. 5, 1900, 174; "How Edison Succeeded," ibid., June 6, 1904, 296; Francis Miller, *Thomas A. Edison: An Inspiring Story for Boys* (Philadelphia: John C. Winston, 1940), 59–60, following 168, 172, 190, 200–201, 203, 239; Lida McCabe, "The Boyhood of Edison," *St. Nicholas: An Illustrated Magazine for Young Folks*, Aug. 1893, 766. On one important source of the success literature's preoccupation with manly vigilance and perseverance, see Charles Darwin, *The Descent of Man and Selection in Relation to Sex*, rev. ed. (Chicago: Rand, McNally, 1874), 559–60; Glenna Matthews, *"Just a Housewife": The Rise and Fall of Domesticity in America* (New York: Oxford University Press, 1987), 116–25, esp. 121.

12. W. K. Dickson and Antonia Dickson, *The Life and Inventions of Thomas Alva Edison* (New York: Thomas Y. Crowell, 1894), 88 (quotation), 91 (quotation), 88–91. Surgical pioneer William Halsted was a contemporary luminary who relied on cocaine for prodigious productivity, beginning in the 1880s. See Gerald Imber, *Genius on the Edge: The Bizarre Double Life of Dr. William Stewart Halsted* (New York: Kaplan, 2010), 55–58, 142, 279.

13. Dickson and Dickson, *Life and Inventions*, 229 (quotation), 232 (quotation), 240 (quotation), 233, 239–40. On the shop culture of the Edison enterprises, see Millard, *Edison and Business*, 22–42.

14. Francis A. Jones, *Thomas Alva Edison: Sixty Years of an Inventor's Life* (New York: Thomas Y. Crowell, 1908), 137 (quotations), 224 (quotation), 301 (quotation), 177, 223–24, 241, 296.

15. Frank L. Dyer and Thomas C. Martin, *Edison: His Life and Inventions*, 2 vols. (New York: Harper and Brothers, 1910), 1:281 (Upton quotation), 1:255–58, 278–81, 299, 332, 400; 2: 633 (Edison quotation), 2:634 (Edison quotation), 2:612, 615, 645, 651–52, 763, 772, 778; Thomas Edison, "Book No. 1," Sept. 11, 1908, in Thomas A. Edison, *The Papers of Thomas Alva Edison*, vol. 1, *The Making of an Inventor, February 1847–June 1873*, ed. Reese V. Jenkins et al. (Baltimore: Johns Hopkins University Press, 1989), 629–32, 641, 644; Edison, "First Batch," June 1909, in Edison, *Papers*, 2:777–78; Edison, "First Batch," June 1909, in Edison, *Papers*, 5:1021; Edison, "First Batch," June 1909, in Thomas A. Edison, *The Papers of Thomas Alva Edison*, vol. 6, *Electrifying New York and Abroad*,

April 1881–March 1883, ed. Paul Israel et al. (Baltimore: Johns Hopkins University Press, 2007), 815. For further heroics after 1910, see Frank L. Dyer, Thomas C. Martin, and William H. Meadowcroft, *Edison: His Life and Inventions*, 2nd. ed., 2 vols. (New York: Harper and Brothers, 1929), 2:782–83, 799. For an eyewitness account of the noisemaker used to stop snoring, see Francis Jehl, *Menlo Park Reminiscences*, vol. 2 (Dearborn, Mich.: Edison Institute, 1938), 607–8.

16. Stross, *Wizard*, 64 (quotation); Samuel Haber, *Efficiency and Uplift: Scientific Management in the Progressive Era, 1890–1920* (Chicago: University of Chicago Press, 1973).

17. "Suggestions on Sleep," *Congregationalist*, Feb. 28, 1895, 323 (quotation); Allan Benson, "Edison on How to Live Long," *Hearst's Magazine*, Feb. 1913, 268 (Edison quotation); untitled item, *Massachusetts Ploughman and New England Journal of Agriculture*, Oct. 28, 1905, 64; Bolton Hall, *The Gift of Sleep* (New York: Moffat, Yard, 1911), 11–13; "Seeking to Solve the Mystery of Sleep and Dreams," *New York Times Magazine*, Oct. 22, 1911, 13; Champ Clark, "The Vacation Period," *Independent*, June 6, 1912, 1248.

18. "Edison's Prophecy: A Duplex, Sleepless, Dinnerless World," *Literary Digest*, Nov. 14, 1914, 967 (Edison quotations), 966 (Edison quotation); Edward Purinton, "What Efficiency Means," *Independent*, July 20, 1918, 96 (quotation); editorial, "Personal Efficiency," ibid., Nov. 30, 1914, 304; Edward Purinton, "The Triumph of the Man Who Acts," ibid., Jan. 17, 1916, 90; "They Say (Recent Opinions, Epigrammatic and Otherwise, by Some of Our Wise and Near-Wise Men and Women)," *Life*, Nov. 26, 1914, 958; H. L. Hollingworth and A. T. Poffenberger, *Applied Psychology* (New York: D. Appleton, 1917), 153–54; *New York Times*, Feb. 11, 1920, 9.

19. Martha Coman and Hugh Weir, "She Married the Most Difficult Husband in the World," *Collier's Weekly*, July 18, 1925, 43 (quotation); *New York Times*, Oct. 19, 1931, 22 (Jones quotation); Thomas A. Edison, *The Diary and Sundry Observations of Thomas Alva Edison*, ed. Dagobert Runes (1948; New York: Greenwood Press, 1968), 58, 178; "Edison's Breakfast," *Youth's Companion*, Feb. 26, 1925, 142; "Do We Sleep Too Much?" *Literary Digest*, Sept. 19, 1925, 25; "Speeding Up Sleep," ibid., Feb. 6, 1926, 26; Frank Stockbridge, "Seven Pioneers in Industry Who Started Turning the World Upside Down," *New McClure's*, 63, 110; Henry Ford with Samuel Crowther, *My Friend Mister Edison* (London: Ernest Benn, 1930), 59–61, 72–75, 84–86. For the Edisonian legacy, see Hannah Lees, "Bedtime Story," *Collier's*, Jan. 14, 1939, 32; "The Ravell'd Sleave," *Industrial Bulletin of Arthur D. Little, Inc.*, Sept. 1943, 2; Greer Williams, "You're Not as Tired as You Think," *Nation's Business*, Dec. 1948, 37; Donald A. Laird, *Increasing Personal Efficiency: The Psychology of Personal Progress*, 4th ed. (New York: Harper and Brothers, 1952), 230; Marguerite Clark, *Why So Tired? The Whys of Fatigue and the Ways of Energy* (New York: Duell, Sloan and Pearce, 1962), 80; Andrew Hamilton, "Do You Need Eight Hours Sleep?" *Science Digest*, July 1964, 25; Ben Glasser, "Sleep Less, Live Better," *Harper's Bazaar*, June 1981, 18; Voice of America, "People in America—March 16, 2003: Thomas Edison," Mar. 14, 2003, http://www.voanews.com/specialenglish/archive/2003-

03/a-2003-03-14-3-1.cfm; Grant Stoddard, "Is Sleep Really Necessary?" *Men's Health*, June 2008, 132.

20. Thomas Kessner, *The Flight of the Century: Charles Lindbergh and the Rise of American Aviation* (New York: Oxford University Press, 2010), 98–121; Joseph J. Corn, *The Winged Gospel: America's Romance with Aviation, 1900–1950* (New York: Oxford University Press, 1983), 17, 21–26; John W. Ward, "The Mythic Meaning of Lindbergh's Flight," in *Myth America: A Historical Anthology*, 2nd ed., ed. Patrick Gerster and Nicholas Cords (St. James, N.Y.: Brandywine Press, 2006), 136–43.

21. *New York Times*, May 21, 1927, 6 (Knight quotation), 1–4, 6.

22. *New York Times*, May 22, 1927, E6 (editorial quotation), 1 (Lindbergh quotation), 5, May 23, 1927, 1 (Lindbergh quotation), 1–3; *Chicago Tribune*, May 22, 1927, 1 (Lindbergh quotation), 2, 4; Kessner, *Flight*, 123.

23. Charles A. Lindbergh, *"We": The Famous Flier's Own Story of His Life and His Transatlantic Flight, Together with His Views on the Future of Aviation* (New York: G. P. Putnam's Sons, 1927), 201 (quotation), 238, 275, 314; Arthur Van Meter, "Lindbergh," in *The Spirit of St. Louis: One Hundred Poems*, ed. Charles Vale (New York: George Doran, 1927), 237 (quotation), 236; Merion Ferguson, "The Last Frontiersman," ibid., 94; *New York Times*, June 12, 1927, 2; "Flight," *Time*, May 30, 1927, 26; "The Man of the Year" and "Heroes," *Time*, Jan. 2, 1928, front cover, 10.

24. Dale Van Every and Morris Tracy, *Charles Lindbergh: His Life* (New York: D. Appleton, 1927), 132 (quotation), 17–18, 83, 87, 90, 120–22, 141–51, 174, 200, 224.

25. Kessner, *Flight*, 224–34.

26. Charles A. Lindbergh, *The Spirit of St. Louis* (New York: Charles Scribner's Sons, 1953), 202 (quotation), 233 (quotation), 362 (quotation), 173–75, 201–3, 232–35, 238, 299, 306, 322, 338–46, 352–62, 374–91, 399–401, 422–24, 451–52; Walter S. Ross, *The Last American Hero: Charles A. Lindbergh* (New York: Harper and Row, 1964), xv–xvi, 107–15, 378; Kessner, *Flight*, 235, 259–60. For further efforts in self-mythologizing, see Charles A. Lindbergh, *Autobiography of Values*, ed. William Jovanovich and Judith Schiff (New York: Harcourt Brace Jovanovich, 1978), 11–12, 77–78.

27. Donald A. Laird, *Increasing Personal Efficiency: The Psychology of Personal Progress* (New York: Harper and Brothers, 1925), 185 (quotation), 192 (quotation), ix, 1, 5; Donald A. Laird, *Increasing Personal Efficiency: The Psychology of Personal Progress*, 4th ed. (New York: Harper and Brothers, 1952), 230–40. On the relationship of business to experts in human relations arising at that time, see Loren Baritz, *The Servants of Power: A History of the Use of Social Science in American Industry* (Middletown, Conn.: Wesleyan University Press, 1960).

28. Donald A. Laird, "Effects of Sleep Loss on Mental Work," *Industrial Psychology* 1 (1926): 427–28; Donald A. Laird and Charles G. Muller, *Sleep: Why We Need It and How to Get It* (New York: John Day, 1930), 6, 7, 15, 113–14, 117–20, 187–204. Laird's survey of 509 leaders in diverse fields found that, on average, they slept almost eight hours. See Donald A. Laird, "A Survey of the Sleep Habits of 509 Men of Distinction," *American Medicine* 39 (1931): 271–75.

29. Donald A. Laird, *How to Sleep and Rest Better* (New York: Funk and Wagnalls, 1937), *passim*, esp. 26–28, 80; Donald A. Laird and Eleanor C. Laird, *The Technique of Getting Things Done: Rules for Directing Will Power, from the Lives of the World's Leaders* (New York: McGraw-Hill, 1947), 192–200; Donald A. Laird and Eleanor C. Laird, *Sound Ways to Sound Sleep* (New York: McGraw-Hill, 1959).

30. Bob Hoffman, *How to Be Strong, Healthy and Happy* (York, Pa.: Strength and Health Publishing, 1938), 36–37 (quotation), 36 (quotation), 36–47, 102–7; Dale Carnegie, *How to Stop Worrying and Start Living* (New York: Simon and Schuster, 1948), 207 (quotation), 208 (quotation), 212; Ray Giles, *Sleep! The Secret of Greater Power and Achievement, with 101 Tips from Famous People* (Indianapolis: Bobbs Merrill, 1938), esp. 13–14; "The Ravell'd Sleave," *Industrial Bulletin of Arthur D. Little, Inc.*, Sept. 1943, 1–2; "Dymaxion Sleep," *Time*, Oct. 11, 1943, 63; "Two Hours Sleep Enough?" *Science Digest*, Dec. 1943, 31–33. On Hoffman and his milieu, see John Fair, *Muscletown USA: Bob Hoffman and the Manly Culture of York Barbell* (University Park: Pennsylvania State University Press, 1999); Elizabeth Toon and Janet Golden, "'Live Clean, Think Clean, and Don't Go to Burlesque Shows': Charles Atlas as Health Advisor," *Journal of the History of Medicine and Allied Sciences* 57 (2002): 39–60, esp. 56. On the continuing hope for faster sleep, see Edwin Diamond, "Long Day's Journey into the Insomniac's Night," *New York Times Magazine*, Oct. 1, 1967, 107.

31. Emma E. Walker, "Pretty Girl Papers," *Ladies' Home Journal*, June 1906, 33 (quotations); Louise Paine Benjamin, "The Best Way to Sleep," ibid., Nov. 1936, 33 (quotation); Laird, *How to Sleep*, 43 (quotation); Ruth Murrin, "Sleeping Beauty," *Good Housekeeping*, Apr. 1933, 89; "Sleep," *New York Times Magazine*, Mar. 12, 1944, 23.

32. William H. Whyte Jr., *The Organization Man* (1956; Philadelphia: University of Pennsylvania Press, 2002), 132 (quotation), 143–45; "Personal Business," *Business Week*, Jan. 5, 1957, 110 (quotation); Lemuel McGee, "The Suicidal Cult of 'Manliness,'" *Today's Health*, Jan. 1957, 28 (quotations), 28–30.

33. Niall Ferguson et al., eds., *The Shock of the Global: The 1970s in Perspective* (Cambridge, Mass.: Belknap Press of Harvard University Press, 2010); R. W. Connell and Julian Wood, "Globalization and Business Masculinities," *Men and Masculinities* 7 (2005): 347–64, esp. 352; Richard T. Pascale and Anthony G. Athos, *The Art of Japanese Management: Applications for American Executives* (New York: Simon and Schuster, 1981); William G. Ouchi, *Theory Z: How American Business Can Meet the Japanese Challenge* (Reading, Mass.: Addison-Wesley, 1981); Katsuo Nishiyama and Jeffrey V. Johnson, "Karoshi—Death from Overwork: Occupational Health Consequences of Japanese Production Management," *International Journal of Health Services* 27 (1997): 625–41.

34. Everett Mattlin, *Sleep Less, Live More* (1979; New York: Ballantine Books, 1980), 9 (quotation), 55 (quotation); Ben Glasser, "Sleep Less, Live Better," *Harper's Bazaar*, June 1981, 16 (quotation), 18 (quotations), 37.

35. Sam Walton with John Huey, *Sam Walton, Made in America: My Story* (New York: Doubleday, 1992), 65–66, 115–17; Thomas J. Peters and Robert H. Waterman Jr., *In Search of Excellence: Lessons from America's Best-Run Companies* (New York: Harper

and Row, 1982), 247; Michael Bergdahl, *What I Learned from Sam Walton: How to Compete and Thrive in a Wal-Mart World* (Hoboken, N.J.: John Wiley and Sons, 2004), 62–63, 66–68; Bob Ortega, *In Sam We Trust: The Untold Story of Sam Walton and How Wal-Mart Is Devouring the World* (New York: Times Business, 1998), 85; Don Soderquist, *The Wal-Mart Way: The Inside Story of the Success of the World's Largest Company* (Nashville: Nelson Business, 2005), 120–21; Bethany Moreton, *To Serve God and Wal-Mart: The Making of Christian Free Enterprise* (Cambridge, Mass.: Harvard University Press, 2009), 62–63, 81–83; Nelson Lichtenstein, *The Retail Revolution: How Wal-Mart Created a Brave New World of Business* (New York: Metropolitan Books, 2009), 58–59, 77, 151; Carrie Tuhy, "The Small Sleep," *Esquire*, Sept. 1985, 136, 139.

36. Tamara Eberlein, "How to Feel Rested on Too Little Sleep," *Redbook*, Apr. 1996, 42 (quotation); Amy Eschliman and Leigh Oshirak, *Balance Is a Crock, Sleep Is for the Weak: An Indispensable Guide to Surviving Working Motherhood* (New York: Avery, 2010), 172 (quotation), 147–48, 155–56, 279–81; Roberta Israeloff, "The Sleep Mystique: Could You Get By on Less?" *Working Woman*, Sept. 1990, 195; U.S. Federal Glass Ceiling Commission, *Good for Business: Making Full Use of the Nation's Human Capital: The Environmental Scan* (Washington: Government Printing Office, 1995), iv; John Seabrook, "Snacks for a Fat Planet: PepsiCo Takes Stock of the Obesity Epidemic," *New Yorker*, May 16, 2011, 56: "[PepsiCo CEO Indra] Nooyi is tall, slim, poised, and looks well rested in spite of the fact that she says she works twenty hours a day, seven days a week. If she sleeps more than four hours, 'I feel like I'm wasting time,' she told me."

37. Donald Trump with Tony Schwartz, *Trump: The Art of the Deal* (New York: Random House, 1987), 3 (quotations); Donald Trump with Meredith McIver, *Trump: Think Like a Billionaire: Everything You Need to Know About Success, Real Estate, and Life* (New York: Random House, 2004), xix (quotation), 92; Donald Trump with Meredith McIver, *Trump: How to Get Rich* (New York: Random House, 2004), xiii (quotation), 7, 13, 91; Jason Lamarche, "Donald Trump's Sleeping Secrets," Apr. 23, 2007 (quotation), *The Business Student*, http://thebusinessstudent.blogspot.com/2007/04/sleep.html; Donald Trump and Bill Zanker, *Think Big and Kick Ass in Business and Life* (New York: Harper Collins, 2007), 46 (quotation), 48 (quotations); Donald Trump with Kate Bohner, *Trump: The Art of the Comeback* (New York: Times Books, 1997), 21, 198, 204; Gwenda Blair, *Donald Trump: Master Apprentice* (New York: Simon and Schuster, 2005), 143.

38. Deacon Jones, "Enshrinement Speech," *Pro Football Hall of Fame*, Aug. 2, 2002 (Allen quotation), http://www.profootballhof.com/hof/member.aspx?PlayerId=14&tab=Speech; Michael A. Messner, "The Meaning of Success: The Athletic Experience and the Development of Male Identity," in *The Making of Masculinities: The New Men's Studies*, ed. Harry Brod (Boston: Allen and Unwin, 1987), 193–209; Donald F. Sabo and Joe Panepinto, "Football Ritual and the Social Reproduction of Masculinity," in *Sport, Men, and the Gender Order: Critical Feminist Perspectives*, ed. Michael A. Messner and Donald F. Sabo (Champaign, Ill.: Human Kinetics Books, 1990), 115–26; John M. Carroll, *Red Grange and the Rise of Modern Football* (Urbana: University of Illinois Press, 2004), 182; Jeff Davis, *Papa Bear: The Life and Legacy of George Halas* (New York: McGraw-

Hill, 2005), 426–27; Jennifer Allen, *Fifth Quarter: The Scrimmage of a Football Coach's Daughter* (New York: Random House, 2000), 1, 94–95, 117, 207; Peter King, "What's This? Redskins Coach Joe Gibbs Came Back to a Different NFL," *Sports Illustrated*, Oct. 25, 2004, 152; *New York Times*, Sept. 27, 2009, Sports Sunday, 1, 7; David Halberstam, *The Education of a Coach* (New York: Hyperion, 2005), 25, 108, 110, 264–65; James Lavin, *Management Secrets of the New England Patriots: From "Patsies" to Triple Super Bowl Champs*, 2 vols. (Stamford, Conn.: Pointer Press, 2005), 1:332.

39. Jon Gruden with Vic Carucci, *Do You Love Football? Winning with Heart, Passion and Not Much Sleep* (New York: HarperCollins, 2003), 4 (quotation), 7, 62–65, 86–87, 117, 140, 155, 232, 241; Justin Peters, "No Sleep until Touchdown," *Slate*, Sept. 8, 2006 (quotation), http://www.slate.com/id/2149181; Kelefa Sanneh, "Monday Night Lights: How Jon Gruden Became America's Football Coach," *New Yorker*, Dec. 12, 2011, 40, 41; *Appleton Post-Crescent* (Wisc.), Sept. 10, 2006, B10 (McCarthy quotations); David Fleming, "Away Games," *ESPN the Magazine*, June 4, 2007, 66–72.

40. Marc Beauchamp, "Asleep on the Job," *Forbes*, May 30, 1988, 293 (quotation), 292–94; Verlyn Klinkenborg, "Awakening to Sleep," *New York Times Magazine*, Jan. 5, 1997, 28 (quotation); *Wall Street Journal*, May 7, 2008, B9; John Carney, "Citi Never Sleeps: The Ad Campaign," May 7, 2008, *Dealbreaker*, http://www.dealbreaker.com/2008/05/citi_never_sleeps_the_ad_campa.php; Everett Mattlin, "Executive Insomnia," *Town and Country*, Feb. 1970, 42–43; Michael M. Lewis, *Liar's Poker: Rising Through the Wreckage on Wall Street* (New York: W. W. Norton, 1989), 29, 68, 171, 186; Walter Kiechel III, "The Executive Insomniac," *Fortune*, Oct. 8, 1990, 183; Peter D. Kramer, *Listening to Prozac* (New York: Penguin Books, 1994), 16–17. On the bureaucratic leadership style, see Richard S. Tedlow, Kim Eric Bettcher, and Courtney A. Purrington, "The Chief Executive Officer of the Large American Industrial Corporation in 1917," *Business History Review* 77 (2003): 687–701.

41. Will Meyerhofer, "Not Worth It," *The People's Therapist*, Apr. 13, 2011 (quotation), http://thepeoplestherapist.com/2011/04/13/not-worth-it/; Deborah L. Rhode, *Balanced Lives: Changing the Culture of Legal Practice* (Chicago: Commission on Women in the Profession, American Bar Association, 2001), 14 (quotation), 11–21; Renee M. Landers, James B. Rebitzer, and Lowell J. Taylor, "Rat Race Redux: Adverse Selection in the Determination of Work Hours in Law Firms," *American Economic Review* 86 (1996): 329–48; Staci Zaretsky, "Lawyers, You Can Sleep When You're Dead," *Above the Law*, Aug. 4, 2011, http://abovethelaw.com/2011/08/lawyers-you-can-sleep-when-youre-dead/; Elie Mystal, "You Guys Aren't Getting a Lot of Sleep, Are You?" ibid., Feb. 24, 2012, http://abovethelaw.com/2012/02/you-guys-arent-getting-a-lot-of-sleep-are-you/. On the growing oversupply of lawyers, see Quintin Johnstone, "An Overview of the Legal Profession in the United States, How That Profession Recently Has Been Changing, and Its Future Prospects," *Quinnipiac Law Review* 26 (2008): 739–48, 790–91; U.S. Bureau of Labor Statistics, *Occupational Outlook Handbook, 2012–13* ed., *Lawyers*, http://www.bls.gov/ooh/legal/lawyers, accessed Nov. 16, 2012.

42. Jerome Groopman, "Eyes Wide Open: Can Science Make Regular Sleep Un-

necessary?" *New Yorker*, Dec. 3, 2001, 54 (quotation); *New York Times*, Dec. 11, 2011, 1 (quotation), 4; *New York Times*, July 6, 2012, A1, A7; Marianne Cooper, "Being the 'Go-To Guy': Fatherhood, Masculinity, and the Organization of Work in Silicon Valley," in *Families at Work: Expanding the Boundaries*, ed. Naomi Gerstel, Dan Clawson, and Robert Zussman (Nashville: Vanderbilt University Press, 2002), 14 (quotation), 7, 9, 20; Ben Mezrich, *The Accidental Billionaires: The Founding of Facebook, a Tale of Sex, Money, Genius and Betrayal* (New York: Doubleday, 2009), 92 (quotation), 92–93, 96, 169, 170, 198, 210, 247; David Kirkpatrick, *The Facebook Effect: The Inside Story of the Company That Is Connecting the World* (New York: Simon and Schuster, 2010), 136, 137, 166; Andrew Torba, "Five Things to Know Before Dating a Tech Entrepreneur," *Tech. li*, Nov. 22, 2011, www.tech.li/2011/11/5-things-to-know-before-dating-a-tech-entrepreneur; Alexandra Jacobs, "Happy Feet," ibid., Sept. 14, 2009, 69; *USA Today*, June 18, 2001, B1, B2; Margot Adler, "In Today's World, the Well-Rested Lose Respect," NPR, Jan. 17, 2008, http://www.npr.org/template/story/story.php?storyId=18155047.

43. Will H. Courtenay, "Constructions of Masculinity and Their Influence on Men's Well-Being: A Theory of Gender and Health," *Social Science and Medicine* 50 (2000): 1388–89 (quotation), 1385–401; Will H. Courtenay, "Behavioral Factors Associated with Disease, Injury, and Death among Men: Evidence and Implications for Prevention," *Journal of Men's Studies* 9 (2000): 81–142; Gunther Peck, "Manly Gambles: The Politics of Risk on the Comstock Lode, 1860–1880," *Journal of Social History* 26 (1993): 701–23.

Chapter 2. In a Drowsy State

Note to epigraph: U.S. House of Representatives, Committee on Interstate and Foreign Commerce, *Hearing . . . on the Bills HR 4438, HR 16676, and HR 18671, to Limit the Hours of Service of Railroad Employees*, 59th Cong., 1st sess., 1906, 3 pts. (Washington, D.C.: Government Printing Office, 1906), 1:10 (Fuller quotation).

1. David R. Roediger and Philip S. Foner, *Our Own Time: A History of American Labor and the Working Day* (New York: Verso, 1989), 43–64; Benjamin Chace et al., "Circular of the Fall River Mechanics," June 1844, in *A Documentary History of American Industrial Society*, ed. John R. Commons et al., 11 vols., vol. 8, *Labor Movement*, ed. John R. Commons (Cleveland: Arthur Clark, 1910), 86–91; Lowell Convention, "Preamble and Resolutions," Mar. 1845, in ibid., 99–106; William Schouler, "The First Official Investigation of Labor Conditions," 1845, in ibid., 133–51; Kathryn Kish Sklar, "'The Greater Part of the Petitioners Are Female': The Reduction of Women's Working Hours in the Paid Labor Force, 1840–1917," in *Worktime and Industrialization: An International History*, ed. Gary S. Cross (Philadelphia: Temple University Press, 1988), 110–20; Marion C. Cahill, *Shorter Hours: A Study of the Movement Since the Civil War* (New York: Columbia University Press, 1932), 112; Elizabeth Brandeis, "Labor Legislation," in John R. Commons et al., *History of Labor in the United States*, 4 vols., vol. 3, *History of Labor in the United States, 1896–1932: Working Conditions, Labor Legislation* (New York: Macmillan, 1935), 97–98, 460, 471–74, 499; Peter C. Baldwin, *In the Watches of the Night: Life*

in the Nocturnal City, 1820–1930 (Chicago: University of Chicago Press, 2012), 21–27, 104–37.

2. Dorothee Schneider, *Trade Unions and Community: The German Working Class in New York City, 1870–1900* (Urbana: University of Illinois Press, 1994), 184–86, 190–91.

3. U.S. Supreme Court, *Lochner v. New York, United States Reports*, vol. 198 (New York: Banks Law Publishing, 1905), 57 (Peckham quotation), 70 (Hirt quotation), 52–74. For further discussion of the sleep-related health problems of bakers, see Charles Iffland, "Reasons Why Night Work Should Be Abolished in Bakeries," *American Federationist*, May 1919, 407–9.

4. U.S. Supreme Court, *Muller v. Oregon, United States Reports*, vol. 208 (New York: Banks Law Publishing, 1908), 421 (Brewer quotation), 415–23; Louis D. Brandeis and Josephine Goldmark, *Women in Industry: Decision of the United States Supreme Court in Curt Muller vs. State of Oregon Upholding the Constitutionality of the Oregon Ten Hour Law for Women and Brief for the State of Oregon* (1908; New York: Arno Press, 1969), esp. 18, 34–35; Sklar, "'Greater Part,'" 121–24. For similar policy discourse regarding endangered children, see Alan Derickson, "Making Human Junk: Child Labor as a Health Issue in the Progressive Era," *American Journal of Public Health* 82 (1992): 1280–90.

5. Annie M. MacLean, *Wage-Earning Women* (New York: Macmillan, 1910), 178 (quotation), 178–79; New York State Factory Investigating Commission, *Second Report*, vol. 1 (Albany: J. B. Lyon, 1913), 193 (quotation), 194 (quotation), 195 (quotation), 193–212; Susan Lehrer, *Origins of Protective Labor Legislation for Women, 1905–1925* (Albany: State University of New York Press, 1987), 24, 38–39; Alice Kessler-Harris, *Out to Work: A History of Wage-Earning Women in the United States* (New York: Oxford University Press, 1982), 191–92; Diane Kirkby, "The Wage-Earning Woman and the State: The National Women's Trade Union League and Protective Labor Legislation, 1903–1923," *Labor History* 28 (1987): 56, 59, 61. For a broader discussion of this reform rhetoric and the contradictions of protective policy, see Alice Kessler-Harris, "The Paradox of Motherhood: Night Work Restrictions in the United States," in *Protecting Women: Labor Legislation in Europe, the United States, and Australia, 1880–1920*, ed. Ulla Wikander, Alice Kessler-Harris, and Jane Lewis (Urbana: University of Illinois Press, 1995), 337–57. On the tradition of engaged social empiricism that studies of nocturnal employment drew upon, see, among others, Martin Bulmer, Kevin Bales, and Kathryn Kish Sklar, eds., *The Social Survey in Historical Perspective, 1880–1940* (Cambridge: Cambridge University Press, 1991); Dorothy Ross, *The Origins of American Social Science, 1865–1905* (Cambridge: Cambridge University Press, 1991), 143–59; Alice O'Connor, *Poverty Knowledge: Social Science, Social Policy, and the Poor in Twentieth-Century U.S. History* (Princeton, N.J.: Princeton University Press, 2001), 25–44.

6. Brandeis, "Labor Legislation," in Commons et al., *History of Labor*, 3: 474–79; Kessler-Harris, *Out to Work*, 191.

7. Louis D. Brandeis and Josephine Goldmark, *The Case Against Nightwork for Women, Revised with New Introduction to March 1, 1918: Court of Appeal, State of New York, the People of the State of New York, Respondent, Against Charles Schweinler Press,*

a Corporation, Defendant-Appellant (New York: National Consumers' League, 1918), 1 (quotation), 1–46 passim; U.S. Supreme Court, *Radice v. People of the State of New York, United States Reports,* vol. 264 (Washington, D.C.: Government Printing Office, 1924), 294 (Sutherland quotation), 292–98; John T. McGuire, "Making the Case for Night Work Legislation in Progressive Era New York, 1911–15," *Journal of the Gilded Age and Progressive Era* 5 (2006): 67–68; Mary Van Kleeck, *Women in the Bookbinding Trade* (New York: Survey Associates, 1913), 151; Allison L. Hepler, *Women in Labor: Mothers, Medicine, and Occupational Health in the United States, 1890–1980* (Columbus: Ohio State University Press, 2000), 53; U.S. Women's Bureau, *Night-Work Laws in the United States: Summary of State Legislation Regulating Night Work for Women,* Bulletin 7 (Washington, D.C.: Government Printing Office, 1920). On the desire to curb night work in order to eliminate the risk of sexual assault faced by women commuting in the dark, see Baldwin, *Watches of the Night,* 194, 198.

8. Florence Kelley, "Wage-Earning Women in War Time," *Journal of Industrial Hygiene* 1 (1919): 276 (anonymous worker quotation), 282 (quotation), 261–83, esp. 273–78; Agnes de Lima, *Night-Working Mothers in Textile Mills, Passaic, New Jersey* (N.p.: National Consumers' League and Consumer's League of New Jersey, 1920), 5 (quotation), 9 (anonymous worker quotation), 8–18; Landon R. Storrs, *Civilizing Capitalism: The National Consumers' League, Women's Activism, and Labor Standards in the New Deal Era* (Chapel Hill: University of North Carolina Press, 2000), 49–51, 65–67, 73–76, 85–87, 155–76, 220–21.

9. U.S. Women's Bureau, *The Employment of Women at Night,* by Mary Hopkins, Bulletin 64 (Washington, D.C.: Government Printing Office, 1928), 39 (quotation), 40 (quotation), 52 (quotation), 1, 13, 18–22, 39–41, 50–52, 56–57; U.S. Women's Bureau, *The Effects of Labor Legislation on the Employment Opportunities of Women,* by Mary N. Winslow, Bulletin 65 (Washington, D.C.: Government Printing Office, 1928), 18–22, 47, 172–73, 285. On the bureau's strategy in the conservative 1920s, see Mark Hendrickson, "Gender Research as Labor Activism: The Women's Bureau in the New Era," *Journal of Policy History* 20 (2008): 482–515.

10. U.S. Women's Bureau, *State Labor Laws for Women with Wartime Modifications, December 15, 1944,* pt. V: *Explanation and Appraisal,* Bulletin 202-V (Washington, D.C.: Government Printing Office, 1946), 8, 10, 14, 24, 63–66; National Industrial Conference Board, *Legal Restrictions on Hours of Work in the United States: A Reference Manual* (New York: National Industrial Conference Board, 1924), 12, 13, 16–19, 44–125; National Industrial Conference Board, *Night Work in Industry* (New York: National Industrial Conference Board, 1927), 11; Brandeis, "Labor Legislation," in Commons et al., *History of Labor,* 3: 495–500; Vanessa H. May, *Unprotected Labor: Household Workers, Politics, and Middle-Class Reform in New York, 1870–1940* (Chapel Hill: University of North Carolina Press, 2011), 3, 77–80, 137–42.

11. "One Day of Rest in Seven," *American Labor Legislation Review,* Dec. 1912, 530 (AALL quotation), 517–33; Pennsylvania, *Laws of the General Assembly . . . , 1913* (Harrisburg: C. E. Aughinbaugh, Printer to the State of Pennsylvania, 1913), 913 (quotation);

John B. Andrews, "One-Day-of-Rest-in-Seven Legislation: An Immediate Issue," *American Labor Legislation Review*, Sept. 1923, 176 (quotation), 175–76; John A. Fitch, "Rest Periods for the Continuous Industries," ibid., Mar. 1913, 53–62; "Hours," ibid., Oct. 1913, 402; Kenneth Fones-Wolf, *Trade Union Gospel: Christianity and Labor in Industrial Philadelphia, 1865–1915* (Philadelphia: Temple University Press, 1989), 51; Annie Polland, "Working for the Sabbath: Sabbath in the Jewish Immigrant Neighborhoods of New York," *Labor: Studies in Working-Class History of the Americas* 6, no. 1 (Summer 2009): 33–56; National Industrial Conference Board, *Legal Restrictions*, 13–14. For union efforts to have Sunday closing laws enforced, see David Brody, *The Butcher Workmen: A Study of Unionization* (Cambridge, Mass.: Harvard University Press, 1964), 11–12, 21. On the week, the work week, the weekend, the Sabbath, and cyclical time, see Eviatar Zerubavel, *The Seven-Day Circle: The History and Meaning of the Week* (Chicago: University of Chicago Press, 1989), esp. 86–95; Eviatar Zerubavel, *Hidden Rhythms: Schedules and Calendars in Social Life* (Berkeley: University of California Press, 1985), 101–37. For one anthropologist's attempt to treat the day-of-rest movement as a throwback to primitive cultures, undercutting productivity and progress itself, see Hutton Webster, *Rest Days: A Study in Early Law and Morality* (New York: Macmillan, 1916), esp. 1: "The custom of refraining from labor on certain occasions is by no means unknown to peoples in the lower stages of culture. . . . A survey of the evidence . . . indicates that the sabbatarian regulations have arisen chiefly, if not wholly, as pure superstitions, the product of an all-too-logical intellect or of a disordered fancy. In the last analysis they are based primarily on fear."

12. U.S. Interstate Commerce Commission, *Seventeenth Annual Report of the Interstate Commerce Commission, December 15, 1903* (Washington, D.C.: Government Printing Office, 1903), 102–4, 344–46; Mark Aldrich, *Death Rode the Rails: American Railroad Accidents and Safety, 1828–1965* (Baltimore: Johns Hopkins University Press, 2009), 42–184. An attempt to limit rail workers to twelve consecutive working hours within a twenty-four-hour period failed to make it through Congress in 1884. See Walter Licht, *Working for the Railroad: The Organization of Work in the Nineteenth Century* (Princeton, N.J.: Princeton University Press, 1983), 177–78n38.

13. *Brotherhood of Locomotive Engineers Monthly Journal*, Apr. 1904, 262–63 (quotation); Edward A. Moseley, "Railroad Accidents in the United States," *American Monthly Review of Reviews*, Nov. 1904, 595 (unnamed newspaper quotation), 596 (quotation), 592–96; John J. Esch, "Should the Safety of Employees and Travellers on Railroads Be Promoted by Legislation?" *North American Review*, Nov. 1904, 675 (quotation), 675–78, 684; Theodore Roosevelt, "President's Annual Message," *Congressional Record* 39 (Dec. 6, 1904), 11 (quotation); U.S. Interstate Commerce Commission, *Eighteenth Annual Report of the Interstate Commerce Commission, December 19, 1904* (Washington, D.C.: Government Printing Office, 1904), 97, 105, 361–66. Another variant of the Progressive agenda-setting process had the ICC picking up a trade journal's analysis of the commission's data. See "Forty-One Rear Collisions," *Railroad Gazette*, Aug. 22, 1902, rpt. in U.S. Interstate Commerce Commission, *Sixteenth Annual Report of the Interstate Commerce*

Commission, December 15, 1902 (Washington, D.C.: Government Printing Office, 1902), 313: "Giving trainmen plenty of rest seems to be well enough understood when there is a discussion with a grievance committee; but as long as the men can get partial relief by sleeping in the caboose on the road everybody seems willing to swallow his principles and go in for a big car-movement record."

14. *Brotherhood of Locomotive Engineers Monthly Journal,* Feb. 1905, 161, Apr. 1905, 333, 340, June 1905, 488, 489, July 1905, 625, Aug. 1905, 682; Paul M. Taillon, *Good, Reliable, White Men: Railroad Brotherhoods, 1877–1917* (Urbana: University of Illinois Press, 2009), 179. On long hours in earlier years, see Licht, *Working for the Railroad,* 174; James H. Ducker, *Men of the Steel Rails: Workers on the Atchison, Topeka and Santa Fe Railroad, 1869–1900* (University of Nebraska Press, 1983), 16–19, 120.

15. U.S. House of Representatives, Committee on Interstate and Foreign Commerce, *Hearing on HR 4438,* 1:7 (Fuller quotation), 10 (Fuller quotations), 3–19; Taillon, *White Men,* 179.

16. House, *Hearing on HR 4438,* 1:28 (Norris quotation), 24–30, 32, 42, 48, 50, 57, 65, 73; U.S. House of Representatives, Committee on Interstate and Foreign Commerce, *Limiting the Hours of Service of Railroad Employees,* 59th Cong., 1st sess., 1906, House Report 4567 (Washington, D.C.: Government Printing Office, 1906), 2, 5, 7–8. For the weaker bill in the other chamber, see U.S. Senate, Committee on Education and Labor, *To Promote the Safety of Employees and Travelers upon Railroads,* 59th Cong., 1st sess., June 9, 1906, Senate Report 4246 (Washington, D.C.: Government Printing Office, 1906), 1–2.

17. U.S. House of Representatives, Committee on Interstate and Foreign Commerce, *Hearing . . . on the Bills Senate Act 5133 and HR 24373 to Limit the Hours of Service of Railroad Employees,* 59th Cong., 2nd sess., 1907 (Washington, D.C.: Government Printing Office, 1907), 22 (Willard quotation), 3–44; *U.S. Statutes at Large* 34 (1907): 1415–17; *Brotherhood of Locomotive Engineers Monthly Journal,* May 1908, 389–91, 437, Oct. 1908, 897–98; Aldrich, *Death Rode the Rails,* 184–85 (Aldrich points out the modest impact of this law on accidents). For examples of the ongoing problem of sleep-induced mishaps, despite the provisions of the law, see U.S. Interstate Commerce Commission, *In Re Investigation of Accident on the New York, New Haven and Hartford Railroad near North New Haven, Conn., September 5, 1913,* by George McGinty (Washington, D.C.: Government Printing Office, 1913), 9–10; Mark Aldrich, "Combating the Collision Horror: The Interstate Commerce Commission and Automatic Train Control, 1900–1939," *Technology and Culture* 34 (1993): 49–51.

18. Jerold S. Auerbach, "Progressives at Sea: The La Follette Act of 1915," *Labor History* 2 (1961): 344–60, esp. 345, 350–51; Leon Fink, *Sweatshops at Sea: Merchant Seamen in the World's First Globalized Industry, from 1812 to the Present* (Chapel Hill: University of North Carolina Press, 2011), 96–97, 107; *U.S. Statutes at Large* 38 (1915): 1164–85, esp. 1164, 1165; Andrew Furuseth, "The Seaman's Law and Its Critics," *American Labor Legislation Review,* Mar. 1916, 61, 65; Frederick L. Hoffman, "Occupational Hazards in the American Merchant Marine," ibid., 72.

19. U.S. Bureau of Air Commerce, *[Part] 61—Scheduled Airline Rules (Interstate)* (Washington, D.C.: Government Printing Office, 1937), 7–8, 11. For corporate policies stricter than the federal standards, see Pan American Airways, "Statement of Policy . . . with Regard to Hours, Rates of Pay and Working Conditions of All Pilots," 8, Aug. 15, 1938, Ross McFarland Collection, box 192, folder 6, Special Collections and Archives, Wright State University Libraries, Dayton, Ohio; Ross A. McFarland et al., "An Analysis of the Physiological and Psychological Characteristics of Two Hundred Civil Air Line Pilots," *Aviation Medicine* 10 (1939): 161.

20. U.S. House of Representatives, Committee on Public Works and Transportation, Subcommittee on Aviation, *Flight Attendant Duty Limitations: Hearing . . . on HR 14*, 102nd Cong., 1st sess., 1991 (Washington, D.C.: Government Printing Office, 1991), 57 (Leon quotation), 55–77; Lee Kolm, "Stewardesses' 'Psychological Punch': Gender and Commercial Aviation in the United States, 1930–1978," in *From Airships to Airbus: The History of Civil and Commercial Aviation*, ed. William F. Trimble, 2 vols. (Washington, D.C.: Smithsonian Institution Press, 1995), 2:112–27; Kathleen M. Barry, *Femininity in Flight: A History of Flight Attendants* (Durham, N.C.: Duke University Press, 2007); Aviation Safety Institute, *A Study of Airline Flight Attendant Sleepiness, Fatigue and Stress* (Worthington, Ohio: Aviation Safety Institute, 1980); Roberta G. Lessor, "Social Movements, the Occupational Arena and Changes in Career Consciousness: The Case of Women Flight Attendants," *Journal of Occupational Behavior* 5 (1984): 44–45; U.S. Federal Aviation Administration, "Petitions for Rulemaking," *Federal Register* 50 (1985): 6185; U.S. Federal Aviation Administration, "Flight Attendant Duty Period Limitations and Rest Requirements," *Federal Register* 59 (1994): 42974–94; Drew Whitelegg, *Working the Skies: The Fast-Paced, Disorienting World of the Flight Attendant* (New York: New York University Press, 2007), esp. 99–125. For the unused mandate to prescribe working-time limitations for cabin-crew members, see *U.S. Statutes at Large* 52 (1938): 1008.

21. U.S. Bureau of Air Commerce, *Scheduled Airline Rules*, 8.

22. On the evolution of overtime-pay law, see, Marc Linder, *The Autocratically Flexible Workplace: A History of Overtime Regulation in the United States* (Iowa City: Fanpihua Press, 2002); Marc Linder, *"Time and a Half's the American Way": A History of the Exclusion of White-Collar Workers from Overtime Regulation, 1868–2004* (Iowa City: Fanpihua Press, 2004); Ronnie J. Steinberg, *Wages and Hours: Labor and Reform in Twentieth-Century America* (New Brunswick, N.J.: Rutgers University Press, 1982).

23. Roediger and Foner, *Our Own Time*, 25, 194–206; Licht, *Working for the Railroad*, 142, 178–79; Michael Kazin, *Barons of Labor: The San Francisco Building Trades and Union Power in the Progressive Era* (Urbana: University of Illinois Press, 1987), 39; Peter Cole, *Wobblies on the Waterfront: Interracial Unionism in Progressive-Era Philadelphia* (Urbana: University of Illinois Press, 2007), 41, 47, 64, 69; Walter Galenson, *The United Brotherhood of Carpenters and Joiners: The First Hundred Years* (Cambridge, Mass.: Harvard University Press, 1983), 187; U.S. National War Labor Board, *Memorandum on the Eight-Hour Working Day* (Washington, D.C.: Government Printing Office, 1918); "Recent Application of the Eight-Hour Day," *Monthly Labor Review*, Sept. 1918,

188–96; Melvyn Dubofsky, *The State and Labor in Modern America* (Chapel Hill: University of North Carolina Press, 1994), 59–60, 71–78.

24. U.S. Women's Bureau, *Employed Women Under NRA Codes*, by Mary Pidgeon, Bulletin 130 (Washington, D.C.: Government Printing Office, 1935), 10–11, 34–44; Storrs, *Civilizing Capitalism*, 109, 308n61–62; Leverett S. Lyon et al., *The National Recovery Administration: An Analysis and Appraisal* (Washington, D.C.: Brookings Institution, 1935), esp. 365–91; Ellis W. Hawley, *The New Deal and the Problem of Monopoly: A Study in Economic Ambivalence* (Princeton, N.J.: Princeton University Press, 1966), 19–146; Stanley Vittoz, *New Deal Labor Policy and the American Industrial Economy* (Chapel Hill: University of North Carolina Press, 1987), 73–134.

25. U.S. Senate, Committee on Education and Labor, and U.S. House of Representatives, Committee on Labor, *Fair Labor Standards Act of 1937: Joint Hearings . . . on S. 2475 and H.R. 7200*, 75th Cong., 1st sess., 1937 (Washington, D.C.: Government Printing Office, 1937), 189 (Perkins quotation), 233–34, 622, 812, 814; American Federation of Labor, *Report of Proceedings of the Fifty-Third Annual Convention, 1933* (Washington, D.C.: Judd and Detweiler, n.d.), 475–76; John S. Forsythe, "Legislative History of the Fair Labor Standards Act," *Law and Contemporary Problems* 6 (1939): 466, 474, 478, 486; *U.S. Statutes at Large* 52 (1938): 1063, 1067–68; Irving Bernstein, *A Caring Society: The New Deal, the Worker and the Great Depression* (Boston: Houghton Mifflin, 1985), 116–45; Benjamin K. Hunnicutt, *Work Without End: Abandoning Shorter Hours for the Right to Work* (Philadelphia: Temple University Press, 1988), esp. 80–81, 310; Storrs, *Civilizing Capitalism*, 177–98. Exceptional universalistic policies to cap hours rather than merely make overwork more expensive to employers appeared in Alaska in the 1910s and in Montana and Pennsylvania in the 1930s. None of these short-lived initiatives was animated to any significant extent by concerns over sleep and rest. See Linder, *Autocratically Flexible Workplace*, 69–241.

26. Harold F. Browne, *Shift Operation Under Defense Conditions* (New York: National Industrial Conference Board, 1941), 5–11; "Round the Clock," *Business Week*, Jan. 10, 1942, 63–64; "All-Out Production: Workers' Health and the Twenty-Four-Hour Schedule," *War Medicine* 2 (1942): 341–42; J. J. Bloomfield, "Industrial Hygiene in War Production," *California and Western Medicine* 57 (1942): 236.

27. Nathaniel Kleitman, *Sleep and Wakefulness as Alternating Phases in the Cycle of Existence* (Chicago: University of Chicago Press, 1939), 437 (quotation), 437–39; Nathaniel Kleitman, "A Scientific Solution of the Multiple Shift Problem," in Industrial Hygiene Foundation, *Proceedings of the Seventh Annual Meeting, 1942* (Pittsburgh: Industrial Hygiene Foundation, n.d.), 20 (quotation), 19–23; J. K. Westerfield, "Management Tackles the Night Shift Problem," *American Business*, Feb. 1942, 20; Nathaniel Kleitman, "Physiological Arrangement of Shifts with Respect to Ages, Interests and Social Activities of Workers," Mar. 1942, Nathaniel Kleitman Papers, box 10, folder 6, Special Collections Research Center, Regenstein Library, University of Chicago; Nathaniel Kleitman to Curtis Collison, Mar. 5, 1942, ibid.; Morris Fishbein to Nathaniel Kleitman, July 9, 1942, ibid.; H. M. Miller to Nathaniel Kleitman, Sept. 23, 1942, ibid.;

Nathaniel Kleitman to Fowler Harper, Feb. 13, 1943, ibid., folder 7; U.S. Department of Labor, Division of Labor Standards, *Arranging Shifts for Maximum Production* (Washington, D.C.: Division of Labor Standards, 1942); V. A. Zimmer to D. E. Foster, July 2, 1943, RG 100: Records of the Bureau of Labor Standards, Division of Labor Standards Classified Central Files, 1941–1945, box 22, folder: Results of Shorter Hours, Archives II, National Archives, College Park, Md.; Waldemar Kaempffert, "Red, White and Blue Shifts," *New York Times Magazine*, Sept. 20, 1942, 14, 27; Waldemar Kaempffert, "Better Hours for War Workers," *Science Digest*, Dec. 1942, 66–70; New York State Department of Labor, *Problems of Shift Rotation: Social and Physiological Aspects*, by Beatrice Mintz (Albany: New York State Department of Labor, 1943), 2, 4. On Kleitman's early career and its immediate scientific context, see Kenton Kroker, *The Sleep of Others and the Transformation of Sleep Research* (Toronto: University of Toronto Press, 2007), 205–37. On the bureaucratic activism of the Division of Labor Standards, see Gerald Markowitz and David Rosner, "More Than Economism: The Politics of Workers' Safety and Health, 1932–1947," *Milbank Quarterly* 64 (1986): 331–54.

28. U.S. Women's Bureau, *Night Work for Women and Shift Rotation in War Plants*, Special Bulletin 6 (Washington, D.C.: Government Printing Office, 1942), 4 (quotation), 7 (quotation), 3–8; Theodore Waters, "Report of the Legal Committee," in Industrial Hygiene Foundation, *Proceedings, 1942*, 72–74; U.S. Women's Bureau, *Employing Women in Shipyards*, by Dorothy K. Newman, Bulletin 192-6 (Washington, D.C.: Government Printing Office, 1944), 35–40. On the female influx into the paid workforce, see, among others, Chester W. Gregory, *Women in Defense Work During World War II: An Analysis of the Labor Problem and Women's Rights* (New York: Exposition Press, 1974); Karen Anderson, *Wartime Women: Sex Roles, Family Relations, and the Status of Women During World War II* (Westport, Conn.: Greenwood Press, 1981), 3–74; Susan Hartmann, *The Home Front and Beyond: American Women in the 1940s* (Boston: Twayne, 1982), 77–99; Ruth Milkman, *Gender at Work: The Dynamics of Job Segregation by Sex During World War II* (Urbana: University of Illinois Press, 1987), 49–64. For a medical critique of women's night work, see Milton Kronenberg, "Women and Wartime Health Problems," *Industrial Medicine* 11 (1942): 336.

29. U.S. Women's Bureau, *Women's Employment in the Making of Steel, 1943*, by Ethel Erickson, Bulletin 192-5 (Washington, D.C.: Government Printing Office, 1944), 20–21, 25, 33; "Survey Shows How Women War Workers Live," *Labor Information Bulletin*, Aug. 1942, 5–6; U.S. Women's Bureau, *Recreation and Housing for Women War Workers: A Handbook on Standards*, by Mary V. Robinson, Bulletin 190 (Washington, D.C.: Government Printing Office, 1942), 7, 21–26; U.S. Women's Bureau, *Progress Report on Women War Workers' Housing, April 1943*, Special Bulletin 17 (Washington, D.C.: Government Printing Office, 1944), 1–10; U.S. Women's Bureau, *State Labor Laws, 1944*, 25–27, 31, 35, 42, 44; Hepler, *Women in Labor*, 79.

30. Anna M. Baetjer, *Women in Industry: Their Health and Efficiency* (Philadelphia: W. B. Saunders, 1946), 15 (quotation), 15–16, 21–28; U.S. Women's Bureau, *Night Work for Women in Hotels and Restaurants*, Bulletin 233 (Washington, D.C.: Government Print-

ing Office, 1949), 2 (quotation), 1–3, 8–11, 29–35, 42–44; Dorothy Sue Cobble, *The Other Women's Movement: Workplace Justice and Social Rights in Modern America* (Princeton: Princeton University Press, 2004), 64, 142–43, 147–48; Storrs, *Civilizing Capitalism*, 240; Hepler, *Women in Labor*, 83–101.

31. U.S. President's Commission on the Status of Women, *American Women: Report of the President's Commission on the Status of Women* (Washington, D.C.: Government Printing Office, 1963), 37–38 (quotation), U.S. President's Commission on the Status of Women, Committee on Protective Legislation, *Report of the Committee on Protective Labor Legislation* (Washington, D.C.: Government Printing Office, 1963), iii, 9–13; Cobble, *Other Women's Movement*, 171–95; Steinberg, *Wages and Hours*, 226–27.

32. Juliet B. Schor, *The Overworked American: The Unexpected Decline of Leisure* (New York: Basic Books, 1993), 107 (quotation); Gary S. Cross, *Time and Money: The Making of Consumer Culture* (New York: Routledge, 1993); Janice Hedges and Edward Sekscenski, "Workers on Late Shifts in a Changing Economy," *Monthly Labor Review*, Sept. 1979, 14–22; Nancy Gordon, "The Prevalence and Health Impact of Shift Work," *American Journal of Public Health* 76 (1986): 1225–28; Stanley Aronowitz, *False Promises: The Shaping of American Working Class Consciousness* (New York: McGraw-Hill, 1973); James O'Toole et al., *Work in America: Report of a Special Task Force to the Secretary of Health, Education, and Welfare* (Cambridge, Mass.: MIT Press, 1973); James O'Toole, ed., *Work and the Quality of Life: Resource Papers for* Work in America (Cambridge, Mass.: MIT Press, 1974).

33. Charles Noble, *Liberalism at Work: The Rise and Fall of OSHA* (Philadelphia: Temple University Press, 1986), 68–98; Nicholas A. Ashford, *Crisis in the Workplace: Occupational Disease and Injury* (Cambridge, Mass.: MIT Press, 1976), 138–233, 299–302.

34. E. Thiis-Evensen, "Shift Work and Health," *Industrial Medicine and Surgery* 27 (1958): 496 (quotation), 493–97; Floyd C. Mann, "Shift Work and the Shorter Workweek," in *Hours of Work*, ed. Clyde E. Dankert, Floyd C. Mann, and Herbert R. Northrup (New York: Harper and Row, 1965), 126 (quotation), 111–27; Paul E. Mott et al., *Shift Work: The Social, Psychological, and Physical Consequences* (Ann Arbor: University of Michigan Press, 1965), 255 (quotation); S. Wyatt and R. Marriott, "Night Work and Shift Changes," *British Journal of Industrial Medicine* 10 (1953): 164–72; Bo Bjerner, Ake Holm, and Ake Swensson, "Diurnal Variation in Mental Performance," ibid., 12 (1955): 103–10; R. T. Wilkinson, "Effects of Up to 60 Hours' Sleep Deprivation on Different Types of Work," *Ergonomics* 7 (1964): 175–86; Anthon Aanonsen, *Shift Work and Health* (Oslo: Scandinavian University Books, 1964). For helpful overviews of the early work, see J. Carpentier and P. Cazamian, *Night Work: Its Effects on the Health and Welfare of the Worker* (Geneva: International Labor Office, 1977); J. Rutenfranz et al., "Biomedical and Psychosocial Aspects of Shift Work: A Review," *Scandinavian Journal of Work, Environment and Health* 3 (1977): 165–82; Great Britain, Health and Safety Executive, Employment Medical Advisory Service, *Shift Work and Health: A Critical Review of the Literature*, by J. M. Harrington (London: Her Majesty's Stationery Office, 1978).

35. P. G. Rentos, "Opening Remarks and Statement of Purpose," in U.S. National

Institute of Occupational Safety and Health (NIOSH), *Shift Work and Health: A Symposium*, DHEW Publication (NIOSH) 76–203 (Washington, D.C.: Government Printing Office, 1976), 3 (quotation), 3–4; Paul E. Mott, "Social and Psychological Adjustment to Shift Work," in ibid., 150 (quotation), 145; Elliott Weitzman, "Group 1 [discussion report]," in ibid., 233 (quotation); Austin Henschel, "NIOSH Point of View," in ibid., 6; Elliott Weitzman, "Circadian Rhythms: Discussion," in ibid., 53–56; Wilse B. Webb, "Social and Psychological Adjustment to Shift Work: Discussion II," in ibid., 158; Torbjorn Akerstedt and Jan Froberg, "Shift Work and Health—Interdisciplinary Aspects," in ibid., 179–80.

36. NIOSH, *Shift Work Practices in the United States*, by Donald L. Tasto and Michael J. Colligan, DHEW (NIOSH) Publication 77–148 (Washington, D.C.: Government Printing Office, 1977); NIOSH, *Health Consequences of Shift Work*, by Donald L. Tasto et al., DHEW Publication (NIOSH) 78–154 (Washington, D.C.: Government Printing Office, 1978); Paul Naitoh, "Circadian Cycles and Restorative Power of Naps," in NIOSH, *The Twenty-Four Hour Workday: Proceedings of a Symposium on Variations in Work-Sleep Schedules*, ed. Laverne C. Johnson et al., DHEW Publication (NIOSH) 81–127 (Washington, D.C.: Government Printing Office, 1981), 693–720. For the efforts to keep the issue alive at NIOSH, see Roger R. Rosa and Michael J. Colligan, "Extended Workdays: Effects of 8-Hour and 12-Hour Rotating Shift Schedules on Performance, Subjective Alertness, Sleep Patterns, and Psychosocial Variables," *Work and Stress* 3 (1989): 21–32; Roger R. Rosa, "Napping at Home and Alertness on the Job in Rotating Shift Workers," *Sleep* 16 (1993): 727–35; Roger R. Rosa, "Toward Better Sleep for Workers: Impressions of Some Needs," *Industrial Health* 43 (2005): 85–87.

37. Noble, *Liberalism at Work*, 173–96; Eula Bingham, "The New Look at OSHA: Vital Changes," *Labor Law Journal* 29 (1978): 487–92; James C. Robinson, *Toil and Toxics: Workplace Struggles and Political Strategies for Occupational Health* (Berkeley: University of California Press, 1991), 108–64; Frank Goldsmith and Lorin Kerr, "Worker Participation in Job Safety and Health," *Journal of Public Health Policy* 4 (1983): 447–66.

38. U.S. Congress, Office of Technology Assessment, *Biological Rhythms: Implications for the Worker* (Washington, D.C.: Government Printing Office, 1991), 25 (quotation), 18–19, 22–25; U.S. President's Commission on the Accident at Three Mile Island, *The Need for Change: The Legacy of TMI: Report of the President's Commission on the Accident at Three Mile Island* (Washington, D.C.: Government Printing Office, 1979); Merrill M. Mitler et al. (Committee on Catastrophes, Sleep and Public Policy, Association of Professional Sleep Societies), "Catastrophes, Sleep, and Public Policy: Consensus Report," *Sleep* 11 (1988): 100–109; Charles Perrow, *Normal Accidents: Living with High-Risk Technologies* (New York: Basic Books, 1984) U.S. House of Representatives, Committee on Science and Technology, Subcommittee on Investigations and Oversight, *Biological Clocks and Shift Work Scheduling: Hearings*, 98th Cong., 1st sess., 1983 (Washington, D.C.: Government Printing Office, 1983); U.S. House of Representatives, Committee on Science and Technology, Subcommittee on Investigations and Oversight, *Biological Clocks and Shift Work Scheduling: Report*, 98th Cong., 2nd sess., 1984 (Washington,

D.C.: Government Printing Office, 1984), esp. iv; U.S. Congress, Office of Technology Assessment, *Safe Skies for Tomorrow: Aviation Safety in a Competitive Environment* (Washington, D.C.: Government Printing Office, 1988); U.S. National Transportation Safety Board, *Marine Accident Report: Grounding of the U.S. Tankship* Exxon Valdez *on Bligh Reef, Prince William Sound near Valdez, Alaska, March 24, 1989* (Washington, D.C.: National Transportation Safety Board, 1990); State of Alaska, Oil Spill Commission, *Spill, the Wreck of the* Exxon Valdez: *Implications for Safe Marine Transportation: Report of the Alaska Oil Spill Commission* (Juneau: Oil Spill Commission, 1990); U.S. National Commission on Sleep Disorders Research, *Wake Up America: Report of the National Commission on Sleep Disorders Research*, 2 vols. (Washington, D.C.: Government Printing Office, 1993, 1994), esp. 1:vi–viii, 26–30, 2:78–112.

39. Timothy B. McCall, "No Turning Back: A Blueprint for Residency Reform," *Journal of the American Medical Association* 261 (1989): 909 (quotations), 909–10; Natalie S. Robins, *The Girl Who Died Twice: Every Patient's Nightmare: The Libby Zion Case and the Hidden Hazards of Hospitals* (New York: Delacorte Press, 1995), esp. 100–112, 201–9; *New York Times*, June 8, 1987, A18; New York State Department of Health, Ad Hoc Advisory Committee on Emergency Services, *Final Report* (Albany: New York State Department of Health, 1987); Robert Levin, "Beyond 'The Men of Steel': The Origins and Significance of House Staff Training Stress," *General Hospital Psychiatry* 10 (1988): 114–21; Executive Council, Association of American Medical Colleges, "Resident Supervision and Hours: Recommendations of the Association of American Medical Colleges," *Journal of Medical Education* 63 (1988): 422–23. For a portrait of physician overwork and sleep disruption in the nineteenth century, see Steven J. Peitzman, "'I Am Their Physician': Dr. Owen J. Wister of Germantown and His Too Many Patients," *Bulletin of the History of Medicine* 83 (2009): 245–70, esp. 252, 256.

40. C. H. Jacques, James C. Lynch, and Judith S. Samkoff, "The Effects of Sleep Loss on Cognitive Performance of Residents," *Journal of Family Practice* 30 (1990): 223–29; Judith S. Samkoff and C. H. Jacques, "A Review of Studies Concerning Effects of Sleep Deprivation and Fatigue on Residents' Performance," *Academic Medicine* 66 (1991): 687–93; Christine Laine et al., "The Impact of a Regulation Restricting Medical House Staff Working Hours on the Quality of Patient Care," *Journal of the American Medical Association* 269 (1993): 374–78; Matthew B. Weinger and Sonia Ancoli-Israel, "Sleep Deprivation and Clinical Performance," ibid., 287 (2002): 955–57; *New York Times*, Feb. 23, 1993, A1, B4; Ian R. Holzman and Scott H. Barnett, "The Bell Commission: Ethical Implications for the Training of Physicians," *Mount Sinai Journal of Medicine* 67 (2000): 136–39; Christopher Landrigan, "Effect of Reducing Interns' Work Hours on Serious Medical Errors in Intensive Care Units," *New England Journal of Medicine* 351 (2004): 1838–48; "Exhausted Doctor to Wake Up Early, Finish Surgery in Morning," *Onion*, Sept. 20, 2007, http://www.theonion.com/articles/exhausted-doctor-to-wake-up-early-finish-surgery-i,5846; N. Fontaine and J. Socrates, "Directive 2000/34/EC of the European Parliament and of the Council of 22 June 2000," *Official Journal of the European Council* L 195 (2000): 41–45, esp. 43; Sanjay Gupta, "Is Your Doctor Too Drowsy?" *Time*,

Mar. 11, 2002, 75; Tracy Ehlers, "The Patient and Physician Safety and Protection Act: Crucial Federal Legislation to Improve the Lives of Residents and Patients," *Connecticut Public Interest Law Journal* 4 (2004): 1–15.

41. Public Citizen et al. to R. David Layne, Apr. 30, 2001, http://www.citizen.org/ publications/release.cfm?ID=6771; Public Citizen, "OSHA Denies Petition to Reduce Work Hours for Doctors-in-Training," Oct. 10, 2002, http://www.citizen.org/pressroom/ release.cfm?ID=1239; Work Group on Resident Duty Hours, Accreditation Council for Graduate Medical Education, "Report," June 11, 2002, http://www.acgme.org/ac-Website/dutyHours/dh_wkgroupreport611.pdf; Christopher Landrigan et al., "Interns' Compliance with Accreditation Council for Graduate Medical Education Work-Hour Limits," *Journal of the American Medical Association* 296 (2006): 1063–70; Accreditation Council for Graduate Medical Education, "Common Program Requirements," 16–19, Sept. 26, 2010, http://acgme-2010standards.org/pdf/Common_Program_Requirements _07012011.pdf; Public Citizen et al. to David Michaels, Sept. 2, 2010, http://www.citizen. org/documents/1917.pdf; Alexander B. Blum et al., "Implementing the 2009 Institute of Medicine Recommendations on Resident Physician Work Hours, Supervision, and Safety," *Nature and Science of Sleep* 3 (2011): 47–85, doi:10.2147/NSS.S19649.

42. House of Delegates, American Nurses Association, "Policy Position 6.73: Opposing the Use of Mandatory Overtime as a Staffing Solution," July 2000, House of Delegates, "House Actions," vol. 1, American Nurses Association Library, Silver Spring, Md.; Pennsylvania State Nurses Association, "The Position of the Pennsylvania State Nurses Association on Mandatory Overtime," Mar. 30, 2001, http://www.psna.org/c_PosStat_ OT.htm; Linder, *Autocratically Flexible Workplace*, 357–90; Washington State Department of Labor and Industries, "Law Restricting Mandatory Overtime for Nurses," Oct. 31, 2003, http://www.lni.wa.gov/WorkplaceRights/files/esa11.pdf; "2005 Legislation: Mandatory Overtime," *ANA Nursing World*, Dec. 2005, http://www.nursingworld.org/ gova/state/2005/mandatory.htm; Pennsylvania State Education Association, "Pennsylvania Bans Mandatory Overtime for Nurses and Health Care Employees," n.d., http:// www.psea.org/general.aspx?id=2914, accessed Dec. 1, 2010; New York State, "Section 167[of Labor Law]," n.d., http://www.labor.state.ny.us/formdocs/wp/Nurse_Overtime _Section_167.pdf, accessed Dec. 1, 2010; Robert Iafolla, "Massachusetts Restricts Nurses' Overtime," *Occupational Safety and Health Reporter*, Nov. 15, 2012, 1012; U.S. Senate, Committee on Governmental Affairs, Subcommittee on Oversight of Government Management, Restructuring, and the District of Columbia, *Finding a Cure to Keep Nurses on the Job: The Federal Government's Role in Retaining Nurses for Delivery of Federally-Funded Health Care Services: Hearing*, 107th Cong., 1st sess., 2001 (Washington, D.C.: Government Printing Office, 2002), 28–29, 32–34, 38; U.S. House of Representatives, Committee on Ways and Means, Subcommittee on Health, *Health Quality and Medical Errors: Hearing*, 107th Cong., 2nd sess., 2002 (Washington, D.C.: Government Printing Office, 2002), 24, 27.

43. Judith Walzer Leavitt, *Typhoid Mary: Captive to the Public's Health* (Boston: Beacon Press, 1997); Allan M. Brandt, *No Magic Bullet: A Social History of Venereal Disease*

in the United States Since 1880 (New York: Oxford University Press, 1985); Nayan Shah, *Contagious Divides: Epidemics and Race in San Francisco's Chinatown* (Berkeley: University of California Press, 2001); Howard Markel, *When Germs Travel: Six Major Epidemics That Have Invaded America Since 1900 and the Fears They Have Unleashed* (New York: Pantheon Books, 2004); Werner Troesken, *Water, Race, and Disease* (Cambridge, Mass.: MIT Press, 2004); Barron H. Lerner, *The Breast Cancer Wars: Hope, Fear, and the Pursuit of a Cure in Twentieth-Century America* (New York: Oxford University Press, 2001); Daniel M. Fox, *Power and Illness: The Failure and Future of American Health Policy* (Berkeley: University of California Press, 1995).

Chapter 3. The Long Turn

Note to epigraph: Alfred Kiefer to Editor, *Survey*, Sept. 21, 1920, John Fitch Papers, box 2, folder 18, Archives Division, Wisconsin Historical Society, Madison.

1. On rotational schemes, see Committee on Work-Periods in Continuous-Industry of the Federated American Engineering Societies, *The Twelve-Hour Shift in Industry* (New York: E. F. Dutton, 1922), 66, 68, 86, 87, 89, 113, 124, 128, 135, 152, 163; Peter C. Baldwin, *In the Watches of the Night: Life in the Nocturnal City, 1820–1930* (Chicago: University of Chicago Press, 2012), 127–29. On health as physical capital, see Tony Coles, "Negotiating the Field of Masculinity: The Production and Reproduction of Multiple Dominant Masculinities," *Men and Masculinities* 12 (2009): 37.

2. Thomas J. Misa, *A Nation of Steel: The Making of Modern America, 1865–1925* (Baltimore: Johns Hopkins University Press, 1995), 4–131; Harold C. Livesay, *Andrew Carnegie and the Rise of Big Business* (New York: HarperCollins, 1975), 77–128; David Brody, *Steelworkers in America: The Nonunion Era* (Urbana: University of Illinois Press, 1998), 1–49, 96–111; Michael Nuwer, "From Batch to Flow: Production Technology and Work-Force Skills in the Steel Industry, 1880–1920," *Technology and Culture* 29 (1988): 808–38. On the pattern into which early iron making fit, see David Montgomery, *Workers' Control in America: Studies in the History of Work, Technology, and Labor Struggles* (New York: Cambridge University Press, 1979), 9–31.

3. Brody, *Steelworkers in America*, 50–79; Paul Krause, *The Battle for Homestead, 1880–1892: Politics, Culture, and Steel* (Pittsburgh: University of Pittsburgh Press, 1992).

4. Kenneth Warren, *Big Steel: The First Century of the United States Steel Corporation, 1901–2001* (Pittsburgh: University of Pittsburgh Press, 2001), 1–63; Misa, *Nation of Steel*, 133–71.

5. Andrew Carnegie, "Results of the Labor Struggle," *Forum*, Aug. 1886, 544 (quotation), 549 (quotation); James H. Bridge, *The Inside History of the Carnegie Steel Company: A Romance of Millions* (New York: Aldine Book, 1903), 189 (Jones quotation), 188–90; Krause, *Battle for Homestead*, 235–37, 241, 246, 250, 305; Brody, *Steelworkers in America*, 35–38; John A. Fitch, *The Steel Workers* (1910; Pittsburgh: University of Pittsburgh Press, 1989), 112–15, 169–71.

6. Charles B. Dew, "Disciplining Slave Ironworkers in the Antebellum South: Coer-

cion, Conciliation, and Accommodation," *American Historical Review* 79 (1974): 412–13; Elizabeth Brandeis, "Labor Legislation," in John R. Commons et al., *History of Labor in the United States*, 4 vols., vol. 3, *History of Labor in the United States, 1896–1932: Working Conditions, Labor Legislation* (New York: Macmillan, 1935), 101; Fitch, *Steel Workers*, 146, 168–69, 180–81, 200; U.S. Senate, Committee on Education and Labor, *Report on Strike at Bethlehem Steel Works, South Bethlehem, Pennsylvania*, 61st Cong., 2nd sess., 1910, Senate Document 521 (Washington, D.C.: Government Printing Office, 1910), 10–11; U.S. House of Representatives, Committee on Investigation of United States Steel Corporation, *United States Steel Corporation: Hearings*, 62nd Cong., 1st and 2nd sess., 1911–12 (Washington, D.C.: Government Printing Office, 1912), 2875–76; Brody, *Steelworkers in America*, 37–39, 78; S. J. Kleinberg, *The Shadow of the Mills: Working-Class Families in Pittsburgh, 1870–1907* (Pittsburgh: University of Pittsburgh Press, 1989), 10; John A. Fitch, "Lackawanna: Swamp, Mill, and Town," *Survey*, Oct. 7, 1911, 938, 945; John A. Fitch, "Birmingham District: Labor Conservation," *Survey*, Jan. 6, 1912, 1528; John A. Fitch, "The Steel Industry and the People in Colorado," *Survey*, Feb. 3, 1912, 1706–7.

7. Brody, *Steelworkers in America*, 170–71; Gerald E. Eggert, *Steelmasters and Labor Reform, 1886–1923* (Pittsburgh: University of Pittsburgh Press, 1981), 47–57; [U.S. Steel], "From Minutes of Presidents' Meeting," Feb. 25, 1910, William Dickson Papers, box 5, folder: United States Steel Corporation, 1910–1911, Historical Collections and Labor Archives, Pennsylvania State University Libraries, University Park; William B. Dickson, "Betterment of Labor Conditions in the Steel Industry," *Iron Trade Review*, Nov. 3, 1910, 818, 821; Fitch, *Steel Workers*, 325–26; Elbert Gary to Stockholders of United States Steel Corporation, Mar. 12, 1912, Fitch Papers, box 3, folder 1; John A. Fitch, "Rest Periods for the Continuous Industries," *American Labor Legislation Review*, Mar. 1913, 57; U.S. House, *United States Steel Corporation*, 2875–76; John A. Fitch, "The Labor Policies of Unrestricted Capital," *Survey*, Apr. 6, 1912, 18; U.S. Bureau of Labor Statistics, *Wages and Hours of Labor in the Iron and Steel Industry in the United States*, Bulletin 151 (Washington, D.C.: Government Printing Office, 1914), 9, 11, 13–16; Mary Heaton Vorse, *Men and Steel* (New York: Boni and Liveright, 1920), 26; "Hours," *American Labor Legislation Review*, Oct. 1913, 402; "Shall Steel-Makers Work Seven Days?" *Survey*, Nov. 4, 1916, 131–33; Alfred Kiefer to Gentlemen, May 4, 1921, Fitch Papers, box 2, folder 18.

8. State of Pennsylvania, "An Act for the Suppression of Vice and Immorality," in *The Statutes at Large of Pennsylvania from 1682 to 1801*, 16 vols. (Harrisburg: William Ray, State Printer, 1903), 9:333 (quotation), 333–38; John A. Fitch, "Bethlehem: The Church and the Steel Workers," *Survey*, Dec. 2, 1911, 1285–98, esp. 1294–97; Brody, *Steelworkers in America*, 117, 155, 197; Fitch, *Steel Workers*, 223–24.

9. Hannah R. Sewall, "Child Labor in the United States," *Bulletin of the Bureau of Labor*, May 1904, 505, 556; Carnegie, "Results of the Labor Struggle," 544; Fitch, *Steel Workers*, 177; Fitch, *Hours of Labor*, 5; Karen Olson, *Wives of Steel: Voices of Women from the Sparrows Point Steelmaking Communities* (University Park: Pennsylvania State University Press, 2005), 38; U.S. Senate, *Report on Conditions of Employment in the Iron and Steel Industry in the United States*, 4 vols., 62nd Cong., 1st sess., 1911, Senate Document

110, vol. 3, *Working Conditions and the Relations of Employers and Employees* (Washington, D.C.: Government Printing Office, 1913), 20, 21, 195–202.

10. John Fitch, "[Interview] Ch-12," Jan. 22, 1908 (unidentified worker quotations), Fitch Papers, box 4, folder 1; Bennie Capozza, "Oral History Interview," with Joe Lodics, Apr. 4, 1974, n.p., United Steelworkers of America Oral History Collection, United Steelworkers of America Archive, Historical Collections and Labor Archives, Pennsylvania State University Libraries, University Park; Margaret F. Byington, *Homestead: The Households of a Mill Town* (1910; Pittsburgh: University of Pittsburgh Press, 1974), 36; Fitch, *Steel Workers*, 14, 201–2; Olson, *Wives of Steel*, 38.

11. L. W., "Homestead as Seen by One of Its Workmen," *McClure's Magazine*, July 1894, 165; Charles A. Gulick Jr., *Labor Policy of the United States Steel Corporation* (New York: Columbia University, 1924), 23; Albert Carter, untitled interview by Major Mason, July 2, 1974, McKeesport, Pa., 2–3, Oral History Collection, box 116, folder: Carter, Albert, Transcripts, Pennsylvania State Archives, Harrisburg; Sewall, "Child Labor," 504, 505; Fitch, "Birmingham District," 1528; Fitch, *Hours of Labor*, 6–8; Fitch, *Steel Workers*, 173; June J. Pilcher, Barbara J. Lambert, and Allen I. Huffcutt, "Differential Effects of Permanent and Rotating Shifts on Self-Report Sleep Length: A Meta-Analytic Review," *Sleep* 23 (2000): 155–63. Two unnamed plants imported the British system invented by Lord Leverhulme, which called for rotation on an eighteen-hour cycle. Workers put in six hours, had twelve hours off, then worked another six hours. Unsurprisingly, this system failed to catch on in this country. See Horace B. Drury, "The Three-Shift System in the Steel Industry," *Bulletin of the Taylor Society* 6 (1921): 24.

12. Stockholders Committee, United States Steel Corporation, "Report," Apr. 25, 1912, in *The Pittsburgh Survey*, ed. Paul U. Kellogg, 6 vols., vol. 3, *Wage-Earning Pittsburgh* (New York: Russell Sage Foundation, 1914), 397–98 (quotation), 396–98; Thomas Bell, *Out of This Furnace* (1941; Pittsburgh: University of Pittsburgh Press, 1976), 167 (quotation); U.S. House, *United States Steel*, 2838 (Brandeis quotation), 2836–38; John A. Fitch, "Old Age at Forty," *American Magazine*, Mar. 1911, 656; Eduardo Furio, untitled interview by Matthew Magda, Apr. 20, 1981, Monessen, Pa., 6–8, Oral History Collection, box 85, folder: Furio, Eduardo, Edited Transcript, Pennsylvania State Archives; B. R. Brachman, untitled interview by [unidentified first name] Kane, Dec. 2, 1974, Bethlehem, 3, box 5, folder: Bethlehem Transcripts, ibid.; Elizabeth Beardsley Butler, "Sharpsburg: A Typical Waste of Childhood," in *Wage-Earning Pittsburgh*, 293–94; Gulick, *Labor Policy*, 23; Olson, *Wives of Steel*, 38; Fitch, *Steel Workers*, 173; Florence Kelley, "Factory Inspection in Pittsburgh," in *Wage-Earning Pittsburgh*, ed. Kellogg, 202–3. For other manifestations of overworked underage steelworkers, see U.S. Immigration Commission, *Reports of the Immigration Commission*, 41 vols., vol. 8, *Immigrants in Industries, Part 2: Iron and Steel Manufacturing*, vol. 1 (Washington, D.C.: Government Printing Office, 1911), 379–80; Stephen Wisyanski, untitled interview by Matthew Magda, Apr. 9, 1981, Monessen, Pa., 6–8, Oral History Collection, box 84, folder: Wisyanksi, Stephen, Edited Transcript, Pennsylvania State Archives.

13. Carnegie, "Results of the Labor Struggle," 545 (quotation); Fitch, *Hours of Labor*,

17 (unidentified executive quotation), 15–17; Arundel Cotter, *The Gary I Knew* (Boston: Stratford, 1928), 40 (quotation); William Hard, "Making Steel and Killing Men," *Everybody's Magazine*, Nov. 1907, 588; Melvin I. Urofsky, *Big Steel and the Wilson Administration: A Study in Business-Government Relations* (Columbus: Ohio State University Press, 1969), 276; U.S. House, *United States Steel*, 2521. For belated industrialists' belated acknowledgment of work-induced sleep problems, see National Industrial Conference Board, *Night Work in Industry* (New York: National Industrial Conference Board, 1927), 16: "The supply of night workers is particularly scarce in the warm summer months because of the difficulty of procuring adequate sleep and rest in hot weather." For a suggestive glimpse of shift work sleep disorder, see ibid., 29: "The men gradually went stale after too long a time on the night shift."

14. Edward S. Slavishak, *Bodies of Work: Civic Display and Labor in Industrial Pittsburgh* (Durham: Duke University Press, 2008), 4 (quotation); Angela Morgan, "Work!" *South Works Review*, May–June 1920, 30 (quotation); Whiting Williams, "Memorandum of Factors in the Problem of the Shorter Day for Steel and Iron Workers," June 1, 1920, 5 (quotation), 6 (quotation), Fitch Papers, box 4, folder 4; William Dickson, "The Steel Worker's Lament," n.d., Dickson Papers, box 2, folder: Memoirs No. 1—continued; Fitch, "Policies of Unrestricted Capital," 18–19; Clayton Patterson, *Review of "The Steel Strike of 1919 by the Commission of Inquiry, Inter-Church World Movement"* (Summit, N.J.: Summit Record, 1921), 106 (quotation), 107; Interchurch World Movement of North America, *Report on the Steel Strike of 1919* (New York: Harcourt, Brace and Howe, 1920), 78–84; Brody, *Steelworkers in America*, 100. On Williams's career, see Daniel A. Wren, *White Collar Hobo: The Travels of Whiting Williams* (Ames: Iowa State University Press, 1987), esp. 24–27, 33–35.

15. Charles R. Walker, *Steel: The Diary of a Furnace Worker* (Boston: Atlantic Monthly Press, 1922), 42 (Fred quotation), 60–61, 116, 150, 272; Bertha Saposs, "Interview with [unnamed] Polish Shearman," n.d. [ca. July 1920], David Saposs Papers, box 26, folder 8, Archives Division, Wisconsin Historical Society, Madison; Bertha Saposs, "Interview with Slavish Worker, Washington Street," n.d. [ca. July 1920], Saposs Papers, box 26, folder 7; Alfred Kiefer to Gentlemen, May 4, 1921, Fitch Papers, box 2, folder 18; Byington, *Homestead*, 87; Charles R. Walker, "The Twelve-Hour Shift," *American Labor Legislation Review*, June 1923, 113.

16. Byington, *Homestead*, 172 (quotation), 148; Bell, *Out of This Furnace*, 48–49 (quotation); Mary Senior, "Interview with Mr. and Mrs. Mike Gessner," July 21, 1920 (quotation), Saposs Papers, box 26, folder 8; Mary Senior, "Interview with Mr. Stuart," July 18, 1920, ibid.; Mary Senior, "Interview with Mr. and Mrs. Funak," July 20, 1920, ibid.; Mary Senior, "Interview with Mr. Massic," n.d. [ca. Aug. 1, 1920], ibid., folder 9; U.S. Bureau of Labor Statistics, *Causes and Prevention of Accidents in the Iron and Steel Industry*, by Lucian W. Chaney, Bulletin 298 (Washington, D.C.: Government Printing Office, 1922), 179; Kleinberg, *Shadow of the Mills*, 10–11.

17. F. Elizabeth Crowell, "Painter's Row," *Charities and the Commons*, Feb. 6, 1909, 904 (quotation), after 904 [unpaginated photos]; Commission, *Reports*, 8:661; Byington,

Homestead, 145; Abraham Epstein, *The Negro Migrant in Pittsburgh* (Pittsburgh: University of Pittsburgh School of Economics, 1918), 8, 12, 13; Peter Gottlieb, *Making Their Own Way: Southern Blacks' Migration to Pittsburgh, 1916–30* (Urbana: University of Illinois Press, 1987), 70. On hotbed arrangements, see Byington, *Homestead*, 145; Fitch, "Lackawanna," 933–34; Immigration Commission, *Reports*, 8:403; U.S. Senate, *Working Conditions and Relations*, 3:442; Sophonisba P. Breckinridge and Edith Abbott, "Chicago Housing Conditions, V: South Chicago at the Gates of the Steel Mills," *American Journal of Sociology* 17 (1911): 164, 166. For other glimpses of the overcrowded sleeping spaces to which many workers resorted during the industrializing era, see Mark Wyman, *Round-Trip to America: The Immigrants Return to Europe, 1880–1930* (Ithaca, N.Y.: Cornell University Press, 1993), 63; Tyler Anbinder, "From Famine to Five Points: Lord Lansdowne's Tenants Encounter North America's Most Notorious Slum," *American Historical Review* 107 (2002): 372, 373. For one U.S. Steel unit's oblivious advice to its employees not to sleep in crowded rooms, see "Timely Warning," *South Works Review*, May–June 1920, 27.

18. Olson, *Wives of Steel*, 20, 22; Epstein, *Negro Migrant in Pittsburgh*, 8, 11–12, 14; Gottlieb, *Making Their Own Way*, 69, 131; Dennis C. Dickerson, *Out of the Crucible: Black Steelworkers in Western Pennsylvania, 1875–1980* (Albany: State University of New York Press, 1986), 56–57; U.S. Senate, *Working Conditions and Relations*, 3:439–40; Kleinberg, *Shadow of the Mill*, 66–71, 73–75; Phillip Bonofsky, "The Life and Death of a Steel Worker," *Masses and Mainstream*, Apr. 1952, 15; Byington, *Homestead*, 46–51; Fitch, "Lackawanna," 933; Immigration Commission, *Reports*, 8: 127–29. In 1916, Mexican railway maintenance workers employed in California protested overcrowd conditions in company housing, which forced them to try to sleep where cooking took place. See Natalia Molina, *Fit to Be Citizens? Public Health and Race in Los Angeles, 1879–1939* (Berkeley: University of California Press, 2006), 67.

19. U.S. House, *United States Steel*, 2912 (Fitch quotations), 3040 (Byington quotation), 3034, 3039–40; Peter Roberts, "Immigrant Wage-Earners," in *Wage-Earning Pittsburgh*, ed. Kellogg, after 48 (Hine quotation), 47; Fitch, "Labor Policies of Unrestricted Capital," 19–20; Immigration Commission, *Reports*, 8:117, 123–27, 294, 296, 551, 774, 776, 9:78–82, 94, 243; Breckinridge and Abbott, "Chicago Housing Conditions," 165.

20. Byington, *Homestead*, 131–38, 143–44, 148; Kleinberg, *Shadow of the Mills*, 81–83; Ewa T. Morawska, *For Bread with Butter: The Life-Worlds of East Central Europeans in Johnstown, Pennsylvania, 1890–1940* (New York: Cambridge University Press, 1985), 127, 130, 351n51; Olson, *Wives of Steel*, 54–55, 65; Fitch, *Steel Workers*, 343; Immigration Commission, *Reports*, 8:104–9, 410, 661. On the arduous work of managing a boarding or lodging business, see Bell, *Out of This Furnace*, 173, 175; Mary Senior, "Interview with Mrs. William Hyslop," July 24, 1920, Saposs Papers, box 26, folder 7; Mary Senior, "Interview with Mrs. Yanek," Aug. 26, 1920, ibid.; Bertha Saposs, "Interview with Mr. Ford," n.d. [ca. Aug. 1920], ibid., folder 9; Olson, *Wives of Steel*, 53.

21. Breckinridge and Abbott, "Chicago Housing Conditions," 145 (quotation), 147; Kleinberg, *Shadow of the Mills*, 65 (quotation), 75–76, 86; Olson, *Wives of Steel*,

24; Henry M. McKiven, *Iron and Steel: Class, Race, and Community in Birmingham, Alabama, 1875–1920* (Chapel Hill: University of North Carolina Press, 1995), 135; Alfred Kiefer to Gentlemen, May 4, 1921, Fitch Papers, box 2, folder 18; Brody, *Steelworkers in America*, 102, 110; Crowell, "Painter's Row," 899, 910; Byington, *Homestead*, 29, 131, 136; Immigration Commission, *Reports*, 9:188.

22. John E. Bodnar, *Workers' World: Kinship, Community, and Protest in an Industrial Society, 1900–1940* (Baltimore: Johns Hopkins University Press, 1982), 89 (Kika quotation); Crowell, "Painter's Row," 902 (quotation); Whiting Williams, *What's on the Worker's Mind, by One Who Put on Overalls to Find Out* (New York: Charles Scribner's Sons, 1920), 23 (quotation); Walker, *Steel*, 44, 55, 58; John Fitch, "[Interview] Ch-1," Dec. 14, 1907, Fitch Papers, box 4, folder 1; Furio, interview, 8; Mary Senior, "Interview with 'Mrs. Frye," July 29, 1920, Saposs Papers, box 26, folder 9.

23. Garland, "Homestead and Its Perilous Trades," 8 [unidentified ex-steelworker quotation], 19; Fitch, *Steel Workers*, 201 (quotation), 14–15, 201–4; Williams, *Worker's Mind*, 28 (quotation); Walker, *Steel*, vi; Bell, *Out of This Furnace*, 32; Vorse, *Men and Steel*, 148, 174; Interchurch World Movement, *Report on Strike*, 65–66; Byington, *Homestead*, 112, 171–73; Fitch, "Old Age at Forty," 656; Bertha Saposs, "Interview with Mrs. Kelley," n.d. [ca. July 1920], Saposs Papers, box 26, folder 7.

24. Fitch, *Steel Workers*, 240–41; U.S. House, *United States Steel*, 3270; Committee on Work-Periods, *Twelve-Hour Shift*, 221–28; Ida Tarbell, "The Golden Rule in Business: Hours," *American Magazine*, Apr. 1915, 30; Walker, "Twelve-Hour Shift," 111. On the provision of formal rest breaks, generally of too little duration to permit any napping, see U.S. Bureau of Labor Statistics, *Welfare Work for Employees in Industrial Establishments in the United States*, Bulletin 250 (Washington, D.C.: Government Printing Office, 1919), 34.

25. Interchurch World Movement, *Report on Strike*, 60 (unidentified open-hearth laborer quotation), 63; Williams, *Worker's Mind*, 15 (quotation), 17, 32, 240–41, 246–47; Williams, "Discussion," 43 (quotation); Whiting Williams, "Memorandum of Factors in the Problem of the Shorter Day for Steel and Iron Workers," June 1, 1920, 5, 6, Fitch Papers, box 4, folder 4; U.S. Senate, *Working Conditions and Relations*, 3:201–2; Walker, *Steel*, 79, 147, 151. At the Scovill Manufacturing Company brass works in Waterbury, Connecticut, where the night shift in the 1910s ran over twelve hours, on-the-job sleeping was widespread. See Frederic S. Lee, *The Human Machine and Industrial Efficiency* (New York: Longmans, Green, 1918), 67. For the persistence through mid-century of night-shift sleeping at one U.S. Steel subsidiary, see John Hoerr, *And the Wolf Finally Came: The Decline of the American Steel Industry* (Pittsburgh: University of Pittsburgh Press, 1988), 300: "Sleeping nooks were plentiful. On the night, 11 P.M. to 7 A.M., more people may have been sleeping in National Tube than in all the hotels of McKeesport."

26. L. W., "Homestead as Seen," 168 (quotation); Paul Willis, "Shop Floor Culture, Masculinity and the Wage Form," *Working-Class Culture: Studies in History and Theory*, ed. J. Clarke, C. Critcher, and R. Johnson (New York: St. Martin's Press, 1979), 196 (quotation), 185–98; D. J. Saposs, "Chat on the Street with American Worker," Aug. 16, 1920,

Saposs Papers, box 26, folder 6; John Wolota, untitled interview by Peter Gottlieb, June 14, 1974, McKees Rocks, Pa., box 115, folder: Wolota, John, Transcripts, Oral History Collection, Pennsylvania State Archives; Alfred Kiefer to Editor, *Survey*, Sept. 21, 1920, Fitch Papers, box 2, folder 18; Alfred Kiefer to Gentlemen, May 4, 1921, ibid.; Mary Senior, "Interview with Mr. and Mrs. Funak," July 20, 1920, Saposs Papers, box 26, folder 8; Walker, *Steel*, 59–60. For shopfloor shenanigans at the end of the twentieth century, see Robert Bruno, *Steelworker Alley: How Class Works in Youngstown* (Ithaca, N.Y.: ILR Press, 1999), 67: "Pranks and high jinxes were as common as steel coil. Al Campbell said, 'Guys had their shoes painted orange when they fell asleep.'" For auto workers' use of the restroom as a refuge for furtive breaks, see Stephen Meyer, "Work, Play, and Power: Masculine Culture on the Automotive Shop Floor, 1930–1960," *Men and Masculinities* 2 (1999): 121–22.

27. Williams, *Worker's Mind*, 29–30 (quotation), 94, 287; Whiting Williams, "Discussion [of Horace Drury, 'The Three-Shift System in the Steel Industry']," *Bulletin of the Taylor Society* 6 (1921): 42 (quotation); "Shall Steel-Makers Work Seven Days?" 133; Olson, *Wives of Steel*, 45, 80–81. For the contrary view that alcohol served as a stimulant, not a sedative, see Fitch, *Steel Workers*, 227. On steelworkers' coffee consumption, see Immigration Commission, *Reports*, 9:84–90; Walker, *Steel*, 43, 70, 73, 74, 114.

28. Crystal Eastman, *Work-Accidents and the Law* (New York: Russell Sage Foundation, 1910), 88–89 (quotation), 149 (quotation), 91, 95, 98; Fitch, *Steel Workers*, 67 (quotation), 63–70; Williams, "Discussion," 43 (quotation); Whiting Williams, "Memorandum of Factors in the Problem of the Shorter Day for Steel and Iron Workers," June 1, 1920, 5, 6, Fitch Papers, box 4, folder 4; Hard, "Making Steel and Killing Men," 586; Garland, "Homestead and Its Perilous Trades," 15, 16; Fitch, *Hours of Labor*, 6; Walker, *Steel*, 51. For a missed opportunity for recognition, one that fell back on blaming much on the carelessness and awkwardness of accident victims without considering at all their sleep-deprived state, see U.S. Bureau of Mines, *Occupational Hazards at Blast-Furnace Plants and Accident Prevention*, by Frederick Willcox, Bulletin 140 (Washington, D.C.: Government Printing Office, 1917). For another missed opportunity based on the mistaken assumption that fatigue developed only over the course of the shift, rather than being a condition that could also impair unrested workers from the outset of their working stint, see Bureau of Labor Statistics, *Causes and Prevention*, 10, 185–89.

29. U.S. Senate, *Report on Conditions of Employment in the Iron and Steel Industry in the United States*, 4 vols., 62nd Cong., 1st sess., 1911, Senate Document 110, vol. 4, *Accidents and Accident Prevention* (Washington, D.C.: Government Printing Office, 1913), 80–81 (quotation), 15, 80–82, 150–54; Kleinberg, *Shadow of the Mills*, 28–31, 39.

30. Vorse, *Men and Steel*, 29 (quotation); U.S. Public Health Service, *A Health Survey of Ten Thousand Male Industrial Workers: Statistical Analysis of Surveys in Ten Industries*, by Rollo H. Britten and L. R. Thompson, Public Health Bulletin 162 (Washington, D.C.: Government Printing Office, 1926), 38, 93, 94, 96, 143, 156–57, 159, 163, 166; Horace Drury, "Three-Shift System," 9; Mary Senior, "Interview with Mr. Clair Hill," July 20, 1920, Saposs Papers, box 26, folder 8; Walker, *Steel*, 150; Walker, "Twelve-Hour Shift,"

112. On sleep deprivation and hypertension, see Kristen L. Knutson et al., "Association Between Sleep and Blood Pressure in Midlife: The CARDIA Sleep Study," *Archives of Internal Medicine* 169 (2009): 1055–61. On shift work sleep disorder, see Christopher Drake et al., "Shift Work Sleep Disorder: Prevalence and Consequences Beyond That of Symptomatic Day Workers," *Sleep* 27 (2004): 1453–62. On health care as a commodity beyond the means of steelworkers, see Byington, *Homestead*, 84, 87.

31. Furio, interview, 8 (quotation); Walker, *Steel*, 60 (Nick quotation), 116; Mary Senior, "Interview with Mr. Jenkins," July 22, 1920, Saposs Papers, box 26, folder 7; Bell, *Out of This Furnace*, 47.

32. Fitch, "Old Age at Forty," 656 (quotation); Byington, *Homestead*, 172 (quotation); Fitch, *Steel Workers*, 62–63; John Fitch, "[Interview] Ch-6," Jan. 10, 1908, Fitch Papers, box 4, folder 1; John Fitch, "[Interview] Ch-9," Jan. 15, 1908, ibid.; John A. Fitch, "Some Pittsburgh Steel Workers," *Charities and the Commons*, Jan. 2, 1909, 555; Fitch, *Hours of Labor*, 12; D. J. Saposs, "Interview with Croatian worker, on Warren, Ohio, car," Aug. 26, 1920, Saposs Papers, box 26, folder 6; Walker, *Steel*, 71–72, 149.

33. Fitch, *Steel Workers*, 63 (quotation); Byington, *Homestead*, 25–26; John Fitch, "Illinois: Boosting for Safety," *Survey*, Nov. 4, 1911, 1158; H. F. Porter, "Industrial Hygiene of the Pittsburgh District," in *Wage-Earning Pittsburgh*, ed. Kellogg, 251, 252.

34. J. W. Schereschewsky, "Trachoma in Steel Mill Workers: An Investigation of the Origin and Prevalence of the Disease Among the Employees of the Youngstown Sheet and Tube Co., Youngstown, Ohio," *Public Health Reports* 29 (1914): 567 (quotation), 565–67.

35. John A. Fitch, "The Long Day," *Survey*, Mar. 5, 1921, 789 (Root quotation), 792–93; Fitch, "Old Age at Forty," 655; Garland, "Homestead and Its Perilous Trades," 16; Charles B. Spahr, *America's Working People*, 2nd ed. (New York: Longmans, Green, 1900), 155; Fitch, *Hours of Labor*, 14; U.S. Senate, *Working Conditions and Relations*, 383; Drury, "Three-Shift System," 8; Walker, *Steel*, 148, 285, 287–88; John Fitch, "Interview with Lodeman," July 23, 1920, Saposs Papers, box 26, folder 8; D. J. Saposs, "Interview with Kowalski," Aug. 19, 1920, ibid., folder 6; Slavishak, *Bodies of Work*, 173. On the relationship between fatigue and sleepiness, see Torbjorn Akerstedt, Lars Torsvall, and Mats Gillberg, "Sleepiness and Shift Work: Field Studies," *Sleep* 5: suppl. 2 (1982): S95–S106; Torbjorn Akerstedt and Kenneth P. Wright Jr., "Sleep Loss and Fatigue in Shift Work and Shift Work Disorder," *Sleep Medicine Clinics* 4 (2009): 260: "'Sleepiness' is not the same thing as 'fatigue,' at least not scientifically. . . . '[S]leepiness' refers to the tendency of falling asleep. Fatigue may include sleepiness, but also states such as physical and mental fatigue. Often, the two concepts are interconnected, but they need not be." For attempts to grapple with workers' fatigue in this era, see Josephine Goldmark, *Fatigue and Industry: A Study in Industry* (New York: Russell Sage Foundation, 1912); Lee, *Human Machine*; Alan Derickson, "Physiological Science and Scientific Management in the Progressive Era: Frederic S. Lee and the Committee on Industrial Fatigue," *Business History Review* 68 (1994): 483–514; Anson Rabinbach, *The Human Motor: Energy, Fatigue, and the Origins of Modernity* (New York: Basic Books, 1990). On neurasthenia

and bourgeois fatigue more broadly, see Edward Shorter, *From Paralysis to Fatigue: A History of Psychsomatic Illness in the Modern Era* (New York: Free Press, 1991).

36. Maurine W. Greenwald and Margo Anderson, eds., *Pittsburgh Surveyed: Social Science and Social Reform in the Early Twentieth Century* (Pittsburgh: University of Pittsburgh Press, 1996); Steven R. Cohen, "The Pittsburgh Survey and the Social Survey Movement: A Sociological Road Not Taken," in *The Social Survey in Historical Perspective, 1880–1940,* ed. Martin Bulmer, Kevin Bales, and Kathryn Kish Sklar (New York: Cambridge University Press, 1991), 245–68; Kate Sampsell-Willmann, *Lewis Hine as Social Critic* (Jackson: University Press of Mississippi, 2009), 58–75. On Progressive empirical inquiries and reform advocacy, see Mary O. Furner, "Knowing Capitalism: Public Investigation and the Labor Question in the Long Progressive Era," in *The State and Economic Knowledge: The American and British Experiences,* ed. Mary O. Furner and Barry Supple (New York: Cambridge University Press, 1990), 241–86; Libby Schwebber, "Progressive Reformers, Unemployment, and the Transformation of Social Inquiry in Britain and the United States, 1880s–1920s," in *States, Social Knowledge, and the Origins of Modern Social Policies,* ed. Dietrich Rueschemeyer and Theda Skocpol (Princeton, N.J.: Princeton University Press, 1996), 163–200; Alice O'Connor, *Poverty Knowledge: Social Science, Social Policy, and the Poor in Twentieth-Century U.S. History* (Princeton, N.J.: Princeton University Press, 2001), 25–44.

37. John F. McClymer, "The Pittsburgh Survey, 1907–1914: Forging an Ideology in the Steel District," *Pennsylvania History* 41 (1974): 169–86; Byington, *Homestead,* 218–32, esp. 225, 227; F. Elisabeth Crowell, "The Housing Situation in Pittsburgh," *Charities and the Commons,* Feb. 6, 1909, 871–81.

38. Fitch, *Steel Workers,* 205–6, 242–43; John A. Fitch, "The United States Steel Corporation and Labor," *Annals of the American Academy of Political and Social Science* 42 (1912): 19; cf. Steven R. Cohen, "The Failure of Fair Wages and the Death of Labor Republicanism: The Ideological Legacy of the Pittsburgh Survey," in *Pittsburgh Surveyed,* ed. Greenwald and Anderson, 50–68.

39. Roy Lubove, "John A. Fitch, *The Steel Workers,* and the Crisis of Democracy," in Fitch, *Steel Workers,* viii–ix; Charles Hill, "Fighting the Twelve-Hour Day in the American Steel Industry," *Labor History* 15 (1974): 21–23; Fitch, "Lackawanna," 929–45; Fitch, "Illinois," 1145–60; Fitch, "Bethlehem," 1285–98; Fitch, "Birmingham District," 1527–40; Fitch, "Steel Industry and Colorado," 1706–20; Fitch, "Labor Policies of Unrestricted Capital," 17–27; [John Fitch] to Paul Kellogg, Oct. 25, 1910, Fitch Papers, box 2, folder 20; Fitch to Kellogg, Feb. 7, 1911, ibid.; Kellogg to Fitch, Mar. 2, 1911, ibid.; Fitch, *Hours of Labor;* Fitch, "Rest Periods," 58–62; U.S. House, *United States Steel Corporation,* 2873ff; Brody, *Steelworkers in America,* 161–63. On the forbidding climate for Progressivism in Pennsylvania, see Paul B. Beers, "Boies Penrose," in *Pennsylvania Kingmakers,* ed. Robert G. Crist (University Park: Pennsylvania Historical Association, 1985), 42–44; Walter Davenport, *Power and Glory: The Life of Boies Penrose* (New York: G. P. Putnam's Sons, 1931), 161–240; Morton Keller, *Regulating a New Society: Public Policy and Social Change in America, 1900–1933* (Cambridge, Mass.: Harvard University Press, 1998), 198. For

indirect evidence suggesting that Fitch may have had a hand in moving the Progressive Party to endorse the eight-hour day for workers in continuous-process industries in its 1912 platform, see John Fitch to Paul Kellogg, Feb. 7, 1911, Fitch Papers, box 2, folder 20; Donald B. Johnson, comp., *National Party Platforms*, rev. ed., 2 vols. (Urbana: University of Illinois Press, 1978), 1:177. On the Wisconsin reform perspective that much influenced Fitch, see Leon Fink, *Progressive Intellectuals and the Dilemmas of Democratic Commitment* (Cambridge, Mass.: Harvard University Press, 1997), 52–113.

40. Urofsky, *Big Steel*, 271–78; Brody, *Steelworkers in America*, 170–71, 197, 212, 235.

41. Whiting Williams, "Memorandum of Factors in the Problem of the Shorter Day for Steel and Iron Workers," June 1, 1920, 9 (quotation), Fitch Papers, box 4, folder 4; William Z. Foster, *The Great Strike and Its Lessons* (New York: B. W. Huebsch, 1920), 95 (National Committee for Organizing Iron and Steel Workers quotation); Carnegie Steel Company, "Time Book," Jan.–Sept. 1919, United States Steel Corporation Duquesne Works, Industrial Relations Department Records, box 14, item 3, Archives of Industrial Society, Archives Service Center, University of Pittsburgh, Pittsburgh; Vorse, *Men and Steel*, 26, 148, 150; Interchurch World Movement, *Report on Strike*, 71; Walker, *Steel*, 69, 153; *Amalgamated Journal*, July 24, 1919, 1, 5, Aug. 7, 1919, 8, Aug. 28, 1919, 30; David Brody, *Labor in Crisis: The Steel Strike of 1919* (Philadelphia: J. B. Lippincott, 1965), 63–111; Urofsky, *Big Steel*, 285–90.

42. *Amalgamated Journal*, Sept. 25, 1919, 12 (Wheeling local quotation), 1, 6, 7, Oct. 16, 1919, 8, Nov. 20, 1919, 8, 19, Nov. 27, 1919, 6, 7; U.S. Senate, Committee on Education and Labor, *Investigating Strike in Steel Industries*, 66th Cong., 1st sess., 1919 (Washington, D.C.: Government Printing Office, 1919), 15 (quotation), 14–15; John Harbert, "Oral History Interview," with Frank Lindh, Aug. 9, 1974, n.p. (quotation), Steelworkers Oral History Collection; John Warady, "Oral History Interview," with Larry Gorski, Apr. 20, 1974, McKeesport, Pa., ibid.; Brody, *Labor in Crisis*, 112–74; Foster, *Great Strike*, 96–233; Walker, *Steel*, 127–28; U.S. Senate, Committee on Education and Labor, *Investigation of Strike in Steel Industries: Hearings . . . Pursuant to S. Res. 188 . . . and S. Res. 202*, 2 vols., 66th Cong., 1st sess., 1919 (Washington, D.C.: Government Printing Office, 1919), 2:546–47, 559, 726–27; Urofsky, *Big Steel*, 324–33; Freeman Patton, untitled interview with Peter Gottlieb, July 11, 1974, Pittsburgh, Oral History Collection, box 115, folder: Patton, Freeman, Transcripts, Pennsylvania State Archives; Dickerson, *Out of Crucible*, 89. For an instance of a strikebreaking railroad manager sleeping on trains, see Olivier Zunz, *Making America Corporate, 1870–1920* (Chicago: University of Chicago Press, 1990), 63.

43. Interchurch World Movement, *Report on Strike*, 12 (quotation), 247 (quotation), 4–5, 11–12, 15, 17, 44–84, 245–50; Department of Industrial Relations, Interchurch World Movement of North America, "Industrial Relations and the Churches," n.d. [ca. Oct. 3, 1919], Interchurch World Movement of North America Records, box 1, folder 3, Ecumenical Library, Interchurch Center, New York; Department of Industrial Relations, Interchurch World Movement of North America, "Working Program of the Industrial Relations Department," Oct. 10, 1919, ibid.; Foster, *Great Strike*, 156–60; Brody, *Labor in Crisis*, 177–78; Daniel Poling, "Still Silent on the Twelve-Hour Day," *New Republic*, Dec.

29, 1920, 133–34; Interchurch World Movement, *Public Opinion and the Steel Strike: Supplementary Reports of the Investigators to the Commission of Inquiry, the Interchurch World Movement* (New York: Harcourt, Brace, 1921), 306–30. For ad hominem conservative attacks on the Interchurch report, see Patterson, *Review*, esp. 1–3, 9, 25, 29, 106–8; Marshall Olds, *Analysis of the Interchurch World Movement Report on the Steel Strike* (New York: G. P. Putnam's Sons, 1923).

44. Drury, "Three-Shift System," 9 (quotations), 2–29; Williams, "Discussion," 42 (quotation), 42–44. For his prior work, see Horace B. Drury, *Scientific Management: A History and Criticism* (New York: Columbia University Press, 1915).

45. S. Adele Shaw, "Three Shifts: The Pioneers and the Problem," *Survey*, Mar. 5, 1921, 809 (quotation), 809–18; Fitch, "Long Day," 783–98; *New York Times*, Mar. 8, 1921, 27.

46. Committee on Work-Periods, *Twelve-Hour Shift*, ix (Harding quotation), 12, 15, 41–42, 45–55, 260, 268–93; "The President's Move Against the Twelve-Hour Day," *Literary Digest*, June 3, 1922, 14–15. On the diagnostic skills necessary in continuous-flow operations, see Nuwer, "Batch to Flow," 811n16, 834–38.

47. Herbert Hoover, *Memoirs*, 3 vols., vol. 2, *The Cabinet and the Presidency, 1920–1933* (New York: Macmillan, 1952), 103 (quotation), 103–4; *New York Times*, Aug. 3, 1923, 8, Aug. 9, 1923, 6, Aug. 15, 1923, 28, Aug. 16, 1923, 2; Frederick MacKenzie, "Steel Abandons the Twelve-Hour Day: A Demonstration of the Power of Public Opinion," *American Labor Legislation Review*, Sept. 1923, 179–86; Gulick, *Labor Policy*, 41–55; Eggert, *Steelmasters*, 50–51; William Dickson, "Can American Steel Plants Afford an Eight-Hour Turn?" *Survey*, Jan. 3, 1914, 376; William Dickson, diary, Sept. 11, 1919, Dickson Papers, box 1. This reform had several determinants, and differences within the historiography are mainly matters of emphasis. For analyses placing relatively less weight on management self-interest, see Hill, "Fighting the Twelve-Hour Day," 19–35, esp. 27–31; Brody, *Steelworkers in America*, 271–75. For the interpretation with which my own is most in accord, see David R. Roediger, "The Limits of Corporate Reform: Fordism, Taylorism, and the Working Week in the United States, 1914–1929," in *Worktime and Industrialization: An International History*, ed. Gary S. Cross (Philadelphia: Temple University Press, 1988), 139–42. On Hooverian corporatism, see Joan Hoff Wilson, *Herbert Hoover: Forgotten Progressive* (Prospect Heights, Ill.: Waveland Press, 1992), 79–121, esp. 94; Ellis W. Hawley, "Herbert Hoover, the Commerce Secretariat, and the Vision of an 'Associative State,' 1921–1928," *Journal of American History* 61 (1974): 116–40. On slow reactions and negligent behavior by the sleep deprived, see Julian Lim and David F. Dinges, "Sleep Deprivation and Vigilant Attention," *Annals of the New York Academy of Science* 1129 (2008): 305–22.

48. S. Adele Shaw, "Now That Jerry Has Time to Live," *Survey*, Sept. 1, 1924, 568–70; Olson, *Wives of Steel*, 38; James Rose, *Duquesne and the Rise of Steel Unionism* (Urbana: University of Illinois Press, 2001), 43; "Average Hours and Earnings in the Iron and Steel Industry, 1913 to 1926," *Monthly Labor Review*, May 1927, 164–65; Carnegie-Illinois Steel Corporation and Steel Workers Organizing Committee, "Agreement," Mar. 2, 1937,

Harold Ruttenberg Papers, box 3, folder 14, Historical Collections and Labor Archives, Pennsylvania State University Libraries, University Park; *New York Times*, Mar. 4, 1937, 1; Jones and Laughlin Steel Corporation and Steel Workers Organizing Committee, *Agreement . . . , Effective May 25, 1937* (n.p., 1937), 3.

49. Committee on Work-Periods, *Twelve-Hour Shift*, 280–82; Lizabeth Cohen, *Making a New Deal: Industrial Workers in Chicago, 1919–1939*, 2nd ed. (New York: Cambridge University Press, 2008), 315; Carnegie-Illinois Steel Corporation and United Steelworkers of America, *Agreement . . . , September 1, 1942* (Pittsburgh: Carnegie-Illinois Steel Corporation, 1942), 14–17; Carnegie-Illinois Steel Corporation, Duquesne Works, "Present Operating Schedule, 38″ and 40″ Mills," Dec. 30, 1942, Duquesne Industrial Relations Records, box 4, folder: Schedules (General Correspondence), 1936–1942; National War Labor Board, "Directive Order of War Labor Board in Case of Globe Steel Tubes Company," Feb. 14, 1944, ibid., box 10, folder: Shift Differentials; [U.S. Steel Corporation], "Electric Furnace 20 Week-40 Hour Schedule," n.d. [ca. Nov. 1947], ibid., box 30, folder: Schedule Survey, November 1947; [U.S. Steel Corporation], "40 Hour Working Schedule—Open Hearth Department," n.d. [ca. 1959], ibid., box 15, folder: Schedules (General Correspondence); Mark McColloch, "Consolidating Industrial Citizenship: The USWA at War and Peace, 1939–46," in *Forging a Union of Steel: Philip Murray, SWOC, and the United Steelworkers*, ed. Paul F. Clark, Peter Gottlieb, and Donald Kennedy (Ithaca, N.Y.: ILR Press, 1987), 57–58; Olson, *Wives of Steel*, 79; U.S. Steel Corporation, "Careers: Plant Operations," n.d. [ca. Jan. 2011], http://www.ussteel.com/corp/people/careers/plant-operations.asp, accessed Feb. 13, 2011. For emerging scientific recognition of adverse effects of rapid rotation, see, among others, Nathaniel Kleitman, *Sleep and Wakefulness as Alternating Phases in the Cycle of Existence* (Chicago: University of Chicago Press, 1939), 437–39; Nathaniel Kleitman, "A Scientific Solution of the Multiple Shift Problem," in Industrial Hygiene Foundation of America, *Proceedings of the Seventh Annual Meeting, 1942* (Pittsburgh: Industrial Hygiene Foundation of America, n.d.), 19–23; Ludwig Teleky, "Problems of Night Work: Influences on Health and Efficiency," *Industrial Medicine* 12 (1943): 776–78; New York, State Department of Labor, *Problems of Shift Rotation: Social and Physiological Aspects*, by Beatrice Mintz (Albany: New York State Department of Labor, 1943). For managerial acknowledgment of the perils of rotation, see Paul J. W. Pigors and Charles A. Myers, *Personnel Administration: A Point of View and a Method* (New York: McGraw-Hill, 1947), 255–56. On the advantage of forward clockwise rotation (and of infrequent rotation), see Charles A. Czeisler, Martin C. Moore-Ede, and Richard M. Coleman, "Rotating Shift Work Schedules That Disrupt Sleep Are Improved by Applying Circadian Principles," *Science* 217 (1982): 460–63.

50. J. Rutenfranz et al., "Biomedical and Psychosocial Aspects of Shift Work," *Scandinavian Journal of Work, Environment and Health* 3 (1977): 165–82; Charles M. Winget, Lewis Hughes, and Joseph LaDou, "Physiological Effects of Rotational Work Shifting: A Review," *Journal of Occupational Medicine* 20 (1978): 204–10; Richard Coleman and Richard Dement, "Falling Asleep at Work: A Problem for Continuous Operations," *Sleep*

Research 15 (1986): 265; Roger R. Rosa, Michael J. Colligan, and Paul Lewis, "Extended Workdays: Effects of 8-Hour and 12-Hour Rotating Shift Schedules on Performance, Subjective Alertness, Sleep Patterns, and Psychological Variables," *Work and Stress* 3 (1989): 21–32; R. T. Wilkinson, "How Fast Should the Night Shift Rotate?" *Ergonomics* 35 (1992): 1425–46; Mark I. Holbrook, Melinda H. White, and Michelle J. Hutt, "Increasing Awareness of Sleep Hygiene in Rotating Shift Workers: Arming Law-Enforcement Officers Against Impaired Performance," *Perceptual and Motor Skills* 79 (1994): 520–22; Maurice Ohayon et al., "Prevalence and Consequences of Sleep Disorders in a Shift Work Population," *Journal of Psychosomatic Research* 53 (2002): 577–83. For suggestions that perseverance through long hours and rough working conditions represented a flawed conception of manliness, see Walker, *Steel*, 156–57; Bruce Nelson, *Divided We Stand: American Workers and the Struggle for Black Equality* (Princeton, N.J.: Princeton University Press, 2001), 153.

Chapter 4. Asleep and Awake at the Same Time

Note to epigraph: Ashley Totten, "Why Pullman Porters Organized," *Interracial Review* 22 (1949): 169.

1. U.S. Commission on Industrial Relations (hereafter cited as CIR), *Final Report and Testimony*, 11 vols. (Washington, D.C.: Government Printing Office, 1916), 10:9650 (Sylvester quotation), 9622–27, 9634.

2. On the evolution of sleep science, see William C. Dement, "History of Sleep Physiology and Medicine," in *Principles and Practice of Sleep Medicine*, 4th ed., ed. Meir H. Kryger, Thomas Roth, and William C. Dement (Philadelphia: Elsevier/Saunders, 2005), 1–12; Kenton Kroker, *The Sleep of Others and the Transformations of Sleep Research* (Toronto: University of Toronto Press, 2007). On lay recognition of work-related disease, see United Auto Workers, *The Case of the Workplace Killers: A Manual for Cancer Detectives on the Job* (Detroit: United Auto Workers, 1980); Herbert K. Abrams, "The Worker as Teacher," *American Journal of Industrial Medicine* 4 (1983): 759–68; Barbara Ellen Smith, *Digging Our Own Graves: Coal Miners and the Struggle over Black Lung Disease* (Philadelphia: Temple University Press, 1987), 42, 53, 104–74; Alan Derickson, *Black Lung: Anatomy of a Public Health Disaster* (Ithaca, N.Y.: Cornell University Press, 1998), 4, 14–15, 22–42, 56–57, 150–74. On occupational stress, see Daniel Walkowitz and Peter Eisenstadt, "The Psychology of Work: Work and Mental Health in Historical Perspective," *Radical History Review* 34 (1986): 7–31; Steven Sauter and Joseph Hurrell Jr., "Occupational Health Psychology: Origins, Content, and Direction," *Professional Psychology: Research and Practice* 30 (April 1999): 117–22; Cary L. Cooper and Philip Dewe, *Stress: A Brief History* (Oxford: Blackwell, 2004).

3. Volumes that have clarified many facets of the rise of the BSCP but have not emphasized the centrality of discontent over hours and rest include Brailsford R. Brazeal, *The Brotherhood of Sleeping Car Porters: Its Origins and Development* (New York: Harper and Brothers, 1946); William H. Harris, *Keeping the Faith: A. Philip Randolph, Milton*

P. Webster, and the Brotherhood of Sleeping Car Porters, 1925–37 (Urbana: University of Illinois Press, 1977); Beth Tompkins Bates, *Pullman Porters and the Rise of Protest Politics in Black America, 1925–1945* (Chapel Hill: University of North Carolina Press, 2001); Jack Santino, *Miles of Smiles, Years of Struggle: Stories of Black Pullman Porters* (Urbana: University of Illinois Press, 1989); Larry Tye, *Rising from the Rails: Pullman Porters and the Making of the Black Middle Class* (New York: Henry Holt, 2004); Jervis B. Anderson, *A. Philip Randolph: A Biographical Portrait* (New York: Harcourt Brace Jovanovich, 1973). Anderson does note both that a reduction in work time was the primary demand of the porters' company-union representatives during the 1924 negotiations and that Milton Webster believed that Pullman's rejection of this demand marked the real beginning of the BSCP. However, his treatment of subsequent organizing does not emphasize the unionists' pursuit of this priority. See Anderson, *Randolph*, 166–67.

4. Marcus Rediker, *Between the Devil and the Deep Blue Sea: Merchant Seamen, Pirates, and the Anglo-American Maritime World, 1700–1750* (New York: Cambridge University Press, 1987), 88 (Barlow quotation), 84, 91, 94, 159–60; Peter C. Baldwin, *In the Watches of the Night: Life in the Nocturnal City, 1820–1930* (Chicago: University of Chicago Press, 2012), 121; George Hunter, "Destitution Among Seamen," *Survey*, Aug. 3, 1912, 614, 617, 618; Eric Arnesen, *Waterfront Workers of New Orleans: Race, Class, and Politics, 1863–1923* (Urbana: University of Illinois Press, 1994), 103, 104; Bruce Nelson, *Workers on the Waterfront: Seamen, Longshoremen, and Unionism in the 1930s* (Urbana: University of Illinois Press, 1988), 14–15, 72, 80,106; Peter Cole, *Wobblies on the Waterfront: Interracial Unionism in Progressive-Era Philadelphia* (Urbana: University of Illinois Press, 2007), 15–18, 72; Joseph F. Spillane, *Cocaine: From Medical Marvel to Modern Menace in the United States, 1884–1920* (Baltimore: Johns Hopkins University Press, 2000), 91–92; David T. Courtwright, "The Hidden Epidemic: Opiate Addiction and Cocaine Use in the South, 1860–1920," *Journal of Southern History* 49 (1983): 67–68; Philip L. Fradkin, *Stagecoach: Wells Fargo and the American West* (New York: Simon and Schuster Source, 2002), 32–35, 39, 62, 63; Carlos A. Schwantes, *Long Day's Journey: The Steamboat and Stagecoach Era in the Northern West* (Seattle: University of Washington Press, 1999), 204–14, 219–20, 231–33, 242. For early notice of mariners' plight, see the classic by Bernardino Ramazzini, *De Morbis Artificum Bernardino Ramazzini Diatriba: Diseases of Workers*, trans. Wilmer Wright (1713; Chicago: University of Chicago Press, 1940), 467: "Sailors are exposed to persistent sleeplessness, for since the safety of all on board is entrusted to their vigilance, hardly any time is allowed for them to snatch sleep except in calm weather now and then, and even when they are asleep they cannot trust it to last but have its unreliability always on their minds." On the persistence of daily rotation at sea (albeit with eight—not the original four—hours off in some intervals) into the twentieth century, see Committee on Work-Periods in Continuous-Industry of the Federated American Engineering Societies, *The Twelve-Hour Shift in Industry* (New York: E. P. Dutton, 1922), 183.

5. Michael O'Malley, *Keeping Watch: A History of American Time* (New York: Viking Press, 1990), 55–98; Licht, *Working for the Railroad*, 162, 174–80; Paul M. Taillon,

Good, Reliable, White Men: Railroad Brotherhoods, 1877–1917 (Urbana: University of Illinois Press, 2009), 20–21, 152; Carlene Stephens, "'The Most Reliable Time': William Bond, the New England Railroads, and Time Awareness in Nineteenth-Century America," *Technology and Culture* 30 (1989): 1–24; Mark M. Smith, *Mastered by the Clock: Time, Slavery, and Freedom in the American South* (Chapel Hill: University of North Carolina Press, 1997); Aaron W. Marrs, "Railroads and Time Consciousness in the Antebellum South," *Enterprise and Society* 9 (2008): 433–56; Reed C. Richardson, *The Locomotive Engineer, 1863–1963: A Century of Railway Labor Regulations and Work Rules* (Ann Arbor: Bureau of Industrial Relations, University of Michigan, 1963), 151–52; *Brotherhood of Locomotive Engineers Monthly Journal*, Nov. 1874, 585. For locomotive engineers using cocaine to stay awake on the job, see Thomas Simonton, "The Increase of the Use of Cocaine Among the Laity in Pittsburgh," *Philadelphia Medical Journal*, Mar. 28, 1903, 556.

6. Melinda Chateauvert, *Marching Together: Women of the Brotherhood of Sleeping Car Porters* (Urbana: University of Illinois Press, 1998), 117; Eric Arnesen, *Brotherhoods of Color: Black Railroad Workers and the Struggle for Equality* (Cambridge, Mass.: Harvard University Press, 2001). Because of a lack of extant evidence, I can offer little insight into the maids' situation. Chateauvert laments that "maids did not articulate a separate set of grievances, despite sexually discriminatory work rules." See *Marching Together*, 19 (quotation). On the role of porters' spouses in union and community organizing, see Paula F. Pfeffer, "The Women Behind the Union: Halena Wilson, Rosina Tucker, and the Ladies' Auxiliary to the Brotherhood of Sleeping Car Porters," *Labor History* 36 (1995): 557–78.

7. CIR, *Final Report*, 10:9553–54; *Messenger*, Aug. 1925, 290; *Pullman News*, May 1923, 11; Susan E. Hirsch, "No Victory at the Workplace: Women and Minorities at Pullman During World War II," in *The War in American Culture: Society and Consciousness During World War II*, ed. Lewis A. Erenberg and Susan E. Hirsch (Chicago: University of Chicago Press, 1996), 241–62, esp. 251; Santino, *Miles of Smiles*, 6–10; Joseph Husband, *The Story of the Pullman Car* (Chicago: A. C. McClurg, 1917), 136–55; Lucius M. Beebe, *Mr. Pullman's Elegant Palace Car: The Railway Carriage That Established a New Dimension of Luxury and Entered the National Lexicon as a Symbol of Splendor* (Garden City, N.Y.: Doubleday, 1961); John White Jr., *The American Railroad Passenger Car* (Baltimore: Johns Hopkins University Press, 1978), 245–85; Ralph L. Barger, *A Century of Pullman Cars*, 2 vols. (Sykesville, Md.: Greenberg, 1988, 1990); Pullman Company, *Instructions for Employees on Cars of the Pullman Company* (n.p., 1914), 72–82; Chateauvert, *Marching Together*, 22. Of course, the porters' range of duties and their concomitant time commitments were essentially those expected of female domestic servants. See Faye E. Dudden, *Serving Women: Household Service in Nineteenth-Century America* (Middletown, Conn.: Wesleyan University Press, 1983), 181–82; David M. Katzman, *Seven Days a Week: Women and Domestic Service in Industrializing America* (Urbana: University of Illnois Press, 108–14. For the similarities with health services, see Susan Reverby, *Ordered to Care: The Dilemma of American Nursing, 1850–1940* (New York: Cambridge University Press, 1987), 29–30, 56, 62, 64, 96, 100.

8. Harris, *Keeping Faith*, 3 (quotation); Stanley Buder, *Pullman: An Experiment in Industrial Order and Community Planning, 1880–1930* (New York: Oxford University Press, 1967); Richard T. Ely, "Pullman: A Social Study," *Harper's New Monthly Magazine*, Feb. 1885, 452–66; Bates, *Porters and Protest*, 40–55; Arnesen, *Brotherhoods of Color*, 86–87. One facet of the firm's paternalism was a monthly newsletter, which carried numerous articles encouraging employees to curtail fatigue and sleep loss by altering their behavior and attitudes. See *Pullman News*, Nov. 1922, 194, Oct. 1926, inside back cover, Dec. 1926, inside back cover, July 1929, inside back cover, Mar. 1931, back cover, Apr. 1931, inside back cover, Mar. 1932, back cover, Jan. 1935, 96.

9. Brazeal, *Brotherhood*, 208; Tye, *Rising*, 86; U.S. House of Representatives, Committee on Interstate and Foreign Commerce, *Hearing . . . on the Bills H.R. 4438, H.R. 16676, and H.R. 18671, to Limit the Hours of Service of Railroad Employees*, 59th Cong., 1st sess., 1906 (Washington, D.C.: Government Printing Office, 1906), 69; *U.S. Statutes at Large* 34 (1907): 1416. On arbitrary control of working time under slavery, see Eugene D. Genovese, *Roll, Jordan, Roll: The World the Slaves Made* (New York: Pantheon Books, 1974), 315–19, 321–22; Robert Starobin, *Industrial Slavery in the Old South* (New York: Oxford University Press, 1970), 37–41. For signs that slaveholders tried to ensure that slaves got adequate sleep, in order to be more productive workers, see James O. Breeden, *Advice Among Masters: The Ideal in Slave Management in the Old South* (Westport, Conn.: Greenwood Press, 1980), 75–77. On the effects of overwork, see Philip Buell and Lester Breslow, "Mortality from Coronary Heart Disease in California Men Who Work Long Hours," *Journal of Chronic Disease* 11 (1960): 615–26; Kate Sparks et al., "The Effects of Hours of Work on Health: A Meta-Analytic Review," *Journal of Occupational and Organizational Psychology* 70 (1997): 391–408; Anne Spurgeon, *Working Time: Its Impact on Safety and Health* (Seoul: International Labor Office and Korean Occupational Safety and Health Research Institute, 2003); U.S. National Institute for Occupational Safety and Health, *Overtime and Extended Work Shifts: Recent Findings on Illnesses, Injuries, and Health Behaviors*, by Claire C. Caruso et al., (Cincinnati: National Institute for Occupational Safety and Health, 2004); A. E. Dembe, "The Impact of Overtime and Long Work Hours on Occupational Injuries and Illnesses: New Evidence from the United States," *Occupational and Environmental Medicine* 62 (2005): 588–97.

10. Tye, *Rising*, 86; Brazeal, *Brotherhood*, 198, 211; U.S. Railroad Administration, *Supplement No. 2 to General Order No. 27* (Washington, D.C.: Government Printing Office, 1918); A. Philip Randolph, "Pullman Porters Have Grievances," *Nation*, Sept. 30, 1925, 357.

11. C. F. Anderson, *Freemen yet Slaves under "Abe" Lincoln's Son; or, Service and Wages of Pullman Porters* (Chicago: Press of the Enterprise Printing House, 1904), 26–27 (quotation), 3–4 (quotation), 26–28, 37; CIR, *Final Report*, 10:9622–27, 9634, 9650.

12. *Black Worker*, Feb. 1939, 4 (Sagittarius [Thomas T. Patterson?] quotation), 3–4; Anderson, *Freemen yet Slaves*, 8, 15; T. T. Patterson, untitled address, in Joseph F. Wilson, *Tearing Down the Color Bar: A Documentary History and Analysis of the Brotherhood of Sleeping Car Porters* (New York: Columbia University Press, 1989), 212; Benjamin Stol-

berg, "The Pullman Peon: A Study in Industrial Race Exploitation," *Nation*, Apr. 7, 1926, 366. On the extended assignments on excursion trains, see Robert E. Turner, *Memories of a Retired Pullman Porter* (New York: Exposition Press, 1954), 101–14.

13. Herbert O. Holderness, *The Reminiscences of a Pullman Conductor, or Character Sketches of Life in a Pullman Car* (Chicago: n.pub., 1901), 208 (quotation), 207; Pullman Palace Car Company, *Regulations for the Guidance of Conductors and Porters, Approved January 1, 1874* (Chicago: C. H. Blakely, 1885), 13; *Pullman News*, June 1922, 43; Pullman Company, *Instructions for Employees on Cars of the Pullman Company* (Chicago: Rogers, 1903), 58; Pullman, *Instructions* (1914), 64–65; Brazeal, *Brotherhood*, 211; *Messenger*, Oct. 1926, 299; Pullman Company, *Instructions for Employees on Cars of the Pullman Company* (n.p., 1921), 65; Pullman Company, *Instructions for Porters Employed on Cars of the Pullman Company* (n.p., 1925), 28–29; *New York Times*, Mar. 4, 1934, 11. On the bronco stools, see CIR, *Final Report*, 10:9579. For surreptitious napping while riding the bronco, see ibid., 9651, 9654. Some runs did make use of a "swing porter" or "relief porter," allowing both the porter and the conductor to sleep at the same time (ibid., 9657).

14. Anderson, *Freemen yet Slaves*, 26 (quotation), 26–28; CIR, *Report*, 10:9558 (Hungerford quotation), 9572–73, 9622–27, 9673; Pullman Company, *Instructions* (1903), 7–8, 57; Holderness, *Reminiscences*, 217; Pullman Company, "Transcript of [Disciplinary] Record" (for numerous porters), n.d. [1933], Pullman Company Archives, record group 6, subgroup 1, ser. 1, box 1, folder 14, Roger and Julie Baskes Department of Special Collections, Newberry Library, Chicago; Santino, *Miles of Smiles*, 23.

15. *Pullman News*, May 1924, 6 (Simmons quotation); Harris, *Keeping Faith*, 14–19; Brazeal, *Brotherhood*, 9–14; Leonard A. Lecht, *Experience Under Railway Labor Legislation* (New York: Columbia University Press, 1955), 76; Representatives of the Porters and Maids and Representatives of the Management of the Pullman Company, "Minutes of the Conference," Mar. 21, 1924, 3–4, 11, Pullman Archives, RG 6, subgroup 1, ser. 4, box 2, folder 54; idem, "Minutes of the Conference," Mar. 22, 1924, 7–10, ibid.; Pullman Company and James Sexton et al., "Agreement between the Pullman Company and Its Porters and Maids, Effective Apr. 1, 1924," Mar. 29, 1924 (unpaginated—see Rule 3), ibid. folder 38; Pullman Company, *Instructions for Porters Employed on Cars of the Pullman Company* (n.p., 1925), 28–29.

16. Totten, "Why Pullman Porters Organized,"169 (quotations), 168–69; International Ladies' Auxiliary, BSCP, "Proceedings of the First [*sic* —Second] Biennial Convention, 1940," 56 (third Totten quotation), BSCP *Records*, pt. 2, reel 1, frame 343; Harris, *Keeping Faith*, 26–116; Brazeal, *Brotherhood*, 15–24; Anderson, *Randolph*, 1–215; Andrew E. Kersten, *A. Philip Randolph: A Life in the Vanguard* (Lanham, Md.: Rowman and Littlefield, 2007), 25–46.

17. *Messenger*, Aug. 1925, 290 (Randolph quotations), 289–90, Sept. 1925, 339 (BSCP advertisement quotation), 312 (Randolph quotation), 313 (cartoon quotation), Nov.–Dec. 1925, 352, Jan. 1926, 10.

18. *Messenger*, June 1926, 174 (Celler quotation), 173, May 1927, 165 (Methodist Federation quotation, rpt. from *Social Service Bulletin*, Apr. 1, 1927), Jan. 1926, 23, Feb. 1926,

56–57, Mar. 1926, 88, 94, Oct. 1926, 315; Stolberg, "Pullman Peon," 365, 366; *Pittsburgh Courier*, May 1, 1926, 1; Boston Citizens' Committee, *The Pullman Porters' Struggle* (Boston: Boston Citizen's Committee, 1928). On the larger effort to forge cross-class and other alliances, especially with the African American middle class, see Bates, *Porters and Protest*, 63; Chateauvert, *Marching Together*, 37–38, 42–46.

19. *Messenger*, Aug. 1925, 290; BSCP, *Pullman Porter*, 8; CIR, *Final Report*, 10:9595; Harris, *Keeping Faith*, 3; Chateauvert, *Marching Together*, 21–23.

20. *Messenger*, Sept. 1925, 312 (Randolph quotation), May 1926, 158 (BSCP quotation), Dec. 1925, 384, March 1926, 89–90, Dec. 1926, 361; *Black Worker*, Nov. 15, 1929, 1, 3; Husband, *Story*, 155–56; Randolph, "Pullman Grievances," 357; Santino, *Miles of Smiles*, 59. On the wide range of personal services delivered by porters, see Pullman, *Instructions* (1903), esp. 17; Pullman, *Instructions* (1914), esp. 1; E. D. Nixon, untitled interview, in Studs Terkel, *Hard Times: An Oral History of the Great Depression* (New York: Pantheon Books, 1970), 117–18; Husband, *Story*, 145; Santino, *Miles of Smiles*, 19; David D. Peralta, *Those Pullman Blues: An Oral History of the African American Railroad Attendant* (New York: Twayne, 1996), xxiv–xxv. On servility as a pose, see Bernard Mergen, "The Pullman Porter: From 'George' to Brotherhood," *South Atlantic Quarterly* 73 (1974): 224–35. For differing interpretations of the strengths, weaknesses, and extent of masculinism in the porters' union, see Bates, *Porters and Protest*, esp. 19–20, 32, 65–74, 87–105, 186–87; Chateauvert, *Marching Together*, esp. 3–6, 15, 18–20; Amy G. Richter, *Home on the Rails: Women, the Railroad, and the Rise of Public Domesticity* (Chapel Hill: University of North Carolina Press, 2005), 129–33; Leon Fink, *Progressive Intellectuals and the Dilemmas of Democratic Commitment* (Cambridge, Mass.: Harvard University Press, 1997), 184–213, esp. 196–97, 203–4, 209–10. On manhood and manhood rights more generally, see Kevin K. Gaines, *Uplifting the Race: Black Leadership, Politics, and Culture in the Twentieth Century* (Chapel Hill: University of North Carolina Press, 1996), 4–5, 52, 112–15, 200; Marlon B. Ross, *Manning the Race: Reforming Black Men in the Jim Crow Era* (New York: New York University Press, 2004); Steve Estes, *I Am a Man! Race, Manhood, and the Civil Rights Movement* (Chapel Hill: University of North Carolina Press, 2005).

21. *Messenger*, July 1926, 218 (Randolph quotations), Oct. 1927, 306 (Bradley quotation), Nov.–Dec. 1925, 352, Nov. 1926, 325; Fink, *Progressive Intellectuals*, 196. The taunt that black men lacked stamina may have been especially stinging, not only because of its patent falseness, as demonstrated by the porters' routine job performance, but also because of the longstanding racist stereotype of an unmanly want of endurance among African Americans. On the latter, see Margaret Humphreys, *Intensely Human: The Health of the Black Soldier in the American Civil War* (Baltimore: Johns Hopkins University Press, 2008), 18–19, 31, 144–45, 149.

22. *Black Worker*, Feb. 1, 1930, 3–4 (quotation), 2, Nov. 15, 1929, 2, 4, Dec. 15, 1929, 3, Jan. 1, 1930, 4, Mar. 1, 1930, 1, May 20, 1935, 3–4, July 1937, 3–4; *American Federationist*, June 1930, 671 (Randolph quotation), 672; *Messenger*, Oct. 1927, 306. On the Pullman safety program, see Chateauvert, *Marching Together*, 23, 24; *Pullman News*, Jan. 1923,

263, Nov. 1926, 219, Nov. 1927, 221, June 1928, 39–41; E. F. Carry to Members of the Pullman Family, Apr. 29, 1926, Pullman Archives, RG 6, subgroup 4, ser. 2, vol. 2. On the firm's efficiency concerns, see Bates, *Porters and Protest*, 44; *Pullman News*, June 1922, 48. For other facets of the uneasy relationship between safety and efficiency, see Donald R. Stabile, "The DuPont Experiments in Scientific Management: Efficiency and Safety, 1911–1919," *Business History Review* 61 (1987): 365–86. On respectability, see Evelyn Brooks Higginbotham, *Righteous Discontent: The Women's Movement in the Black Baptist Church, 1880–1920* (Cambridge, Mass.: Harvard University Press, 1993), 14–15, 185–229; Gaines, *Uplifting the Race*, esp. 3–8, 67–99. Allan Spear and James Grossman have characterized Pullman porters as middle class, mainly because of their relatively well-off status in the African American community in the early twentieth century; Kevin Gaines has argued that this was fundamentally a proletarian occupation; Beth Bates has explored most deeply the relations between status and class. See Allan H. Spear, *Black Chicago: The Making of a Negro Ghetto, 1890–1920* (Chicago: University of Chicago Press, 1967), 23n29; James R. Grossman, *Land of Hope: Chicago, Black Southerners, and the Great Migration* (Chicago: University of Chicago Press, 1991), 129; Gaines, *Uplifting the Race*, 15; Bates, *Porters and Protest*, 18–25.

23. A. Philip Randolph, "Statement of Pullman Porters' Position in Fight for Recognition, Living Wage, and Better Working Rules with Pullman Company," Aug. 18, 1927, BSCP, *Records, Series A: Holdings of the Chicago Historical Society and the Newberry Library, 1925–1969*, microfilm ed., ed. William H. Harris, 50 reels (Bethesda, Md.: University Publications of America, 1990–94), pt. 1, reel 2, frames 348–51; *Messenger*, Aug. 1925, 289–90, Oct.–Nov. 1925, 367, Jan. 1926, 10, Oct. 1926, 295, April 1927, 131, June 1927, 205; *Black Worker*, Nov. 15, 1929, 1; Pullman Company and Order of Sleeping Car Conductors, *Agreement, 1922* (n.p., 1922), 3; BSCP, *The Pullman Porter* (New York: BSCP, 1927), 8, 10–12. For Frank Walsh's earlier critique of the loss of rest indirectly due to tipping and his interest in ending the practice, see CIR, *Final Report*, 10:9585.

24. *Messenger*, July 1925, 254 (Randolph quotation), Nov. 1926, 347 (Schuyler quotations), Sept. 1925, 312–13; Feb. 1926, 38, Oct. 1926, 295; BSCP, "Digest of an Argument by the Brotherhood of Sleeping Car Porters in Support of Their Recognition by the Pullman Company," n.d. [ca. 1926], 50 (quotation), A. Philip Randolph Papers, box 15, folder: Pullman Porters and Maids Digest and Argument for Working Agreement, Manuscript Division, Library of Congress, Washington.

25. *Messenger*, July 1925, 254 (Randolph quotation), Feb. 1926, 38; Randolph, "Pullman Porters Have Grievances," 357 (quotation); BSCP, *Pullman Porter*, 10 (quotation), 9 (quotation).

26. *Messenger*, Oct. 1926, 318 (anonymous porter quotation), 306, Feb. 1926, 38 (Randolph quotation), Feb. 1927, 61 (anonymous Minneapolis porter quotation); Pullman and Sleeping Car Conductors, *Agreement, 1922*, 3; BSCP, *Pullman Porter*, 10; BSCP, "Digest of an Argument by the Brotherhood of Sleeping Car Porters in Support of Their Recognition by the Pullman Company," n.d. [ca. 1926], 21, Randolph Papers, box 15, folder: Pullman Porters and Maids Digest and Argument for Working Agreement.

27. Pullman Company [and Plan of Employee Representation], *Agreement, Effective June 1, 1929* (n.p., 1929), 6 (quotation), 4; Porters and Maids Wage Conference, "Minutes," June 1, 1929, 4 (Simmons quotation), 1, May 21, 1929, 10, May 23, 1929, 8–10, May 31, 1929, 1–2, Pullman Archives, RG 6, subgroup 1, ser. 4, box 3A, folder 74; Brazeal, *Brotherhood*, 200.

28. *Black Worker*, Feb. 1, 1930, 2 (Sagittarius quotations), 4, Nov. 15, 1929, 4, Dec. 1, 1929, 3, Mar. 1, 1930, 3.

29. *Messenger*, Oct. 1926, 318 (anonymous porter quotations); Randolph, "Porters Fight Paternalism," 670, 672. For car designs indicating a narrow couch in the men's room, see Barger, *Century of Pullman Cars*, 2: 37, 39, 44, 49, 55, 59, 65–67, 70, 81, 86, 88, 92, 94; White, *American Cars*, 171, 256, 275, 276. Dining-car workers often had to try to sleep on dining tables. See Arnesen, *Brotherhoods of Color*, 21.

30. *Pittsburgh Courier*, Feb. 20, 1926, 2 (Lancaster quotation); CIR, *Final Report*, 10:9577–78, 9610; *Pullman News*, Sept. 1922, 141–42, Oct. 1922, 179; Turner, *Memories*, 101–2; Tye, *Rising*, 56, 59, 89, 135, 140; *Black Worker*, Dec. 1, 1929, 1, Aug. 1, 1930, 4; BSCP, *Pullman Porter*, 7; BSCP, "Digest of an Argument by the Brotherhood of Sleeping Car Porters in Support of Their Recognition by the Pullman Company . . . ," n.d. [ca. 1926], 28, 30, Randolph Papers, box 15, folder: Pullman Porters and Maids Digest and Argument for Working Agreement; Chateauvert, *Marching Together*, 25, 51; Anderson, *Randolph*, 179–80. On segregation in public transportation, see C. Vann Woodward, *The Strange Career of Jim Crow*, commemorative ed. (New York: Oxford University Press, 2002), 14, 18–19, 23–24, 116–17.

31. Harris, *Keeping Faith*, 117–216; Brazeal, *Brotherhood*, 23–114, 198–207; Lecht, *Experience*, 79–85; Arnesen, *Brotherhoods of Color*, 126–27.

32. [BSCP], "Proposed Agreement Between the Pullman [Company], Incorporated, and the Brotherhood of Sleeping Car Porters to Take Effect October 1, 1935," n.d. [ca. July 1935], 3, 5, C. L. Dellums Papers, carton 21, folder: Agreement Data, Bancroft Library, University of California, Berkeley; H. R. Lary, "History of the Mediation Dispute Between the Pullman Company and the Brotherhood of Sleeping Car Porters," n.d. [ca. June 27, 1937], BSCP *Records*, pt. 3, reel 10, frame 548; *New York Times*, Mar. 4, 1934, 11.

33. H. R. Lary, "Minutes of Proceedings," Apr. 6, 1937, 3 (quotation), BSCP *Records*, pt. 3, reel 10, frame 408; H. R. Lary, "Minutes of Proceedings," Apr. 5, 1937, 3–4, ibid., frames 401–2; H. R. Lary, "Minutes of Proceedings," Apr. 9, 1–3, ibid., frames 417–19.

34. R. F. Cole, "Compromise Proposal," Apr. 19, 1937, 1, ibid., frames 447–48; [H. R. Lary], untitled minutes, Apr. 21, 1937, 1–2, ibid., frames 449–50; Pullman Company and BSCP, "Agreement, Effective October 1, 1937," 2, Aug. 25, 1937, ibid., frame 745.

35. C. L. Dellums to A. Philip Randolph, Apr. 21, 1937 (quotation), Dellums Papers, carton 4, folder: Outgoing, Randolph, A. Philip, 1934–38; BSCP, "Proposed Agreement . . . to Take Effect October 1, 1935," n.d. [ca. July 1935], 8, Pullman Archives, RG 6, subgroup 1, ser. 4, box 18, folder 504; [H. R. Lary], untitled minutes, May 5, 1937, BSCP *Records*, pt. 3, reel 10, frame 461; [H. R. Lary], untitled minutes, May 10, 1937, ibid. frame 472; Pullman Company, untitled timesheets, Dec. 1936, ibid., frame 514.

36. [H. R. Lary], untitled minutes, May 3, 1937, BSCP *Records*, pt. 3, reel 10, frame 457; [H. R. Lary], untitled minutes, May 5, 1937, ibid., frames 459–61; Lary, "History," n.d. [June 27, 1937], 8–10, 13, BSCP *Records*, pt. 3, reel 10, frames 554–56, 559; H. R. Lary to J. F. Lane, July 2, 1937, ibid., frame 583; Lary to Lane, July 13, 1937, ibid., frame 595; Robert Cole, "Mediator Cole's Final Compromise Proposal," July 13, 1937, ibid., frame 618; B. H. Vroman et al. to Champ Carry, July 23, 1937, ibid., frame 650; [Pullman negotiator], untitled minutes, July 29, 1937, ibid., frame 672; Robert Cole, "Mediator Cole's Final Compromise Proposal," July 13, 1937, ibid., frame 618; Pullman and BSCP, "Agreement, 1937," 2–3, ibid., frames 745–46; [Pullman negotiator], "Credits for Hours Worked," June 11, 1937, Pullman Archives, RG 6, subgroup 1, ser. 4, box 18, folder 506; Chateauvert, *Marching Together*, 84.

37. BSCP, "Proposed Agreement, 1935," n.d. [ca. July 1935], 6, Dellums Papers, carton 21, folder: Agreement Data; Dellums to Randolph, April 21, 1937, ibid., carton 4, folder: Outgoing, Randolph, A. Philip, 1934–38; Lary, "History," n.d. [ca. June 27, 1937], 15, BSCP *Records*, pt. 3, reel 10, frame 561; Robert Cole, "Mediator Cole's Final Compromise Proposal," July 13, 1937, ibid, frame 617; Pullman and BSCP, "Agreement, 1937," 12, ibid., frame 755.

38. [Lary], minutes, May 5, 1937 (Cole quotation), BSCP *Records*, pt. 3, reel 10, frame 462; Lary, "History," n.d. [ca. June 27, 1937], 9, ibid., frame 555; W. L. Merriam to Champ Carry, Aug. 6, 1937, ibid., frame 708; Pullman and BSCP, "Agreement, 1937," 3, ibid., frame 746.

39. For glimpses of the bargaining process, see Harris, *Keeping Faith*, 213–15; Bates, *Porters and Protest*, 126; Brazeal, *Brotherhood*, 200; Tye, *Rising*, 161–62. On the favorable context, see, among others, Sidney Fine, *Sit-Down: The General Motors Strike of 1936–1937* (Ann Arbor: University of Michigan Press, 1969); Nelson, *Workers on Waterfront*; Robert H. Zieger, *The CIO, 1935–1955* (Chapel Hill: University of North Carolina Press, 1995), 22–89; Dana Frank, "Girl Strikers Occupy Chain Store, Win Big: The Detroit Woolworth's Strike of 1937," in Howard Zinn, Dana Frank, and Robin D. G. Kelley, *Three Strikes: Miners, Musicians, Salesgirls, and the Fighting Spirit of Labor's Last Century* (Boston: Beacon Press, 2001), 57–118; Christopher L. Tomlins, "AFL Unions in the 1930s: Their Performance in Historical Perspective," *Journal of American History* 65 (1979): 1021–42.

40. Oakland Division, BSCP, minutes, Sept. 12, 1939, Dellums Papers, carton 32, untitled vol.; A. Philip Randolph to Benjamin McLaurin, Aug. 5, 1940, BSCP Records, box 122, folder: Agreements, Pullman, Manuscript Division, Library of Congress, Washington; M. B. Osburn and A. Philip Randolph, "Supplemental Agreement," Aug. 8, 1949, 1, ibid., box 54, folder: Agreements, Pullman (1); Eastern, Western and Southeastern Carriers' Conference and Employees' National Conference Committee, "Agreement," Mar. 19, 1949, 3, ibid., box 121, folder: Agreements; T. D. McNeal to Officers and Members, Southwestern Zone, BSCP, Dec. 26, 1963, BSCP Records, box 94, folder: Shorter Work Month Movement; Pullman Company and BSCP, "Agreement . . . , Revised Effective July 1, 1965," Dec. 11, 1964, 7, BSCP *Records*, pt. 1, reel 12, frame 714.

On the Fair Labor Standards Act and its many exemptions, including that for railroad employees, see *U.S. Statutes at Large* 52 (1938): 1060–69, esp. 1067–68; Irving Bernstein, *A Caring Society: The New Deal, the Worker, and the Great Depression* (Boston: Houghton Mifflin, 1985), 116–45, esp. 137–39, 142; Marc Linder, *The Autocratically Flexible Workplace: A History of Overtime Regulation in the United States* (Iowa City: Fanpihua Press, 2002), 243–301.

41. Halena Wilson to Dear Sister, Jan. 19, 1940 (quotation), BSCP *Records*, pt. 2, reel 1, frame 202; BSCP, *Report of Proceedings of Third Biennial Convention and Seventeenth Anniversary Celebration, 1942* (St. Louis: Advocate Press, n.d.), 92 (Spokane Division quotations), 92–93; Lucas Fisher et al. to Mr. Dellums, Sept. 11, 1944 (quotation), ibid., carton 21, folder: Southern Pacific Agreement, 1944; *Black Worker*, Jan. 1941, 1, Apr. 1949, 1; BSCP, *Report of Proceedings of the Fifth Biennial Convention and Twenty-First Anniversary Celebration, 1946* (n.p., n.d.), 26, 36, 84, 193–94; BSCP, *Report of Proceedings of the Sixth Biennial Convention and Twenty-Third Anniversary Celebration, 1948* (n.p., n.d.), 146, 217; BSCP, *Report of Proceedings of the Seventh Biennial Convention and Silver Jubilee Celebration, 1950* (n.p., n.d.), 41; A. Philip Randolph, address, 1952, in Wilson, *Tearing*, 54–55; BSCP, *Report of Proceedings of the Second Triennial Convention and Thirty-First Anniversary, 1956* (n.p., n.d.), 175; BSCP, "Pullman Porters Seek Shorter Work Month," Mar. 12, 1962, BSCP Records, box 94, folder: Shorter Work Month; U.S. Emergency Board No. 155, *Report to the President* (Washington, D.C.: Government Printing Office, 1963), 7.

42. *Black Worker*, Nov. 1937, 3, Jan. 1938, 1, 4, Feb. 1938, 1, Apr. 1938, 1, 3, Oct. 1947, 3; Southwestern Zone, BSCP, "Report of Proceedings," Apr. 29, 1949, 36–37, BSCP *Records*, pt. 1, reel 10, frame 298; Fact Finding Committee, New York Division, BSCP, "Report," n.d. [ca. 1939], 14, ibid., reel 5, frame 664; unidentified porters, "Memorandum to Mr. M. P. Webster," Nov. 11, 1940, ibid., frame 992; H. A. Rock to D. LaRoche, Sept. 26, 1939, Randolph Papers, box 5, folder: Agreements, 1939; BSCP, *Proceedings, 1946*, 81; P. A. Smith to S[idney] Melton, Oct. 4, 1951, Pullman Archives, RG 6, subgroup 1, ser. 7, box 20, folder 285; Melton to Smith, Dec. 5, 1951, ibid.; C. L. Dellums to A. Philip Randolph, Jan. 4, 1937 [*sic*—1938], Dellums Papers, carton 4, folder: Outgoing, Randolph, A. Philip, 1934–38; Randolph to Dellums, Jan. 11, 1938, ibid.; Oakland Division, BSCP, minutes, Mar. 8, 1938, ibid., carton 32, untitled vol.; Dellums to H. C. Lincoln, Dec. 29, 1952, ibid., carton 10, folder: Pullman Time Sheets, 1953; Lincoln to Dellums, Feb. 17, 1953, ibid.

43. Fact Finding Committee, New York Division, BSCP, "Report," n.d. [ca. 1939], I (quotation), I–V, Randolph Papers, box 5, folder: Agreements, 1939; Pullman Company, *Instructions for Car Service Employees* (Chicago: Pullman Press, 1939), 6; Lyn Hughes, *An Anthology of Respect: The Pullman Porters National Historic Registry of African-American Railroad Employees* (Chicago: Hughes-Peterson, 2007), 231. For the classic analysis of the stressful nature of this type of situation, see Robert A. Karasek Jr., "Job Demands, Job Decision Latitude, and Mental Strain: Implications for Job Redesign," *Administrative Sciences Quarterly* 24 (1979): 285–308.

44. T. W. Jones to D. LaRoche, June 14, 1939 (quotations), Randolph Papers, box 5, folder: Agreements, 1939; C. S. Wells to [International] Executive Board, BSCP, June 4, 1947, Dellums Papers, carton 24, folder: National Executive Board; Pullman Company and BSCP, "Agreement . . . , Revised Effective June 1, 1941," Apr. 18, 1941, BSCP Records, box 54, folder: Agreements, Pullman (1); Pullman Company and BSCP, "Supplemental Agreement," Aug. 8, 1949, 4, ibid.; BSCP, "Bulletin on Revision of Agreement," n.d. [ca. Apr. 18, 1941], 4, ibid., box 122, folder: Agreements, Pullman Company; BSCP, *Proceedings, 1942*, 88; BSCP, *Proceedings, 1944*, 151; BSCP, *Report of Proceedings of the First Triennial Convention and Twenty-Eighth Anniversary, 1953* (n.p., n.d.), 188; BSCP, *Proceedings, 1956*, 177; M. P. Ayers to Milton P. Webster, Apr. 5, 1961, BSCP *Records*, pt. 1, reel 11, frame 808; Pullman Company and BSCP, "Agreement," n.d. [ca. July 1, 1965], 7–8, ibid., reel 12, frame 714.

45. Safety and Compensation Department, Pullman Company, "Injury—Porter C. E. Bigbee—Portland," n.d. [ca. Apr. 1935] (quotation), Pullman Archives, RG 6, subgroup 4, ser. 3, box 23, folder 290; BSCP, *Proceedings, 1944*, 151 (Jacksonville Division quotation), 150–52; Safety and Compensation Department, Pullman Company, "Injury—Porter Elmer Brown—Chicago Eastern District," n.d. [ca. Apr. 1931], Pullman Archives., box 22, folder 277; Safety and Compensation Department, Pullman Company, "Injury—Porter J. C. LeSeuer—Milwaukee Agency," n.d. [ca. Oct. 1939], ibid., box 24, folder 303; Safety and Compensation Department, Pullman Company, "Injury—Porter C. R. Collins—New Orleans," n.d. [ca. Feb. 1940], ibid., folder 304; Safety and Compensation Department, Pullman Company, "Injury—Porter E. Patterson—Penn Terminal," n.d. [ca. Aug. 1942], ibid., folder 311; Safety and Compensation Department, Pullman Company, "Injury—Porter James Curruthers—Chicago North," n.d. [ca. Oct. 1941], ibid., box 1, folder 6; Safety and Compensation Department, Pullman Company, "Injury—Porter I. Hammond—Washington," n.d. [ca. Jan. 1944], ibid., box 2, folder 14; *Black Worker*, Feb. 1945, 4, 1, July 1947, 3; Arnold Cherry, "Brotherhood of Sleeping Car Porters Questionnaire," n.d. [ca. 1941], Dellums Papers, carton 24, folder: Questionnaire Returns; Clarence Jackson, "Brotherhood of Sleeping Car Porters Questionnaire," n.d. [ca. 1941], ibid.; Hughes, *Anthology of Respect*, 190; Arthur C. McWatt, "'A Greater Victory': The Brotherhood of Sleeping Car Porters in St. Paul," *Minnesota History* 55 (1997): 213; G. R. Ross et al. to Fact Finding Committee, New York Division, BSCP, n.d. [ca. 1939], Randolph Papers, box 5, folder: Agreements, 1939; Pullman Company, *Instructions for Employees on Cars of the Pullman Company* (n.p., 1952), 11–12; Portland Division to C. L. Dellums, n.d. [ca. 1940], Dellums Papers, carton 24, folder: Contract Negotiations of 1941. At about this time, dining-car employees organized under the Hotel and Restaurant Employees International Alliance negotiated abolition of the odious practice of sleeping on dining tables without any mattress. See Arnesen, *Brotherhoods of Color*, 21, 101.

46. BSCP, *Proceedings, 1948*, 163 (Los Angeles Division quotation), 163–64; BSCP, *Proceedings, 1946*, 73–74; Pullman Company and BSCP, "Agreement . . . , Effective January 1, 1953," Nov. 25, 1952, 5, Pullman Archives, RG 6, subgroup 1, ser. 4, box 19, folder

540; G. W. Bohannon to A. J. Uttich, Jan. 14, 1953, ibid., folder 539; *Black Worker*, April 1955, 4.

47. Arnesen, *Brotherhoods of Color*; Taillon, *Good Men*, 32–33, 57–59, 154–55; Brazeal, *Brotherhood*, 4, 139.

48. Harry Guilbert to My Valentine, Feb. 12, 1929, Pullman Archives, RG 6, sub-group 4, ser. 2, vol. 3. On the discriminatory nature of the health system during the period under consideration, see W. Michael Byrd and Linda A. Clayton, *An American Dilemma*, vol. 2, *Race, Medicine and Health Care in the United States, 1900–2000* (New York: Routledge, 2002), 35–290; David McBride, *From TB to AIDS: Epidemics Among Urban Blacks Since 1900* (Albany: State University of New York Press, 1991), 1–157; Edward H. Beardsley, *A History of Neglect: Health Care for Blacks and Mill Workers in the Twentieth-Century South* (Knoxville: University of Tennessee Press, 1987), 11–41, 77–100. For a case of disease invisibility in the Jim Crow era, see Keith Wailoo, *Dying in the City of the Blues: Sickle Cell Anemia and the Politics of Race and Health* (Chapel Hill: University of North Carolina Press, 2001), 55–106.

49. Safety and Compensation Department, Pullman Company, "File Record of Disability Payments," 1954–55," Pullman Archives, RG 6, subgroup 3, ser. 2, boxes 1–2, folders 1–24; Safety and Compensation Department, Pullman Company, injury reports, 1930–53, ibid., subgroup 4, ser. 3, boxes 22–26. For insights into the experience and meanings of illnesses involving exhaustion, see Arthur Kleinman, *The Illness Narratives: Suffering, Healing, and the Human Condition* (New York: Basic Books, 1988), esp. 100–120; Robert A. Aronowitz, *Making Sense of Illness: Science, Society, and Disease* (New York: Cambridge University Press, 1998), 19–38. On historians' inattention to working-class male bodies, see Ava Baron, "Masculinity, the Embodied Male Worker, and the Historian's Gaze," *International Labor and Working-Class History* 69 (2006): 143–60. On the ascendance of the respectable breadwinner role and its part in replacing producerist with consumerist masculinity, see Martin Summers, *Manliness and Its Discontents: The Black Middle Class and the Transformation of Masculinity, 1900–1930* (Chapel Hill: University of North Carolina Press, 2004); Paul M. Taillon, "'What We Want Is Good, Sober Men': Masculinity, Respectability, and Temperance in the Railroad Brotherhoods, c. 1870–1910," *Journal of Social History* 36 (2002): 319–38, esp. 325–27; cf. Michael McCoyer, "'Rough Mens' in 'the Toughest Places I Ever Seen': The Construction and Ramifications of Black Masculine Identity in the Mississippi Delta's Levee Camps, 1900–1935," *International Labor and Working-Class History* 69 (2006): 57–80. On white stereotyping of black physicality, see Mark M. Smith, *How Race Is Made: Slavery, Segregation, and the Senses* (Chapel Hill: University of North Carolina Press, 2006).

50. For other organizing campaigns that have drawn on the intertwined themes of workplace risks and disrespect, see Kathleen M. Barry, "'Too Glamorous to Be Considered Workers': Flight Attendants and Pink-Collar Activism in Mid-Twentieth-Century America," *Labor* 3, no. 3 (2006): 127; Joan T. Beifuss, *At the River I Stand*, 2nd ed. (Memphis: St. Lukes Press, 1990), 37–40, 57, 228, 257, 286, 451, 453; Estes, *I Am a Man*, 131–51; Leon Fink, *The Maya of Morganton: Work and Community in the Nuevo New South*

(Chapel Hill: University of North Carolina Press, 2003), 27–28, 53–55, 70–71, 91, 138; Human Rights Watch, *Blood, Sweat, and Fear: Workers' Rights in U.S. Meat and Poultry Plants* (New York: Human Rights Watch, 2005), esp. 85–86; Steven H. Lopez, *Reorganizing the Rust Belt: An Inside Study of the American Labor Movement* (Berkeley: University of California Press, 2004), xviii, 41–46, 160–61, 194–95; Fred Brooks, "New Turf for Organizing: Family Child Care Providers," *Labor Studies Journal* 29 (2005): 45–64; Katherine Sciacchitano, "Finding the Community in the Union and the Union in the Community: The First-Contract Campaign at Steeltech," in *Organizing to Win: New Research on Union Strategies*, ed. Kate Bronfenbrenner et al. (Ithaca, N.Y.: ILR Press, 1998), 150–63. On organizing for respect, see Kate Bronfenbrenner, "The Role of Union Strategies in NLRB Certification Elections," *Industrial and Labor Relations Review* 50 (1997): 195–212.

Chapter 5. Six Days on the Road

Note to epigraph: Robert Krueger, *A Gypsy on 18 Wheels: A Trucker's Tale* (New York: Praeger, 1975), 45 (unidentified trucker quotation).

1. Lawrence J. Ouellet, *Pedal to the Metal: The Work Lives of Truckers* (Philadelphia: Temple University Press, 1994), 154 (quotation), 80, 134–36, 154–97, 217, 223; Virginia Scharff, *Taking the Wheel: Women and the Coming of the Motor Age* (Albuquerque: University of New Mexico Press, 1992); Cotton Seiler, *Republic of Drivers: A Cultural History of Automobility in America* (Chicago: University of Chicago Press, 2008), 50–62; Dale F. Belman, Francine Lafontaine, and Kristen A. Monaco, "Truck Drivers in the Age of Information: Transformation Without Gain," in *Trucking in the Age of Information*, ed. Belman and Chelsea White III (Burlington, Vt.: Ashgate, 2005), 186; Shane Hamilton, *Trucking Country: The Road to America's Wal-Mart Economy* (Princeton, N.J.: Princeton University Press, 2008), 196–97; John A. Jakle and Keith A. Sculle, *Motoring: The Highway Experience in America* (Athens: University of Georgia Press, 2008), 174–75, 177, 179–81.

2. On the romantic image of owner-operators, see Warner Brothers Pictures, *They Drive by Night*, directed by Raoul Walsh (1940; Burbank, Calif.: Warner Home Video, 2003); James H. Thomas, *The Long Haul: Truckers, Truck Stops, and Trucking* (Memphis: Memphis State University Press, 1979), 3–11; Jane Stern, *Trucker: A Portrait of the Last American Cowboy* (New York: McGraw-Hill, 1975); Hamilton, *Trucking Country*, 43. On owner-driver cabbies, see Biju Mathew, *Taxi! Cabs and Capitalism in New York City* (New York: New Press, 2005), 5, 8, 62–63, 68, 70, 72, 77; 51, 54–57; Graham R. Hodges, *Taxi! A Social History of the New York City Cabdriver* (Baltimore: Johns Hopkins University Press, 2007), 4–5, 17–18, 32–33, 50–59, 66–69, 85, 89–91, 98–99, 132–36, 179. For another independent operator contending with long hours and short sleep, see Arthur E. Hertzler, *The Horse and Buggy Doctor* (New York: Harper and Brothers, 1938), 65, 70–74, 77–78, 87, 93.

3. Steve Fraser and Gary Gerstle, eds., *The Rise and Fall of the New Deal Order, 1930–1980* (Princeton, N.J.: Princeton University Press, 1989); Patrick J. Akard, "Corporate

Mobilization and Political Power: The Transformation of U.S. Economic Policy in the 1970s," *American Sociological Review* 57 (1992): 597–615.

4. Jakle and Sculle, *Motoring*, 181 (quotation); Hamilton, *Trucking Country*; Thaddeus Russell, *Out of the Jungle: Jimmy Hoffa and the Remaking of the American Working Class* (Philadelphia: Temple University Press, 2003); David Witwer, *Corruption and Reform in the Teamsters Union* (Urbana: University of Illinois Press, 2008); Arthur A. Sloane, *Hoffa* (Cambridge, Mass.: MIT Press, 1991); Dan La Botz, *Rank-and-File Rebellion: Teamsters for a Democratic Union* (New York: Verso, 1990). On employment growth, see Belman, Lafontaine, and Monaco, "Truck Drivers," 183–86.

5. William R. Childs, *Trucking and the Public Interest: The Emergence of Federal Regulation, 1914–1940* (Knoxville: University of Tennessee Press, 1985), 7–43; B. Starr McMullen, "The Evolution of the U.S. Motor Carrier Industry," in *Trucking in the Age of Information*, ed. Belman and White, 6–8; Thomas, *Long Haul*, 99; Frederic Paxson, "The Highway Movement, 1916–1935," *American Historical Review* 51 (1946): 236–53; Mr. X, "Memoirs of Mr. X," interview with Harry Woods, Oct. 9, 1974, Chicago, 9, 11, *New York Times Oral History Program: Woods Highway Truck Library* (Glen Rock, N.J.: Microfilming Corporation of America, 1975); Harold Barger, *The Transportation Industries, 1889–1946: A Study of Output, Employment, and Productivity* (New York: National Bureau of Economic Research, 1951), 53.

6. Barger, *Transportation Industries*, 223–24; "Memoirs of Bert Glupker," interview with Harry Woods, n.d. [ca. 1973], Grand Rapids, Mich., 8, 11–12, *Woods Truck Library*; [International Brotherhood of Teamsters] *Official Magazine*, Nov. 1931, 9 (Tobin quotation), 11 (Tobin quotation), 9–11, Oct. 1932, 12, May 1933, 15, Aug. 1933, 10.

7. Ellis W. Hawley, *The New Deal and the Problem of Monopoly: A Study in Economic Ambivalence* (Princeton, N.J.: Princeton University Press, 1966), 19–146; Leverett S. Lyon et al., *The National Recovery Administration: An Analysis and Appraisal* (Washington, D.C.: Brookings Institution, 1935), esp. 11, 30, 306, 900; Irving Bernstein, *A Caring Society: The New Deal, the Worker, and the Great Depression* (Boston: Houghton, Mifflin, 1985), 119.

8. National Recovery Administration, "Code of Fair Competition for the Trucking Industry: Transcript of the Hearing and Appendix," Nov. 16, 1933, 220–35, RG 9: Records of the National Recovery Administration, Records Maintained by the Library Unit, Transcripts of Hearings, 1933–35, box 194, vol. 3, Archives II, National Archives, College Park, Md.; Meyer H. Fishbein, "The Trucking Industry and the National Recovery Administration," *Social Forces* 34 (1955): 171–79; J. R. Halladay, *Partner in Progress: The Story of the American Trucking Associations* (Alexandria, Va.: American Trucking Associations, 1994), 2–4.

9. U.S. National Recovery Administration, *Code of Fair Competition for the Trucking Industry as Approved on February 10, 1934, by President Roosevelt* (New York: Traffic Publishing, 1934), 14–15; Childs, *Trucking and Public*, 108–9.

10. Childs, *Trucking and Public*, 109–18; Wayne Broehl, *Trucks, Troubles, and Triumph: The Norwalk Truck Line Company* (New York: Prentice-Hall, 1954), 52–53;

Thomas, *Long Haul*, 82; *American Trucking Associations News Bulletin*, Jan. 14, 1935, 1; A. D. Rathbone to Benjamin Eynon, Apr. 12, 1935, RG 9, Records of Code Authorities, Records of the Pennsylvania State Code Authority for the Trucking Industry, General Subject File, Mar. 1934–May 1935, box 2, folder: Code Interpretations; G. H. Becker and D. H. O'Connell, "History of the Code of Fair Competition for the Trucking Industry," n.d. [ca. 1936], ibid., Code Histories, box 46, vol. A; *Official Magazine*, June 1935, 13, 14.

11. U.S. Federal Coordinator of Transportation, *Regulation of Transportation Agencies: Letter from the Chairman of the Interstate Commerce Commission* (Washington, D.C.: Government Printing Office, 1934), 5 (quotation), 14–15, 24, 26, 32, 227, 239; Claude M. Fuess, *Joseph B. Eastman: Servant of the People* (New York: Columbia University Press, 1952), 181, 228–29; Childs, *Trucking and Public*, 119–28.

12. U.S. Senate, Committee on Interstate Commerce, *To Amend the Interstate Commerce Act: Hearings . . . on S. 1629, . . . Motor Carrier Act, 1935*, 74th Cong., 1st sess., 1935 (Washington, D.C.: Government Printing Office, 1935), 72, 82, 98, 327, 407, 417–23; U.S. House of Representatives, Committee on Interstate and Foreign Committee, [unnamed] Subcommittee, *Regulation of Interstate Motor Carriers: Hearing . . . on H.R. 5262 and H.R. 6016*, 74th Cong., 1st sess., 1935 (Washington, D.C.: Government Printing Office, 1935), 423–30; J. B. E[astman] to Rep. Sam Pettengill, July 31, 1935, RG 133: Records of the Federal Coordinator of Transportation, Records of the Labor Relations Section, Legislation File, 1934–1936, box 1, folder: S. 1629 Amendment, Archives II, National Archives, College Park, Md.; J. B. E[astman], "Memorandum on Hours-of-Service Provisions of S. 1629," n.d. [ca. July 31, 1935], ibid.; *U.S. Statutes at Large* 49 (1936): 543–67, esp. 546, 566; Childs, *Trucking and Public*, 128–41.

13. *Official Magazine*, Aug. 1929, 13, Oct. 1932, 12, Aug. 1933, 10, June 1935, 13–15; J. Stannard Baker, "Driver Fatigue—Its Importance and the Remedy," in National Safety Council, *Transactions of the Twenty-Fourth Annual Safety Congress, 1935*, 2 vols. (Chicago: The Council, 1936), 2: 40–41; James S. Baker and Oscar M. Gunderson, *Too Long at the Wheel: A Study of Exhaustion and Drowsiness as They Affect Traffic Accidents* (Chicago: National Safety Council, 1935), 4 (quotation), 19 (quotations), 28 (quotation), 6, 9, 16–48.

14. U.S. Federal Coordinator of Transportation, *Hours, Wages, and Working Conditions in the Intercity Motor Transportation Industries*, 3 parts (Washington, D.C.: The Coordinator, 1936), II:xv, xviii–xix, xxi, 53, 56–57, 86, 94, 99, 110, 120–21.

15. Ibid., II:54, 91–93, 99–100, 102–4, 107, 111–15, 117–18.

16. Ibid., II:73 (quotation), 1, 103, 105, 109, 111–14; III:xiii (quotation), ix, 1–47, 75–118.

17. *Official Magazine*, Mar. 1937, 13 (Tobin quotation), 12–13, Apr. 1937, 2; John Rogers to Commissioner Eastman, Nov. 3, 1936, Joseph Eastman Papers, box 18, unidentified folder, Archives and Special Collections, Frost Library, Amherst College, Amherst, Mass.; Joseph Eastman to John Lawrence, Dec. 16, 1936, ibid., box 44, folder 1; Joseph Eastman to William Green, Feb. 20, 1937, ibid.; U.S. ICC, *50th Annual Report of the Interstate Commerce Commission, November 1, 1936* (Washington, D.C.: Government Printing Office, 1936), 83; U.S. ICC, *51st Annual Report of the Interstate Commerce*

Commission, November 1, 1937 (Washington, D.C.: Government Printing Office, 1937), 81; *Chicago Journal of Commerce*, Feb. 10, 1937, 13, Feb. 11, 5, Feb. 12, 1937, 10; "Truck Hours of Service," *Traffic World*, Feb. 13, 1937, 339–40.

18. *Chicago Journal of Commerce*, Feb. 9, 1937, 4, Feb. 10, 1937, 13, Feb. 12, 1937, 10; *New York Times*, July 25, 1937, 149.

19. "Motor Hours of Service," *Traffic World*, July 17, 1937, 125–26; *New York Times*, July 16, 1937, 6, July 25, 1937, 149.

20. "Motor Hours," 125 (Snow quotation), 125–26; "Motor Hours of Service," *Traffic World*, Aug. 28, 1937, 477; "Motor Hours of Service," ibid., Sept. 18, 1937, 620; "Motor Hours of Service," ibid., Oct. 23, 1937, 925; *New York Times*, July 25, 1937, 149, Sept. 5, 1937, 136.

21. U.S. ICC, *Hours of Service Regulations: Rules and Regulations Governing the Maximum Hours of Drivers of Motor Vehicles Operated by Common and Contract Carriers, Effective July 1, 1938* (Washington, D.C.: Government Printing Office, 1938), 668 (quotation), 669 (quotation), 665–93.

22. William Green to Joseph Eastman, Jan. 6, 1938 (quotation), International Brotherhood of Teamsters, Chauffeurs, Warehousemen, and Helpers of America Records, microfilm copy, reel 68, segment: General Correspondence, 1938, Archives Division, Wisconsin Historical Society, Madison; Eastman to Green, Jan. 7, 1938 (quotation), Eastman Papers, box 19, unnamed folder; ICC, *Hours Regulations, Effective July 1, 1938*, 673 (quotation); U.S. ICC, *Hours of Service Regulations: Rules and Regulations Governing the Maximum Hours of Drivers of Motor Vehicles Operated by Common and Contract Carriers, Effective October 1, 1938* (Washington, D.C.: Government Printing Office, 1938); U.S. ICC, *Hours of Service Regulations: Rules and Regulations Governing the Maximum Hours of Drivers of Motor Vehicles Operated by Common and Contract Carriers, Revised Issue, Effective March 1, 1939* (Washington, D.C.: Government Printing Office, 1938); U.S. ICC, *Motor Carrier Safety Regulations, Revised: Rules and Regulations Governing Qualifications of Employees and Safety of Operation and Equipment of Common Carriers and Contract Carriers of Passengers and Property, and of Private Carriers of Property, by Motor Vehicle* (Washington, D.C.: Government Printing Office, 1941), 73–84, 93–97.

23. ICC, *Hours Regulations, Effective July 1, 1938*, 670 (quotations); Thomas Parran to Joseph Eastman, May 6, 1938 (quotation), RG 443: Records of the National Institutes of Health, General Records of the National Institute of Health, 1930–48, Records Relating to NIH Divisions, box 181, folder: Fatigue Study; Stephen Gibbons and W. M. Splawn, "Agreement Between Interstate Commerce Commission and Treasury Department (Public Health Service) Respecting Study of Driver Fatigue," n.d. [ca. June 4, 1938] (quotations), ibid.; Eastman to Parran, Apr. 25, 1938, Eastman Papers, box 19, unnamed folder. For the IBT's demands for this study, see "Motor Hours" Oct. 23, 1937, 925; ICC, *Hours Regulations, Effective Oct. 1, 1938*, 1–2; *Official Magazine*, June 1938, 2–3, Jan. 1939, 14.

24. M. Collins to Joseph Eastman, July 17, 1940, RG 90: Records of the Public Health

Service, General Records, 1897–1944, General Classified Records, 1936–44, box 430, folder: Interstate Commerce Commission; U.S. ICC, *52d Annual Report of the Interstate Commerce Commission, November 1, 1938* (Washington, D.C.: Government Printing Office, 1938), 93, 94. On the relationship between fatigue and sleepiness, see Torbjorn Akerstedt and Kenneth P. Wright Jr., "Sleep Loss and Fatigue in Shift Work and Shift Work Disorder," *Sleep Medicine Clinics* 4 (2009): 260: "'Sleepiness' is not the same thing as 'fatigue,' at least not scientifically. . . . 'Sleepiness' refers to the tendency of falling asleep. Fatigue may include sleepiness, but also states such as physical and mental fatigue. The issue of the differential definition of sleepiness and fatigue has been subject to a constant debate. One clinically useful distinction between fatigue and sleepiness is that cognitive and muscle fatigue symptoms may be reduced by sedentary activity or rest without sleeping, where subjective sleepiness and the propensity for sleep are often exacerbated by sedentary activity or rest."

25. U.S. PHS, *Fatigue and Hours of Service of Interstate Truck Drivers*, by Benjamin F. Jones et al., Public Health Bulletin 265 (Washington, D.C.: Government Printing Office, 1941), 24 (quotation), xiii, 20–25; R. R. Sayers to Director, National Institute of Health, Oct. 25, 1939 (quotation), RG 443, General Records of the National Institute of Health, 1930–48, Records Relating to NIH Divisions, box 181, folder: Ind[ustrial] Hyg[iene] Div[ision];Robert Olesen to Major General Commandant, U.S. Marine Corps, Aug. 19, 1938, ibid., folder: Fatigue Study; Sayers to Ross MacFarland, Jan. 11, 1940, MacFarland Collection, box 36, folder 8; L. R. Thompson to W. R. Miles, Feb. 24, 1940, RG 90, General Records, 1897–1944, General Classified Records, 1936–44, box 430, folder: Interstate Commerce Commission; W. F. Draper to. E. S. Adams, Apr. 3, 1941, ibid.

26. PHS, *Fatigue and Hours*, 57 (quotation), 12 (National Safety Council quotation), 12–13, 41–80; National Safety Council, *How Long on the Highway?* (Chicago: National Safety Council, 1937), esp. 2, 14, 22–26. For a map displaying the road not taken, see Edward Godfrey, "Role of the Health Department in the Prevention of Accidents," *American Journal of Public Health* 27 (1937): 152–55; Edward Press, "Epidemiological Approach to Accident Prevention," ibid. 38 (1948): 1442–45; John E. Gordon, "The Epidemiology of Accidents," ibid. 39 (1949): 504–15; Rollo H. Britten and Isidore Altman, "Illness and Accidents Among Persons Living Under Different Housing Conditions," *Public Health Reports* 56 (1941): 609–41, esp. 631–35. For a sharp critique of the PHS research design for its focus on fatigue and for failing to mount an epidemiological analysis comparing the driving and sleeping times of drivers who had had accidents with those of drivers who were accident free, see H. M. Johnson, "Index-Numerology and Measures of Impairment," *American Journal of Psychology* 56 (1943): 552–54. On disregard of workers' health interests by Sayers and others in the PHS and the U.S. Bureau of Mines, in contrast to the attitude of the Department of Labor, see Alan Derickson, *Black Lung: Anatomy of a Public Health Disaster* 81, 94–98, 103; Alan Derickson, "'On the Dump Heap': Employee Medical Screening in the Tri-State Zinc-Lead Industry, 1924–1932," *Business History Review* 62 (1988): 656–77; Gerald Markowitz and David Rosner, "More Than

Economism: The Politics of Workers' Safety and Health, 1932–1947," *Milbank Quarterly* 64 (1986): 331–54.

27. PHS, *Fatigue and Hours*, 87 (quotation), 81–87, v–x. For dissemination of this authoritative nonguidance, see "Causes and Effects of Fatigue Among Interstate Truck Drivers," *Monthly Labor Review*, Sept. 1941, 667–69; R. R. Sayers, "Major Studies of Fatigue," *War Medicine* 2 (1942): 812–13.

28. Federal Coordinator, *Hours, Wages*, III:xiii–iv; John R. Commons, "Types of American Labor Organization—The Teamsters of Chicago," *Quarterly Journal of Economics* 19 (1905): 408–10, 414; IBT, *Proceedings of the Eleventh Convention, First Day, September 14, 1925* (Seattle: Alaska Printing, n.d.), 29–30; IBT, *Reports of Officers, Thirteen Convention, 1935* (n.p., n.d.), 6, 69–70; *Official Magazine*, Feb. 1929, 16, Mar. 1929, 6, Aug. 1929, 13, Jan. 1936, 7, Oct. 1936, 13; Farrell Dobbs, *Teamster Rebellion* (New York: Monad Press, 1972), 23–24, 45; "Union Scales of Wages and Hours of Motortruck Drivers, May 15, 1936," *Monthly Labor Review*, May 1937, 1246–47.

29. James R. Hoffa, *The Trials of Jimmy Hoffa: An Autobiography* (Chicago: Henry Regnery, 1970), 84 (quotation), 84–86; Russell, *Jungle*, 23–44; *Northwest Organizer*, July 15, 1936, 2, Feb. 1937, 1–2, June 10, 1937, 3; Farrell Dobbs, *Teamster Power* (New York: Monad Press, 1973), 144–48, 169–70; C. F. Curtis and L. A. Stone to John Clinton, May 3, 1939, IBT Records, reel 10, segment: Dobbs, Farrell, 1939; Farrell Dobbs to Thomas Hughes, May 15, 1939, ibid.; Samuel E. Hill, *Teamsters and Transportation: Employee-Employer Relationships in New England* (Washington, D.C.: American Council on Public Affairs, 1942), 120–21.

30. Donald Garnel, *The Rise of Teamster Power in the West* (Berkeley: University of California Press, 1972), 213–14, 329; Local 120, IBT, and Compliance Committee of St. Paul Employers of Truck Drivers, "Agreement," n.d. [ca. June 1, 1935], 1, U.S. Bureau of Labor Statistics Collective Bargaining Agreements Collection, box 83, folder: Teamsters, Kheel Center for Labor-Management Documentation and Archives, Catherwood Library, Cornell University, Ithaca, N.Y.; "Union Scales of Hours," 1247, 1253–57; Federal Coordinator, *Hours, Wages*, III:145, 149–51; *Northwest Organizer*, Apr. 22, 1937, 3–4, May 20, 1937, 1, Sept. 1, 1938, 3; Local 407, IBT, and Cleveland Group of Certified and Permit Motor Carriers, *Agreement* (n.p., n.d. [1937]), 6.

31. Operators Area Committee and Union Area Committee, IBT, *Articles of Agreement, November 1, 1939, to November 15, 1941, Over-the-Road Motor Freight* (n.p., n.d.), 6 (quotation), 6–7; *Official Magazine*, Aug. 1937, 17 (Tobin quotation); Local 120, IBT, and Compliance Committee of St. Paul Employers of Truck Drivers, "Agreement," n.d., 2 [ca. June 1, 1935], Exhibit B [attachment ca. June 1, 1936], BLS Agreements Collection, box 83, folder: Teamsters; *Northwest Organizer*, Dec. 31, 1936, 2; Dobbs, *Teamster Power*, 179, 207, 234–35; Garnel, *Rise in West*, 190–92, 235; Hill, *Teamsters and Transportation*, 157–58; Local 20, IBT, and Toledo Group of Certificated and Permit Motor Carriers, "Labor Contract," Dec. 29, 1936, 5, ibid., folder: Teamsters Prior to 1939.

32. *International Teamster*, Sept. 1942, inside front cover (quotation), Oct. 1942, inside front cover (quotations), May 1942, 7, Nov. 1942, 15–16, Mar. 1943, 10, July 1943,

18–19, Oct. 1943, 2–3, Sept. 1944, 9–10; U.S. Office of Defense Transportation, *America's Trucks: Keep 'Em Rolling* (Washington, D.C.: Government Printing Office, [1942]), 2; Fuess, *Eastman*, 285; National War Labor Board, "Directive Order: Case No. 4648, Case No. 4448," Feb. 7, 1948, RG 202: Records of the National War Labor Board, Records Relating to Dispute Cases, 1943–45, box 2432, folder: Central States Government Inquiries, Archives II, National Archives, College Park, Md.; National War Labor Board, "Opinion: Case No. 4648, Case No. 4448," Feb. 7, 1944, ibid.; Local 557, IBT, "Brief of Local Union No. 557: Case No. 111-14475-JB," Mar. 29, 1945, ibid., Documents Submitted by Companies and/or Unions, 1943–45, box 2468, folder: Anchor Motor Freight Company; Central States Drivers Council, IBT, "Petition for Reconsideration Filed on Behalf of Employees: Case No. 4648, Case No. 4448," n.d. [ca. Mar. 1, 1944], IBT Records, reel 62, segment: Central States Drivers Council, 1944, January–July. On sleep deprivation in the armed forces during World War II, see Alan Derickson, "'No Such Thing as a Night's Sleep': The Embattled Sleep of American Fighting Men from World War II to the Present," *Journal of Social History* 47 (2013).

33. Emanuel Bloch to Malcolm Ross, Aug. 25, 1944 (quotation), RG 228: Records of the Committee on Fair Employment Practice, Records of Region V, box 5, folder: Teamsters Local 299 . . . , [Case] 5-UR-1269, National Archives at Chicago; Edward Cushman to Robert Goodwin, Aug. 9, 1944, ibid.; Daniel Donovan to George M. Johnson, Aug. 18, 1943, ibid.; Festus Hairston, "Discrimination in War Industries," Dec. 9, 1942, ibid., folder: Teamsters Local 299 . . . , [Case] 5-UR-1269, Complaint of Festus Hairston; G. James Fleming to Johnson, Jan. 26, 1943, ibid.; Edward Swan to Hairston, July 12, 1945, ibid.; Jack Burke to Johnson, Aug. 18 and 26, 1943, ibid., folder: Teamsters Local 299 . . . , [Case] 5-UR-1269, Complaint of George E. Johnson; Donovan to James Fleming, Feb. 5, 1943, ibid.; Fleming to Donovan, Apr. 24, 1943, ibid.; Boris Shishkin to Daniel Tobin, Aug. 28, 1943, ibid; Thomas Flynn to Shishkin, July 21, 1943, RG 228, Records of the Legal Division, Records Relating to Hearings, 1941–1946, box 355, folder: International Brotherhood of Teamsters, Chauffeurs, etc., Local 299, Archives II, National Archives, College Park; President's Committee on Fair Employment Practice, "Case No. 84," June 2, 1945, 6–7, 22, 70–71, 198–201, 210–12, 225–33, ibid., unidentified folder; *Detroit Free Press*, Jan. 7, 1945, sec. 1, 3. Leading me to this episode was Russell, *Jungle*, 122–25. The IBT's discriminatory policy receives attention in Richard D. Leone, *The Negro in the Trucking Industry* (Philadelphia: Industrial Research Unit, University of Pennsylvania, 1970), 20–22, 28–30. For the local context, see Robert Shogan and Tom Craig, *The Detroit Race Riot: A Study in Violence* (Philadelphia: Chilton Books, 1964). For comparable union obstruction in the merchant marine, see Eileen Boris, "'You Wouldn't Want One of 'Em Dancing with Your Wife': Racialized Bodies on the Job in World War II," *American Quarterly* 50 (1998): 85.

34. Joseph Padway, "Validity of Article 25 Related to Owner-Operators," Dec. 11, 1941, 3 (quotation), 4 (quotation), IBT Records, reel 82, segment: Owner-Operator Trucks, 1941, 1949–1950; Commons, "Teamsters of Chicago," 400–402, 415–17, 419, 427–28; Arwen Mohun, *Steam Laundries: Gender, Technology, and Work in the United*

States and Great Britain, 1880–1940 (Baltimore: Johns Hopkins University Press, 1999), 241–43, 246; Witwer, *Corruption*, 72; Hamilton, *Trucking Country*, 44, 51; Garnel, *Rise in West*, 267; *Official Magazine*, Feb. 1935, 16, Apr. 1937, 5; Local 120, IBT, and Executive Committee, St. Paul Employers of Truck Drivers, "Articles of Agreement," July 1, 1937, 2, BLS Agreements Collection, box 83, folder: Teamsters Prior to July 1939; *Northwest Organizer*, June 23, 1938, Sept. 1, 1938, 8; *International Teamster*, Mar. 1945, 10.

35. Central States Drivers Council, IBT, "Minutes of Meeting," Aug. 15, 1945, 7 (Hoffa quotation), IBT Records, reel 63, segment: Central States Drivers Council, Minutes of Meetings, 1943–1949; U.S. Senate, Committee on Interstate and Foreign Commerce, *Amendment to Interstate Commerce Act (Trip Leasing): Hearings . . . on H.R. 3203, Part 2*, 83rd Cong., 2nd sess., 1954 (Washington, D.C.: Government Printing Office, 1954), 377 (Wheeler quotation), 381, 406, 413; Glenn C. Altschuler and Stuart M. Blumin, *The GI Bill: The New Deal for Veterans* (New York: Oxford University Press, 2009), 150, 155, 177; Dan Moldea, *The Hoffa Wars: Teamsters, Rebels, Politicians, and the Mob* (New York: Charter Books, 1978), 45–47, 192–93, 209–10; Hamilton, *Trucking Country*, 69–98; Sloane, *Hoffa*, 18–20; *International Teamster*, Aug. 1946, 28, Apr. 1950, 9, Aug. 1950, 19–22, Feb. 1952, 9–11, Mar. 1952, 11–13; Central States Drivers Council, IBT, and Central States Employers Association Negotiating Committee, *The Central States Area Over-the-Road Motor Freight Agreement* (Chicago: n.pub., [1945]), 10–13; Thomas Flynn to All Local Union, Central States Area, n.d. [ca. Aug. 1946], IBT Records, reel 62, segment: Central States Drivers Council, 1946, July–Dec.; Burton K. Wheeler, Edward K. Wheeler, and Robert G. Seaks, *Before the Interstate Commission, Ex Parte MC-43, Lease and Interchange of Vehicles by Motor Carrier: Brief on Behalf of the International Brotherhood of Teamsters, Chauffeurs, Warehousemen and Helpers of America* (Washington, D.C.: Wilson-Epes, 1949); Alfred Maund, "Peons on Wheels: The Long-Haul Trucker," *Nation*, Nov. 14, 1953, 393–94; *Wall Street Journal*, May 27, 1958, 1, 16; Michael H. Agar, *Independents Declared: The Dilemmas of Independent Trucking* (Washington, D.C.: Smithsonian Institution Press, 1986), 38–69; U.S. Senate, Committee on Commerce, Subcommittee on Surface Transportation, *National Transportation Policy: Report of the Committee on Commerce . . . , by Its Special Study Group on Transportation Policies in the United States*, 87th Cong., 1st sess., 1961 (Washington, D.C.: Government Printing Office, 1961), 512–14; Transportation Association of America, *The Illegal For-Hire Trucking Problem*, rev. ed. (Washington, D.C.: Transportation Association of America, 1963), 1–6.

36. U.S. Senate, Committee on Interstate and Foreign Commerce, Subcommittee on Domestic Land and Water Transportation, *Study of Domestic Land and Water Transportation: Hearings . . . Pursuant to S. Res. 50*, 81st Cong., 2nd sess., 1950 (Washington, D.C.: Government Printing Office, 1950), 1243 (Nordan quotation); Harry Henderson, "Hell on Wheels," *Argosy*, July 1951, 22 (quotation), 92, 95–97; U.S. Senate, *Amendment*, 422 (Vickery quotation), 429 (Voss quotation), 417–34; Wheeler, Wheeler, and Seaks, *Before Commission*, 32, 34, 42–44, 46; Otto Riemer, *Hammer Down: A True Story About Trucking* (Winona, Minn.: Apollo Books, 1985), 1–3, 9; *International Team-*

ster, Sept. 1953, 16; *Wall Street Journal*, May 27, 1958, 16; Robert C. Fellmeth et al., *The Interstate Commerce Omission: The Public Interest and the ICC: The Ralph Nader Study Group Report on the Interstate Commerce Commission and Transportation* (New York: Grossman, 1970), 205, 386.

37. U.S. House of Representatives, Committee on Interstate and Foreign Commerce, *Traffic Safety: Hearings . . . on H.R. 13228*, 89th Cong., 2nd sess., 1966 (Washington, D.C.: Government Printing Office), 353 (Hoffa quotation), 369 (Hoffa quotation); *International Teamster*, July 1953, 25–26, Jan.–Feb. 1958, 21, Aug. 1958, 22–25, Oct. 1961, 11, Sept. 1963, 5–7, Apr. 1970, 6, June 1970, 5–6; Charles R. Perry, *Deregulation and the Decline of the Unionized Trucking Industry* (Philadelphia: Industrial Relations Unit, Wharton School, University of Pennsylvania, 1986), 17–18; Ralph C. James and Estelle D. James, *Hoffa and the Teamsters: A Study of Union Power* (Princeton, N.J.: D. Van Nostrand, 1965), 135–36; La Botz, *Rank-and-File Rebellion*, 166–68; Sloane, *Hoffa*, 201–5; Western Motor Freight Division, Western Conference of Teamsters, IBT, and Arizona Truck Operators' League et al., "Western States Area Over-the-Road Supplemental Agreement" in IBT and Trucking Employers, Inc., *National Master Freight Agreement and Western States Area Over-the-Road Supplemental Agreement . . . , 1964* (n.p., n.d.), 77, 91–92.

38. William Chaffee and R. W. Case to Chief, Chicago District, Jan. 29, 1954 (quotation), RG 88: Records of the Food and Drug Administration, General Subject Files, 1938–1974, box 1860, file 511.09-.67, Archives II, National Archives, College Park, Md.; Central States Drivers Council, IBT, and Central States Area Employers Association et al., *Central States Area Over-the-Road Motor Freight Agreement . . . , 1949* (n.p., n.d.), 17–18, 29; Freight Division, New York State Teamsters Joint Council, IBT, and New York State Employers Trucking Association, *Over-the-Road Motor Freight Agreement . . . , 1958* (n.p., n.d.), 21; Peter Browning, *Working for Wages: On the Road in the Fifties* (Lafayette, Calif.: Great West Books, 2003), 7; Agar, *Independents*, 38; Henderson, "Hell," 22, 93; Stern, *Trucker*, 110, 113, 129; Riemer, *Hammer*, 4–5; Central States Drivers Council, IBT, and Central States Area Employers Association, "Memorandum of Agreement: 1952 Contract Negotiations," n.d. [ca. Feb. 1952], 8, IBT Records, reel 63, segment: Central States Drivers Council, 1952; Carolina Freight Council, IBT, and Winston-Salem Employers Negotiating Committee et al., *Over-the-Road Agreement . . . , 1955* (n.p., n.d.), 25; Freight Division, New York State Joint Council, IBT, and New York State Employers Association, "Over-the-Road Supplemental Agreement," in IBT and Trucking Employers, Inc., *National Master Freight Agreement and Over-the-Road Supplemental Agreement . . . , 1964* (n.p., n.d.), 70; Sloane, *Hoffa*, 242–43; *New York Times*, Jan. 2, 1964, 31; House, *Traffic Safety*, 350, 356; *International Teamster*, Apr. 1961, 26–27, Feb. 1967, 9; IBT and Trucking Employers, Inc., *National Master Freight Agreement and Over-the-Road Supplemental Agreement . . . , 1967* (n.p., n.d.). On sleeper innovations, see "Aluminum Sleeper Cab Lifts Payload 219 Pounds," *Transport Topics*, Jan. 17, 1955, 9; "Improved Sleeper Berth on COE [Cab-over-Engine] Models Introduced by International Harvester," ibid., Dec. 5, 1955, 13; Thomas, *Long Haul*, 129–31.

39. Evan Wylie, "The Frightening Menace of 'Pep' Drugs," *Coronet*, July 1959, 100 (quotation); Earl Green and Carl Montgomery, "Six Days on the Road," *Virtual Truck Route*, 1963, http://www.virtualtruckroute.com/music_lyrics_sixdaysontheroad.html; O. D. Shipley, "The Benzedrine Problem," *Drivers' Digest*, Dec. 1955, 5–6; U.S. House, *Traffic Safety*, 880; Lester Grinspoon and Peter Hedblom, *The Speed Culture: Amphetamine Use and Abuse in America* (Cambridge, Mass.: Harvard University Press, 1975), 17–26; Lin Root, "They Stay Awake—to Die," *Today's Health*, Oct. 1960, 32–33, 65; Carl Baeurlen to Chief, Buffalo District, Oct. 6, 1953, RG 88, General Subject Files, 1938–1974, box 1860, file 511.09-.67; W. R. Moses to Chief, New Orleans District, Dec. 6, 1954, ibid., file 511.09-.66.

40. Henderson, "Hell on Wheels," 23 (quotation); U.S. Senate, Committee on Labor and Public Welfare, Subcommittee on Alcoholism and Narcotics, *Amphetamine Abuse Among Truckdrivers: Hearing . . . on Elimination of Amphetamine Abuse Among Truckdrivers*, 92nd Cong., 1st sess., 1971 (Washington, D.C.: Government Printing Office, 1971), 30 (Leavitt quotations), 30–31, 46, 55–57, 65–66; Leonard Blanton to Chief, Atlanta District, Mar. 26, 1953, RG 88, General Subject Files, 1938–1974, box 1860, file 511.09-.67; William Chaffee to Chief, Chicago District, Jan. 11, 1954, ibid.; Senate, *Amendment*, 419–20, 424–27, 435; Bernie Swart, "Drugs: The Deadly Highway Menace," *Fleet Owner*, May 1964, 78, 81, 83; Fellmeth et al., *Commerce Omission*, 203.

41. Arthur Davis, "Transcript of Interview with Robert Palmer, FDA Inspector, and Chief Inspector [T. C.] Maraviglia," June 28, 1955, 8 (quotation), 4 (quotation), 7, RG 88, General Subject Files, 1938–1974, box 1997, file 511.09-.67; Alfred Barnard to Office of the Commissioner, Dec. 10, 1953, ibid., box 1860, file 511.09-.67; Joseph Gebhart to Chief, St. Louis District, Feb. 10, 1956, ibid., box 2164, file 511.09-.67; F. D. Clark to G. D. Sontheimer, Jan. 8, 1958, ibid., box 2695, file 511.09-.67; F. D. Clark to Chiefs, Chicago, Cincinnati, and Detroit Districts, June 12, 1959, ibid., box 2694, file 511.09-.67; Franklin Clark to John Coffland, Aug. 4, 1959, ibid.; Margaret Kreig, *Black Market Medicine* (New York: Bantam Books, 1968), 236–37; "FDA Moves to Stamp Out Sale of Drugs to Truck Drivers," *Business Week*, Oct. 29, 1955, 42; "Benny Is My Co-Pilot," *Time*, June 11, 1956, 50; John Lagemann, "Don't Stay Awake to Die," *Popular Science*, Oct. 1956, 108–11; Arthur Flemming, "Amphetamine Drugs," *Public Health Reports* 75 (1960): 49–50; Charles O. Jackson, "The Amphetamine Democracy: Medicinal Abuse in the Popular Culture," *South Atlantic Quarterly* 74 (1975): 316–18; John P. Swann, "FDA and the Practice of Pharmacy: Prescription Drug Regulation Before the Durham-Humphrey Amendment of 1951," *Pharmacy in History* 36 (1994): 64–66. The association between truck stops and stimulants began, of course, with their provision of coffee, the mainstay analeptic. See Baker and Gunderson, *Too Long*, 21, 28–29; Hill, *Teamsters and Transportation*, 105; Henderson, "Hell on Wheels," 21; Andrew Hurley, *Diners, Bowling Alleys, and Trailer Parks: Chasing the American Dream in Postwar Consumer Culture* (New York: Basic Books, 2001), 80–82.

42. Arthur Davis, "Death in Small Doses," *Saturday Evening Post*, Jan. 21, 1956, 89 (quotation), 25; Swart, "Drugs," 77 (quotation); John Van Allen to Chief Inspec-

tor, Philadelphia District, Sept. 24, 1958, RG 88, General Subject Files, 1938–1974, box 2695, file 511.09-.67; Joseph Burris, "Memorandum of Telephone Conversation," Dec. 2, 1958, ibid.; Samuel Alfend to J. D. Replogle, Apr. 14, 1958, ibid.; Harold Lee to Chief, New Orleans District, June 22, 1959, ibid., box 2694, file 511.09-.67; W. G. Thuss, "Drivers, Drugs, and Death," *Alabama Trucker*, Feb. 1957, 5, 7; *Philadelphia Inquirer*, July 27, 1958, 1B; *Kansas City Star* (Mo.), Dec. 30, 1958, pp. 1, 2; *Patriot* (Harrisburg, Pa.), May 4, 1962, 1, 5. For industry attempts to minimize the amphetamine-accident connection, see Goley Sontheimer, "Safety Is No Accident," *Transport Topics*, Aug. 17, 1959, 78; U.S. Senate, Committee on Commerce, Subcommittee on Surface Transportation, *Control of Illegal Interstate Motor Carrier Transportation (Amendments to Interstate Commerce Act): Hearings . . . on S. 2560 and S. 2764*, 87th Cong., 2nd sess., 1962 (Washington, D.C.: Government Printing Office, 1962), 69.

43. U.S. ICC, *67th Annual Report, November 2, 1953* (Washington, D.C.: Government Printing Office, 1954), 66; U.S. ICC, *68th Annual Report, November 1, 1954* (Washington, D.C.: Government Printing Office, 1954); Joseph North Jr. to Chief, Baltimore District, Mar. 5, 1957, RG 88, General Subject Files, 1938–1974, box 2695, file 511.09-.67; Fellmeth et al., *Commerce Omission*, 193; 91, 98; U.S. ICC, *71st Annual Report, Fiscal Year Ended June 30, 1957* (Washington, D.C.: Government Printing Office, 1957), 117, 118; U.S. ICC, *73d Annual Report, Fiscal Year Ended June 30, 1959* (Washington, D.C.: Government Printing Office, 1959), 146; Senate, *National Transportation Policy*, 536–37.

44. Franz Halberg, "Temporal Coordination of Physiologic Function," *Cold Spring Harbor Symposia on Quantitative Biology* 25 (1960): 289–310 (the whole volume of the journal was devoted to biological clocks); Martin C. Moore-Ede, Frank M. Sulzman, and Charles A. Fuller, *The Clocks That Time Us: Physiology of the Circadian Timing System* (Cambridge, Mass.: Harvard University Press, 1982), 1–29; *International Teamster*, July 1960, 9; U.S. ICC, "Part 195—Hours of Service of Drivers: Qualifications and Maximum Hours of Service of Employees of Motor Carriers and Safety of Operation and Equipment," *Federal Register* 27 (1962): 3553–55. The IBT's retreat was comparable to the United Auto Workers' contemporaneous surrender of its role in protecting working conditions. See Nelson Lichtenstein, "UAW Bargaining Strategy and Shop-Floor Conflict: 1946–1970," *Industrial Relations* 24 (1985): 360–81, esp. 365.

45. Mark H. Rose, Bruce E. Seely, and Paul F. Barrett, *The Best Transportation System in the World: Railroads, Trucks, Airlines, and American Public Policy in the Twentieth Century* (Columbus: Ohio State University Press, 2006), 137–203; Steven Brill, *The Teamsters* (New York: Simon and Schuster, 1978) ; La Botz, *Rebellion*, 138, 198–205; Perry, *Deregulation*, 59–68; D. Daryl Wyckoff and David H. Maister, *The Owner-Operator: Independent Trucker* (Lexington, Mass.: Lexington Books, 1975), 1–10, 55, 61–65; U.S. House of Representatives, Committee on Small Business, Subcommittee on Special Small Business Problems, *Regulatory Problems of the Independent Owner-Operator in the Nation's Trucking Industry, Part 2: Hearings*, 95th Cong., 1st sess., 1977 (Washington, D.C.: Government Printing Office, 1977); Hamilton, *Trucking Country*, 187–229; Thomas, *Long Haul*, 5, 136–37.

46. U.S. House of Representatives, Committee on Small Business, Subcommittee on Activities of Regulatory Agencies, *Regulatory Problems of the Independent Owner-Operator in the Nation's Trucking Industry, Part 1: Hearings*, 94th Cong., 2nd sess., 1976 (Washington, D.C.: Government Printing Office, 1976), 317 (Johnston quotation), 317–18, 460; U.S. Department of Transportation, Bureau of Motor Carrier Safety, *A Study of the Relationships Among Fatigue, Hours of Service, and Safety of Operations of Truck and Bus Drivers*, by William G. Harris et al. (Washington, D.C.: U.S. Department of Transportation, 1972), x–xi, 54, 69–73; Harry Maurer, "Organizing the 'Gypsies,'" *Nation*, Jan. 11, 1975, 11–15; Wyckoff and Maister, *Owner-Operator*, 56, 64; U.S. Senate, Committee on Commerce, Science and Transportation, *Truck Safety Act of 1978: Hearing . . . on S. 2970*, 95th Cong., 2nd sess., 1978 (Washington, D.C.: Government Printing Office, 1978), 29, 31; D. Daryl Wyckoff, *Truck Drivers in America* (Lexington, Mass.: Lexington Books, 1979), 30, 70, 72, 110, 113–14; Riemer, *Hammer*, 28.

47. Susan B. Van Hemel and William C. Rogers, "Survey of Truck Drivers' Knowledge and Beliefs Regarding Driver Fatigue," *Transportation Research Record* 1640 (1998): 67 (quotation); Michael H. Belzer, *Sweatshops on Wheels: Winners and Losers in Trucking Deregulation* (New York: Oxford University Press, 2000), 189 (quotations), 28–30; Rose, Seely, and Barrett, *Best System*, 203–4, 214–19; Perry, *Deregulation*, 69–110; Michael H. Belzer, "Collective Bargaining After Deregulation: Do the Teamsters Still Count?" *Industrial and Labor Relations Review* 48 (1995): 636–55; U.S. Senate, Committee on Commerce, Science, and Transportation, Subcommittee on Surface Transportation, *Oversight of the Motor Carrier Act of 1980: Hearing*, 99th Cong., 1st sess., 1985 (Washington, D.C.: Government Printing Office, 1986), 17–18, 49–51, 60; Agar, *Independents Declared*, 91–97, 171–73; U.S. Office of Technology Assessment, *Gearing Up for Safety: Motor Carrier Safety in a Competitive Environment* (Washington, D.C.: Government Printing Office, 1988), 50–51; Elisa R. Braver et al., "Long Hours and Fatigue: A Study of Tractor-Trailer Drivers," *Journal of Public Health Policy* 13 (1992): 341–66; Dale L. Belman, Kristen A. Monaco, and Taggert J. Brooks, *Sailors of the Concrete Sea: A Portrait of Truck Drivers' Work and Lives* (East Lansing: Michigan State University Press, 2005).

48. Riemer, *Hammer*, 31 (quotation), 22–23, 31–32, 91; Alex Tresniowski et al., "Nightmare at the Truck Stop," *People*, May 1, 2006, 90 (Maldonado quotation); Braver et al., "Long Hours," 353, 361; Belman, Monaco, and Brooks, *Sailors*, 65–67, 118; U.S. National Transportation Safety Board, *Safety Study: Fatigue, Alcohol, Other Drugs, and Medical Factors in Fatal-to-the-Driver Heavy Truck Crashes*, 2 vols. (Washington, D.C.: National Transportation Safety Board, 1991), 1:v, 12–14, 70, 83, 85, 2:63–65, 111–12, 121–23, 151–52, 159–60, 181–82, 227–30, 247–48, 253–54, 267–69, 367–68; John K. Lauber and Phyllis J. Kayten, "Sleepiness, Circadian Dysrhythmia, and Fatigue in Transportation System Accidents," *Sleep* 11 (1988): 503–12.

49. U.S. House of Representatives, Committee on Public Works and Transportation, Subcommittee on Surface Transportation, *Commercial Motor Carrier Safety: Hearing*, 96th Cong., 2nd sess., 1980 (Washington, D.C.: Government Printing Office, 1980), 31 (Gaibis quotation), 31–32; William C. Dement, "History of Sleep Medicine," *Neurologic*

Clinics 23 (2005): 945–65; John W. Shepard Jr. et al., "History of the Development of Sleep Medicine in the United States," *Journal of Clinical Sleep Medicine* 1 (2005): 61–82; Merrill M. Mitler et al., "The Sleep of Long-Haul Truck Drivers," *New England Journal of Medicine* 337 (1997): 755–61; *New York Times*, Sept. 11, 1997, A22; Andrew J. Solomon et al., "Healthcare and the Long Haul: Long Distance Truck Drivers—A Medically Underserved Population," *American Journal of Industrial Medicine* 46 (2004): 463–71. Because of its sheer magnitude, it is impossible (and unnecessary) to provide comprehensive documentation of the body of scientific studies of work and sleep since 1980. For projects examining truckers' situation (albeit without explicitly identifying shift work sleep disorder as part of that situation), see Robin P. Hertz, "Tractor-Trailer Driver Fatality: The Role of Nonconsecutive Rest in a Sleeper Berth," *Accident Analysis and Prevention* 20 (1988): 431–39; Anne McCartt et al., "Factors Associated with Falling Asleep at the Wheel Among Long-Distance Truck Drivers," ibid., 32 (2000): 493–504; U.S. Federal Highway Administration, and Canada, Transport Canada, *Commercial Motor Vehicle Driver Fatigue and Alertness Study* (Washington, D.C.: Federal Highway Administration, 1996).

50. Gregory Belenky et al., *Potential Hours-of-Service Regulations for Commercial Drivers: Report of the Expert Panel on Review of Federal Highway Administration Candidate Options for Hours of Service Regulations* (Ann Arbor: Transportation Research Institute, University of Michigan, 1998), 15 (quotation); NTSB, *Safety Study*, 1:75; U.S. DOT, Office of Motor Carrier Safety, *An Annotated Literature Review Relating to Proposed Revisions to the Hours-of-Service Regulation for Commercial Motor Vehicle Drivers*, by Deborah M. Freund (Washington, D.C.: Office of Motor Carrier Safety, 1999), esp. 46–49, 56–58, 69–72, 81–83, 86–88, 103–14, 121–22; Ronald R. Knipling, "Update on the U.S. FHWA Commercial Driver Fatigue Research and Technology, Rulemaking, Educational Outreach, and Enforcement Program," in *Managing Fatigue in Transportation: Proceedings of the 3d Fatigue in Transportation Conference, 1998*, ed. Laurence Hartley (Kidlington, Eng.: Pergamon, 1998), 299–314; U.S. Federal Highway Administration, *Commercial Motor Vehicle Driver Fatigue, Alertness, and Countermeasures Survey*, by C. Abrams, T. Schultz, and C. D. Wylie (Washington, D.C.: Federal Highway Administration, 1997), 9–10. For criticism of DOT's sluggishness in improving its hours rules, see U.S. NTSB, *Evaluation of U.S. Department of Transportation Efforts in the 1990s to Address Operator Fatigue* (Washington, D.C.: National Transportation Safety Board, 1999), v, 1–2, 19, 22–23.

51. U.S. Federal Motor Carrier Safety Administration, "Hours of Service of Drivers; Driver Rest and Sleep for Safe Operations: Final Rule," *Federal Register* 68 (2003): 22456–517.

52. U.S. House of Representatives, Committee on Transportation and Infrastructure, Subcommittee on Ground Transportation, *Oversight of the Office of Motor Carriers: Hearings*, 106th Cong., 1st sess., 1999 (Washington, D.C.: Government Printing Office, 1999), 173 (Claybrook quotation), 168–69, 172–73; Belzer, *Sweatshops on Wheels*, 166 (quotation), 166–67; "D.C. Circuit Overturns Hours-of-Service Rules, Says FMCSA

Did Not Consider Drivers' Health," *Labor Relations Week*, July 22, 2004, 1013 (Sentelle quotation); Gregory M. Saltzman and Michael H. Belzer, "The Case for Strengthened Motor Carrier Hours of Service Regulations," *Transportation Journal* 41 (2002): 51–71; U.S. National Institute for Occupational Safety and Health, *Truck Driver Occupational Safety and Health: 2003 Conference Report and Selective Literature Review*, by Gregory M. Saltzman and Michael H. Belzer, DHHS (NIOSH) Publication 2007-120 (Cincinnati: National Institute for Occupational Safety and Health, 2007), 29. For the trucking industry's efforts to escape the terms of the Fair Labor Standards Act, see U.S. Senate, Committee on Education and Labor, and U.S. House of Representatives, Committee on Labor, *Fair Labor Standards Act of 1937: Joint Hearings . . . on S. 2475 and H.R. 7200*, 75th Cong., 1st sess., 1937 (Washington, D.C.: Government Printing Office, 1937), 744, 999–1004, 1006.

53. U.S. Federal Motor Carrier Safety Administration, "Hours of Service of Drivers: Final Rule," *Federal Register* 70 (2005): 49991 (quotations), 49978–50073; Judith Stone et al. to Ray LaHood, Mar. 9, 2009 (quotation, italics in original), http://www.citizen.org/documents/LahoodHOSletter.pdf; Peter Orris et al., *Literature Review on Health and Fatigue Issues Associated with Commercial Motor Vehicle Driver Hours of Work* (Washington, D.C.: Transportation Research Board, 2005); U.S. Court of Appeals for the District of Columbia, Owner-Operator Independent Drivers Association, Inc, Petitioner, v. Federal Motor Carrier Safety Administration, Respondent, July 24, 2007, http://www.truckinjurylawyerblog.com/Extending%20Hours%20of%20 Service%20Rejected%20by%2011th%20Circuit.pdf; *New York Times*, July 25, 2007, A15; Bonnie I. Robin-Vergeer, "Hours-of-Service: Missed Opportunities, Illegal Shortcuts," *Journal of Transportation Law, Logistics and Policy* 74 (2007): 466–89, esp. 484–85; Public Citizen, "Safety Advocates Ask Court to Overturn Bush 'Midnight Regulation," Mar. 9, 2009, http://www.saferoads.org/files/file/SafetyAdvocatesAskCo urttoOverturnBush'MidnightRegulation'.pdf.

54. U.S. Federal Motor Carrier Safety Administration, "Hours of Service of Drivers: Notice of Proposed Rulemaking," *Federal Register* 75 (2010): 82174 (quotation), 82170–98; U.S. Federal Motor Carrier Safety Administration, "Electronic On-Board Recorders and Hours of Service Supporting Documents: Notice of Proposed Rulemaking," ibid., 76 (2011): 5537–55.

55. NIOSH, *Truck Driver Conference*, 77 (quotations), 57–80; W. Karl Sieber, "Truck Driver Safety and Health," *NIOSH Science Blog*, Nov. 19, 2007 (quotation), http://198.246.98.21/niosh/blog/nsb111907_truck.html; Yorghos Apostolopoulos et al., "Worksite-Induced Morbidities Among Truck Drivers in the United States," *AAOHN Journal* 58 (2010): 285–96.

Conclusion

Note to epigraphs: *New York Times*, Jan. 17, 1999, sec. 4, 17 (Postrel quotation); Pierre Bourdieu, *Acts of Resistance: Against the Tyranny of the Market*, trans. Richard Nice (New York: New Press, 1998), 34 (quotation).

1. Beryl Bender Birch, *Power Yoga: The Total Strength and Flexibility Workout* (New York: Simon and Schuster, 1995); Stefanie Syman, *The Subtle Body: The Story of Yoga in America* (New York: Farrar, Straus and Giroux, 2010), 268–92; Emily Martin, *Flexible Bodies: Tracking Immunity in American Culture —From the Days of Polio to the Age of AIDS* (Boston: Beacon Press, 1994), esp. 143–59; Charles Perrow, *Normal Accidents: Living with High-Risk Technologies* (New York: Basic Books, 1984), esp. 89–100; Bo Carlsson, "Flexibility and the Theory of the Firm," *International Journal of Industrial Organization* 7 (1989): 179–203; Xavier de Groote, "The Flexibility of Production Processes: A General Framework," *Management Science* 40 (1994): 933–45; Bennett Harrison, *Lean and Mean: The Changing Landscape of Corporate Power in the Age of Flexibility* (New York: Basic Books, 1994); Eileen Appelbaum and Rosemary Batt, *The New American Workplace: Transforming Work Systems in the United States* (Ithaca, N.Y.: ILR Press of Cornell University Press, 1994); Dailun Shi and Richard L. Daniels, "A Survey of Manufacturing Flexibility: Implications for E-Business Flexibility," *IBM Systems Journal* 42 (2003): 414–27; Nelson Lichtenstein, *The Retail Revolution: How Wal-Mart Created a Brave New World of Business* (New York: Metropolitan Books, 2009); Spencer Johnson, *Who Moved My Cheese? An Amazing Way to Deal with Change in Your Work and in Your Life* (New York: G. P. Putnam's Sons, 1998).

2. Bourdieu, *Acts of Resistance*, 29–44, 81–87; Heather K. Scott, "Reconceptualizing the Nature and Health Consequences of Work-Related Insecurity for the New Economy: The Decline of Workers' Power in the Flexibility Regime," *International Journal of Health Services* 34 (2004): 143–53; Thomas M. Beers, "Flexible Schedules and Shift Work: Replacing the '9-to-5' Workday?" *Monthly Labor Review*, June 2000, 33–40; Harriet B. Presser, *Working in a 24/7 Economy: Challenges for American Families* (New York: Russell Sage Foundation, 2005), 11–58; Lonnie Golden, "Better Timing? Work Schedule Flexibility Among U.S. Workers and Policy Directions," in *Working Time: International Trends, Theory and Policy Perspectives*, ed. Lonnie Golden and Deborah M. Figart (New York: Routledge, 2000), 212–31; Lonnie Golden, "Flexible Work Schedules: What Are We Trading Off to Get Them?" *Monthly Labor Review*, Mar. 2001, 50–67; Karen S. Lyness et al., "It's All About Control: Worker Control over Schedule and Hours in Cross-National Context," *American Sociological Review* 77 (2012): 1023–49. For evidence of limited employee leverage over flexibility in even privileged positions, see Andrew Ross, *No-Collar: The Humane Workplace and Its Hidden Costs* (Philadelphia: Temple University Press, 2004), 10, 18, 81, 143–46; *New York Times*, May 27, 2009, B1, B4; Joan C. Williams, *Reshaping the Work-Family Debate: Why Men and Class Matter* (Cambridge, Mass.: Harvard University Press, 2010), 45, 52–56.

3. Katherine A. Stamatakis, George A. Kaplan, and Robert E. Roberts, "Short Sleep Duration Across Income, Education, and Race/Ethnic Groups: Population Prevalence and Growing Disparities During 34 Years of Follow-Up," *Annals of Epidemiology* 17 (2007): 951 (quotation), 948–55; Presser, *24/7 Economy*, 20–34, 219–20; Christopher L. Drake et al., "Shift Work Sleep Disorder: Prevalence and Consequences Beyond That of Symptomatic

Day Workers," *Sleep* 27 (2004): 1453–62. For the source of my notion of a "sleep divide," see Jerry A. Jacobs and Kathleen Gerson, *The Time Divide: Work, Family, and Gender Inequality* (Cambridge, Mass.: Harvard University Press, 2004). On the broader matrix of inequalities and their implications, see Richard G. Wilkinson, *Unhealthy Societies: The Afflictions of Inequality* (New York: Routledge, 1996); Norman Daniels, Bruce Kennedy, and Ichiro Kawachi, *Is Inequality Bad for Our Health?* (Boston: Beacon Press, 2000).

4. Torbjorn Akerstedt and Lars Torsvall, "Napping in Shift Work," *Sleep* 8 (1985): 105–9; David F. Dinges et al., "The Benefits of a Nap During Prolonged Work and Wakefulness," *Work and Stress* 2 (1988): 139–53; M. H. Bonnet, "Dealing with Shift Work: Physical Fitness, Temperature, and Napping," ibid., 4 (1990): 261–74; David F. Dinges and Roger J. Broughton, eds., *Sleep and Alertness: Chronobiological, Behavioral, and Medical Aspects of Napping* (New York: Raven Press, 1989); Claudio Stampi, ed., *Why We Nap: Evolution, Chronobiology, and Functions of Polyphasic and Ultrashort Sleep* (Boston: Birkhauser, 1992); James B. Maas, *Power Sleep: The Revolutionary Program That Prepares Your Mind for Peak Performance* (New York: HarperPerennial, 1999), 128–32; Ross A. Pigeau and Robert G. Angus, "Modafinil and Amphetamine Versus Naps in Sustained Operations," in *Countermeasures for Battlefield Stressors*, ed. Karl Friedl et al. (Baton Rouge: Louisiana State University Press, 2000), 206–27; Mark R. Rosekind et al., "Alertness Management: Strategic Naps in Operational Settings," *Journal of Sleep Research* 4 (1995): suppl. 2: 62–66; M. Mila Macchi et al., "Effects of an Afternoon Nap on Nighttime Alertness and Performance in Long-Haul Drivers," *Accident Analysis and Prevention* 34 (2002): 825–34; Pierre Philip et al., "The Effects of Coffee and Napping on Nighttime Highway Driving," *Annals of Internal Medicine* 144 (2006): 785–91; Vinnet Arora, "The Effects of On-Duty Napping on Intern Sleep Time and Fatigue," *Annals of Internal Medicine* 144 (2006): 792–98.

5. Arianna Huffington, "Sunday Roundup," *Huffington Post*, Apr. 25, 2011, http://www.huffingtonpost.com/arianna-huffington/air-traffic-control_b_852903.html; Alan Derickson, "Physiological Science and Scientific Management in the Progressive Era: Frederic S. Lee and the Committee on Industrial Fatigue," *Business History Review* 68 (1994): 483–514; Vern Baxter and Steve Kroll-Smith, "Normalizing the Workplace Nap: Blurring the Boundaries Between Public and Private Space and Time," *Current Sociology* 53 (2005): 33–55; Camille W. Anthony and William A. Anthony, *The Art of Napping at Work: The No-Cost, Natural Way to Increase Productivity and Satisfaction* (Burdett, N.Y.: Larson, 1999); Susan B. Van Hemel and William C. Rogers, "Survey of Truck Drivers' Knowledge and Beliefs Regarding Driver Fatigue," *Transportation Research Record*, no. 1640 (1998): 69, 72.

6. Lonnie Golden, "Forced Overtime in the Land of the Free," in *Take Back Your Time: Fighting Overwork and Time Poverty in America*, ed. John de Graaf (San Francisco: Berrett-Koehler, 2003), 33–34; Presser, *24/7 Economy*, 222–23; AFL-CIO, "Control over Work Hours and Alternative Work Schedules," Spring 2001, http://aflcio.org/issues/safety/upload/workhours.pdf; Stephen Hirschfeld, "New Poll Shows Many Americans Are Convinced Unions Are Key to Improving Working Conditions," *Employment Law Alliance*, Sept. 5, 2006, http://www.employmentlawalliance.com/pdf/ELAUnionsD309_01_2006.pdf; Pam Tau Lee and Niklas Krause, "The Impact of a

Worker Health Study on Working Conditions," *Journal of Public Health Policy* 23 (2002): 268–85; Department of Occupational Safety and Health, AFL-CIO, and National Labor College, *Safety and Health for Union Organizers: Facilitator's Guide* (Washington, D.C.: AFL-CIO, 2005); Department of Occupational Safety and Health, AFL-CIO, and National Labor College, *Safety and Health for Union Organizers: Resource Guide* (Washington, D.C.: AFL-CIO, 2005).

7. Johannes Morsink, *The Universal Declaration of Human Rights: Origins, Drafting and Intent* (Philadelphia: University of Pennsylvania Press, 1999), 334 (United Nations quotation), 185–90; Rick Fantasia and Kim Voss, *Hard Work: Remaking the American Labor Movement* (Berkeley: University of California Press, 2004), 28 (quotation), 27–28; Deidre McCann, *Working Time Laws: A Global Perspective* (Geneva: International Labor Office, 2005), 24, 38–41, 69–78; Jody Heymann et al., *The Work, Family, and Equity Index: Where Does the United States Stand Globally?* (Boston: Project on Global Working Families, Harvard School of Public Health, 2004), 1; International Labor Office, *Hours of Work: From Fixed to Flexible?* (Geneva: International Labor Office, 2005); Juliet B. Schor, "Worktime in Contemporary Context: Amending the Fair Labor Standards Act," *Kent Law Review* 70 (1994): 157–72, esp. 164–65, 171. In 2004, an undetected clerical error in the lawmaking process briefly gave workers in Virginia the right to refuse to work on their chosen Sabbath. For the hysterical response by employers, see *New York Times*, July 2, 2004, A13; "Injunction Stays Virginia 'Day of Rest' Law Which Guaranteed Weekend Day Off," *Labor Relations Week*, July 8, 2004, 964. In 2010, the state of New York enacted a Domestic Workers' Bill of Rights that assured those personal services employees one day in seven off, unless the parties agreed to a seventh consecutive work day, to be compensated at the time-and-a-half rate. See New York State Department of Labor, "Domestic Workers' Bill of Rights," http://www.labor.ny.gov/legal/domestic-workers-bill-of-rights.shtm, accessed Nov. 17, 2012. For glimpses into contemporary domestic servants' sleep problems, see *New York Times*, Mar. 8, 2004, A21, July 22, 2012, 20; Pierrette Hondagneu-Sotelo, *Domestica: Immigrant Workers Cleaning and Caring in the Shadows of Affluence* (Berkeley: University of California Press, 2007), 31–32, 142, 145–46, 178, 217. For an attempt to build on the precedent of the New York Domestic Workers' Bill of Rights, see San Francisco Department of Public Health, *A Health Impact Assessment of California Assembly Bill 889: The California Domestic Work Employee Equality, Fairness, and Dignity Act of 2011*, by Megan Gaydos et al., May 2011, esp. 5, 42–54, http://www.sfphes.org/component/jdownloads/finish/33/78.

8. U.S. NIOSH, *Shift Work and Health: A Symposium*, ed. P. G. Rentos and Robert D. Shepard (Washington, D.C.: Government Printing Office, 1976); U.S., NIOSH, *Health Consequences of Shift Work*, by Donald L. Tasto et al. (Washington, D.C.: Government Printing Office, 1978); U.S. NIOSH, *The Twenty-Four Hour Workday: Proceedings of a Symposium on Variations in Work-Sleep Schedules*, ed. Laverne C. Johnson et al. (Cincinnati: National Institute for Occupational Safety and Health, 1981); U.S. NIOSH, *Work-Related Roadway Crashes: Challenges and Opportunities for Prevention*, by Stephanie G. Pratt (Cincinnati: National Institute for Occupational Safety and

Health, 2003); U.S. NIOSH, *Overtime and Extended Work Shifts: Recent Findings on Illnesses, Injuries and Health Behaviors* (Cincinnati: National Institute for Occupational Safety and Health, 2004); Roger R. Rosa, "Toward Better Sleep for Workers: Impressions of Some Needs," *Industrial Health* 43 (2005): 85–87; Claire C. Caruso et al., "Long Working Hours, Safety, and Health: Toward a National Research Agenda," *American Journal of Industrial Medicine* 49 (2006): 930–42. For attempts to draw OSHA into this area, see Public Citizen et al. to R. David Layne, Apr. 30, 2001, http://www.citizen.org/ publications/release.cfm?ID=6771; Public Citizen, "OSHA Denies Petition to Reduce Work Hours for Doctors-in-Training," Oct. 10, 2002, http://www.citizen.org/pressroom/ release.cfm?ID=1239; Charles M. Preston et al. to David Michaels, Sept. 2, 2010, http:// www.citizen.org/documents/1917.pdf. For a provocative call for more investigation of the consequences of flexible work and employment schemes, see J. Benach and C. Muntaner, "Precarious Employment and Health: Developing a Research Agenda," *Journal of Epidemiology and Community Health* 61 (2007): 276–77.

9. For historical inquiries that shed light on overwork and sleep difficulties of women workers, see, among others, Thomas Dublin, *Women at Work: The Transformation of Work and Community in Lowell, Massachusetts, 1826–1860* (New York: Columbia University Press, 1981), 78, 80; Tera W. Hunter, *To 'Joy My Freedom: Southern Black Women's Lives and Labors After the Civil War* (Cambridge, Mass.: Harvard University Press, 1997), 52–57; Faye E. Dudden, *Serving Women: Household Service in Nineteenth-Century America* (Middletown, Conn.: Wesleyan University Press, 1983), 181–82, 196; David M. Katzman, *Seven Days a Week: Women and Domestic Service in Industrializing America* (Urbana: University of Illinois Press, 1981), 108–14; Rebecca Sharpless, *Cooking in Other Women's Kitchens: Domestic Workers in the South, 1865–1960* (Chapel Hill: University of North Carolina Press, 2010), 65–71, 90–92; Vanessa H. May, *Unprotected Labor: Household Workers, Politics, and Middle-Class Reform in New York, 1870–1940* (Chapel Hill: University of North Carolina Press, 2011), 37–40, 47–50, 77–80, 122, 137–42; Susan Reverby, *Ordered to Care: The Dilemma of American Nursing, 1850–1940* (New York: Cambridge University Press, 1987), 29–30, 56, 62, 64, 96, 100; Stephen H. Norwood, *Labor's Flaming Youth: Telephone Operators and Worker Militancy, 1878–1923* (Urbana: University of Illinois Press, 1990), 45–46; Vicki L. Ruiz, *Cannery Women, Cannery Lives: Mexican Women, Unionization, and the California Food Processing Industry, 1930–1950* (Albuquerque: University of New Mexico Press, 1987), 125–28.

10. Sandy Graham, "Are Your Employees Dead Tired?" *Safety and Health*, Mar. 1995, 65.

Index

Acknowledgments

Conventionally, authors acknowledge the members of their immediate family last in the roll call of contributors. But my wife and daughters have waited long enough. I thank my daughters, Katherine and Elizabeth, for their unfailing support of this project, even when the end was nowhere in sight. My wife, Peg, provided my first insights into severe sleep deprivation when we got married during the year (1977) of her medical internship, a grueling rite of professional passage designed to forge indefatigable ironmen. This book is dedicated to her as a small token of appreciation for all her tireless loving encouragement and editorial acumen.

I am very grateful to a host of archivists and other research facilitators. I benefited greatly from the exertions of staff members at the Historical Collections and Labor Archives, Penn State University Libraries; Archives II, National Archives; the National Archives at Chicago; the Manuscript Division, Library of Congress; the Bancroft Library, University of California, Berkeley; the Archives and Special Collections, Frost Library, Amherst College; the Archives Division, Wisconsin Historical Society; the Ecumenical Library, Interchurch Center; the Archives Service Center, University of Pittsburgh; the Baskes Department of Special Collections, Newberry Library; the Kheel Center for Labor Management Documentation and Archives, Catherwood Library, Cornell University; the Special Collections Research Center, Regenstein Library, University of Chicago; the Pennsylvania State Archives; and the Special Collections and Archives, Wright State University Libraries.

A different version of Chapter 4 first appeared as "'Asleep and Awake at the Same Time': Sleep Denial among Pullman Porters," in the fall 2008 issue of *Labor: Studies in Working Class History of the America*, the journal of the Labor and Working Class History Association. I thank the association and Duke University Press for permission to reprint most of that article here.

Penn State University has provided considerable support for this project over the years. I very much appreciate the diligent efforts of my research assistants, Kanika Suri and Suzanne Martin, and a travel grant from the Research Office of the College of the Liberal Arts. Ongoing collegial encouragement came from many nearby sources, including Bill Blair, Paul Clark, Dan Letwin, Jim Quigel, Adam Rome, and Nan Woodruff.

In the wider, overlapping circles of friends and colleagues, I have incurred many debts. I am much obliged to readers of part or all of the manuscript—Eric Arnesen, David Brody, Sue Cobble, Leon Fink, Lonnie Golden, Sandy Jacoby, David McBride, Robert Proctor, Ron Numbers, Pam Susi, Richard Valelly, Jim Weeks, Michael Zuckerman, and the press's anonymous reviewers. For helpful comments on paper presentations, as well as various clues, warnings, and encouragement, I thank William Childs, William Dement, Peter Gottlieb, Bill Kojola, Karen Levy, Jill Lorenz, Elaine McCrate, Marge Murphy, David Roediger, Drew Whitelegg, and David Witwer. My wily editor, Peter Agree, offered an abundance of sage advice that I have valued highly. I am also much indebted to Kathleen Kageff and Noreen O'Connor-Abel for their careful copyediting.